WHAT DOES A WOMAN DO
WHEN HER ONE GREAT LOVE IS GONE FOREVER?

The great love in Sheilah Graham's life was F. Scott Fitzgerald. After his sudden, tragic death she was left numb and shattered. Her only desire was to leave Hollywood, where she had known so much joy and heartache, and go East to seek out others who had loved Scott—his daughter, his editor, his agent, his friends. But then Sheilah put aside her heartache and took up a new life . . . a life that led through an assignment as correspondent in bomb-blasted England, through a wartime romance and marriage that gave her two children, and finally through a new career in Hollywood that propelled her into glittering success as the $5000-a-week queen of moviedom gossip columnists. Despite the glitter and the countless celebrities who crowd these pages, her story is compelling, honest and human.

"The my-life-is-an-open-book approach with a page-turning guaranty. Read on . . ." VIRGINIA KIRKUS

Also by Sheilah Graham

❧ BELOVED INFIDEL

❧ Published by Bantam Books

Sheilah Graham

The Rest of The Story

This low-priced Bantam Book
has been completely reset in a type face
designed for easy reading, and was printed
from new plates. It contains the complete
text of the original hard-cover edition.
NOT ONE WORD HAS BEEN OMITTED.

THE REST OF THE STORY
A Bantam Book / published by arrangement with
Coward-McCann, Inc.

PRINTING HISTORY
Coward-McCann edition published May 1964
2nd printing.........May 1964
Bantam edition published June 1965

Cover photo by John Engstead.

The quotation on page 206 from T. S. Eliot's "The Love
Song of J. Alfred Prufrock" (Collected Poems 1909-1962) is used
by permission of the publisher, Harcourt, Brace & World, Inc.

Bantam Books are published by Bantam Books, Inc., a subsidiary
of Grosset & Dunlap, Inc. Its trade-mark, consisting of the words
"Bantam Books" and the portrayal of a bantam, is registered in the
United States Patent Office and in other countries. Marca Registrada.
Bantam Books, Inc., 271 Madison Avenue, New York, N. Y. 10016.

PRINTED IN THE UNITED STATES OF AMERICA

For Wendy and Robert

I

IT was a frantic year for me, the year of 1941. Forgetting is as important as remembering, he had told me once, and if I were to survive, although this did not seem important then, there was much to forget. The man must be forgotten. I had to put him away in the farthest recess of my mind, and in that first year, I produced him only to comfort his daughter and his friends. His photograph in the checked jacket that I have seen so many times since, with the sad lost smile, must be put away and never looked at again. The books he had given me—I loved the books as though they were him. The letters, the poems, the telegrams, the records, the silver jug he had given me for my birthday in September—no one had ever given me a silver jug or anything like it for a birthday—the paintings, the large Degas in the white frame, the Marie Laurencin pastel—the presents he had given me to make me feel that I, his student in The F. Scott Fitzgerald College of One, was also a collector of art, although he was poor and they were copies. I put them in storage with my other mementos of him when I gave up my apartment, and that is when I sold the green armchair in which he had been sitting when he died—and the second-hand furniture we had bought together in Barker's basement. I sold everything then for a very few dollars, and left Hollywood forever, I was sure.

It was ten years before I was emotionally capable of talking about the death of Scott Fitzgerald. I was lunching at Romanoff's in Beverly Hills, with Jean Dalrymple, the producer, who always reminds me of Queen Victoria in her middle period, and balding, short, round Freddie Finklehoff, a writer. Perhaps they introduced the subject or I did, I'm not sure now, but I found myself talking of Scott with calm detachment. I told them what a charming, amusing person he was and what a pity he had died before completing his book, *The Last Tycoon.* I remember thinking, *How steady your voice is. You see, you can talk about him.* They listened quietly with great interest and I thought, *It is not as difficult as I expected. Perhaps it is possible to tell them how he died.* This was a dangerous area, but worth testing. If I put my voice in a higher key, I was sure I could do it. The trick was to talk as though I had known Scott only slightly. "It was about three in the afternoon. We were in the living room of my apartment in Hollywood. He was eating a chocolate bar; he always craved candy when he was on the wagon," I said, with a sort of amused hardness, "and he was jotting down football plays in the *Princeton Alumni Weekly.* And then," I said with more difficulty, "something pulled him up from the green armchair, he clutched the mantelpiece and fell to the floor and died." And suddenly, quite dreadfully, in the fashionable, crowded restaurant, I was weeping as chokingly as I am now, writing this.

The fact is, I will never get over Scott Fitzgerald. The shock of witnessing the immediate death of someone you love leaves a permanent scar. No one, except my children, has ever meant as much to me. I will never, ever forget this gracious, moral man.

But it would be absurd to say that I have been in mourning for the past twenty-three years. Everyone who knows me would smile at the idea. My life during these years has been too extraordinary. I've had too much happen to me, good and bad, but mostly overwhelmingly good, for me ever to feel too sorry for myself. Although I sometimes wish that my life had been more conventional and calm.

But when Scott died, I could not think of a good reason for living. At first there was a leftover flame which kept me going. But as the weeks passed the bright glow of anguish faded and I had nothing. There was no one to consult, no one to consider, no one to worry about, no one to ask me how I was, what I was going to do. I was free. But where should I go? Where should I go now that I was free to go anywhere? I wanted to go home, and home was England.

In 1938, when Scott had realized that World War II was inevitable, he had advised me to become an American citizen. Scott was to sponsor me and shortly before he died, I had taken out my first papers. Now there seemed no reason for me to change citizenship. Perhaps, I thought, I could do some good for England if I went there and wrote stories about the war for my newspaper syndicate. The more I

thought of it, it seemed the one thing to do. Scott had promised me we would go to Europe if *The Last Tycoon* were
a success. He would invade Ernest Hemingway's territory
and write about this new kind of war, he had said with a
half-smile. He had called me a lone wolf, but I had friends
in England. Johnny, Major John Gillam, my ex-husband, was
in England. I had divorced him in 1937, but that had not
interrupted our close relationship. The Mitfords were there,
and Lord Donegall was there. He had written me in September 1939, "We are not having much fun in this country.
Do you think you could drop me a line?" And a man to
whom I had once been engaged had sent a message: "I don't
want to be dramatic, but if you never hear from me again
you will at any rate know that there has never been anyone
but you." I would not be so desperately lost and restless in
England, and there would be excitement and danger.

Chiefly, I knew I had to get away from Hollywood. In a
letter to Johnny, dated February 22, 1941, I wrote, "I would
not want to live my life, what is left of it, in Hollywood. I
flew to New York a month ago and told John Wheeler I
would like to work for him in London. Wheeler reminded me
my Hollywood contract did not expire until July 12th. He's
given me until May to think it over. I am lucky to have
John Wheeler as a friend, although when it's a matter of
business, he can be a little harder than the next man."

I left for New York the day after Christmas, and Sid Perel-
man was on the same train, accompanying the body of his
brother-in-law, Nathanael West, who had been killed with
his wife, Eileen, in an automobile accident in Encino, the
day after Scott died. I had liked Nat but not Eileen. They
had come to Scott's house in Encino the previous summer;
Eileen had made fun of Scott when he had shown them his
scrapbooks with the dance cards and invitations and the
dark and red and gold locks of hair of the girls he had
known, and all the mementos he had kept. Scott was a great
keeper of things that had happened. Eileen had called Scott
a snob and said that he cared only for the rich. I had read
"The Rich Boy," but I had never seen Scott on the fringe
of rich people's lives, and it came as a great surprise to me
later when everyone, it seemed, was rediscovering him, to
read so much about his admiration for the rich.

It was exciting in New York. The city was gay, and the
atmosphere, as always, bursting with great energy, and men
and women in uniform, although America was not to be in

the war for almost another year. The Army and the Navy and the Air Force were mobilizing and this was a time of frenzied preparation for the war. Everyone seemed prosperous and the theatres were crowded. The film houses did a landslide business. Everyone was out. Everyone was living as hard as possible. Everyone wanted to have fun. No one wanted a sad face around the table, so I set my mouth in a perpetual smile, and I think I fooled some of the people, except those who knew about Scott. There was always the thought, *Perhaps I will meet someone like Scott; there must be another man like him.*

I was not ready at that time to bury Scott, and I walked fast like a woman with a message, visiting the people I had met with him. Scottie came up from Vassar. We talked at length about her father in my room at the Gotham Hotel. She was very pretty. Ash-blond hair, with Scott's eyes and forehead and Zelda's complexion and mouth and lovely legs. She had shed the fat that had annoyed her so much when I first met her four years before in Hollywood, when she was fifteen, although Scott had been pleased with her chubbiness—"This isn't the age for her to be *too* popular with boys."

Scottie made no apologies for the battles she had had with her father. He had tried to anticipate everything that would happen in her life and prepare her for it, to protect her, and Scottie had found this unnecessary, annoying and constricting. She was sorry, as I was, that he had not finished his book before he died. We were both really angry about this.

I told her she would realize when she was a bit older that the long-distance supervision of her activities was because her father had loved her very much. She looked a little disbelieving, but she did not want to hurt my feelings and conceded, "It's possible." She assured me she had always respected her father's writing ability. I told her how proud he had been of the two or three pieces she had written. She knew this, despite their argument at the Brown Derby in Hollywood on her last visit. "If you want to write," he had told her, "you must use another name. You cannot trade on my reputation." He had not forgiven his wife, Zelda, for using the same characters and places in his *Tender Is the Night* for her novel, *Save Me the Waltz*. "Don't worry, I won't," Scottie had promised him tartly, and she used the name of Frances Scott for her stories, two of which appeared in *The New Yorker*.

But mostly, Scottie talked about me; what was I going to do? I told her that I was leaving Hollywood and she was pleased. "I don't see how you could have lived there in the first place. It's so unreal, and without Daddy—" There wasn't much money, she said, "And I'm going to leave Vassar." "Oh, no, you mustn't do that." I was shocked and disturbed. "This is what your father wanted above all things, for you to finish your education at Vassar." I did not tell her he believed that if Zelda had, as an adolescent, followed through with whatever she started and if she had known how to discipline herself, perhaps she would not have become mentally ill.

Zelda was with her mother in Montgomery, Alabama, when Scott died, but she would soon be going back to the sanitarium in Asheville, North Carolina. Her doctor had told Scott that Zelda's form of illness did not usually survive middle age, and Zelda was now in her early forties. For the first time I hoped she would die. Her insanity was too great a burden for a nineteen-year-old girl. "Your mother won't live very long," I told Scottie. And when poor Zelda died dreadfully in the sanitarium fire a few years later, Scottie reminded me with great awe, "You told me she wouldn't live very long." I tried to look wise, as one who can read the future.

During one of our talks, Scottie, who was practical for all her vagueness when she couldn't be bothered with a name or a telephone number, asked me, "Sheilah, if that old Ford of Daddy's is around, perhaps you could arrange to send it east. I could use it." I made some inquiries, but I never did find out what happened to the car. It must have fallen apart and expired on some junk heap. I learned from Frances Kroll, his secretary, that Scott had not finished paying for it, at the rate of $20 a month.

I saw Scott's editor, Maxwell Perkins. I had met him with Scott in his office upstairs at Scribner's on Fifth Avenue, and Max invited me for tea at the Ritz. I liked this gentle, quiet man. He was enthusiastic over what Scott had written of *The Last Tycoon*. "It promised to be the most brilliant book he ever did. I think Stahr, though incomplete, is his best character. I read the manuscript fast the first time, then I read it again and found so vastly much more in it than in the fast reading. That does not often happen—only in cases of large dimension not at first perceived. It would break a man's heart to see what this book could have been and that it wasn't finished. Practically speaking, I don't know what to do."

He wasn't sure, he said, but Scribner's might publish it in its half-finished state, perhaps with *The Great Gatsby.* And I thought, *How happy this would make Scott.* On May 20, 1940, he had written to Mr. Perkins suggesting they reissue *The Great Gatsby,* which was out of print. But the editor, believing there would not be a sale, had replied, "This is not the right time for it." Perhaps later, after *The Last Tycoon* was finished. At that time, neither his publisher nor his agent nor his friends seriously believed that Scott was capable of the long, lonely dedication of writing a book. A "Pat Hobby" story in *Esquire* perhaps, but not a Scott Fitzgerald book.

Now Scribner's was considering publishing his less than half-finished novel. Mr. Perkins liked the first chapter especially. He told me, "It's so good, it could be something all by itself." Scott had sent this chapter to *Collier's* Magazine, hoping they would give him the big advance they had promised, to make it possible for him to finish the book without the energy-draining necessity of going back to a film studio, writing scripts that were always rewritten by inferior writers. But *Collier's* had rejected that first chapter, over which Scott had labored so long and with such care, and which I had thought was superb.

I brought Frances and Albert Hackett, who were now living in New York, the poem Scott had written after he had been called in the middle of a dinner party at their house in Hollywood to report to Metro. Scott was working at the time on *Marie Antoinette* for Norma Shearer.

Sing a song for Sheilah's supper, belly void of rye;
Gone before the cocktail, back for the pie.
Stromberg sent for Poppa, though Papa hadn't et,
To do what Jesus couldn't—
Save Marie Antoinette. . . .

Jesus hadn't saved Scott either. He was replaced as usual by another writer in the Metro stable of highly paid puppet authors.

The Gerald Murphys, who had been Scott's friends for so long, took me to lunch at the Louis XIV Café by the ice-skating rink in Rockefeller Center. I looked a sight, my eyes red, my face swollen with so much weeping. The Murphys were enormously kind to me. They showed me a telegram Scott had sent them in March of 1938 when I had flown to New York without him. "Will you give her a call?" he had asked them. "Of course, Sheilah has many friends in New York, but it can be lonely arriving at Newark alone."

They assured me that I had done a great deal to make Scott happy. It was Scott who had made me happy, I told them. It was Scott who had done so much for me. I remember the white, cold sunshine on the big windows of the restaurant and I was not unhappy. I was with the Murphys, who had loved Scott, and we talked of him and he was alive. I have seen this with people who have lost a loved one. The dead are living again when they are talked about. Perhaps this is the way all of us are alive, otherwise, isn't it a dream? When people who love you talk about you, you are there in a smile and a laugh and in the stories about you, and there is warmth and love.

I spent a weekend with the Harold Obers in Scarsdale. Harold was Scott's agent and he was extremely sad because Scott had quarreled with him in the last months of his life. Scott was always needing more money and Harold finally had to say, "No, I can't give you any more." Scott wrote him an angry letter, fired him as agent, and scratched his name out of his will as executor. Max Perkins' name was substituted for Mr. Ober's, and this made the will illegal. It was decided that only Judge John Biggs, who was a friend from Scott's Princeton days, should act as executor. I saw Judge Biggs on several occasions. He told me there was little money. "But he had a big insurance policy for Zelda and Scottie. What happened to that?" I asked. "He borrowed against it to such an extent that there's less than $30,000 left. Of course we'll have to use all of it for Zelda's maintenance." I told Judge Biggs how much Scott had wanted Scottie to finish her education at Vassar. He contacted the Murphys and several of Scott's friends. They raised the money and Scottie did finish her education at Vassar.

✎ CHAPTER TWO

ON February 1, 1941, Lord Donegall cabled from London. He had heard of Scott's death and hoped I was not too miserable. I replied, THIS PART OF WORLD INTOLERABLE NOW. AM HOPING TO GET WAR CORRESPONDENT JOB IN LONDON, SO FAR UNSUCCESSFULLY. It was kind of him to be concerned.

I wrote to John Wheeler on my return from New York. I told him I was sure I wanted to leave Hollywood. His reply was emphatic: "You must wait." I was English, he reminded me, and if I went to England I could be kept there indefinitely. Was that what I wanted? I did not know, but I did want to go to England. He tried another tactic: "I can't guarantee that your column will be available should you want it back." And then, with an explosion of exasperation and concerned curiosity, "Why do you want to get killed?" I did not really want to get killed. I wanted to do something violently different. There were still nightly raids on London, but not with the intensity of the Battle of Britain.

"I want to go," I hammered away during the following months. It was a good idea, I pointed out, for an Englishwoman, someone who knew England as well as I did, to write about the war effort by Englishwomen. I would have good contacts, I reminded him: I knew several editors on Fleet Street, there were Lord Beaverbook, the Mitfords—Unity Mitford, the Aryan Dream Girl, was in Hitler's disfavor and had been shot under mysterious circumstances—perhaps I could get the true story. Also, I had made a reputation as a journalist in this country and my stories would be read, I felt, with interest. I reminded him that up to that time, no one had written about the dedicated women's effort in the war in England. Well, he wrote back, with less vehemence, he was not very optimistic, but he would think about it. That was the most to which he would commit himself.

All I could think of was how to get to England. I felt guilty at not being there. I was raised with a "What is there I would not do for you, England, my own?" I was in America, safe, rich, comfortable America, while England was being blasted to bits.

I redoubled my efforts. John Wheeler finally agreed I could go to England for NANA, provided I would be assured of an exit visa. "I'll have no trouble on this point," I told him. "Douglas Williams, a friend of mine, is in charge of visas for correspondents."

But friends sometimes are the people who do not help you when you need them. Douglas Williams could not, or would not, guarantee me an exit visa. John Wheeler was glad and informed me, "I tried, you cannot go." He should have known I don't give up that easily. I immediately cabled Lord Beaverbrook.

NORTH AMERICAN NEWSPAPER ALLIANCE WANTS SEND ME ENGLAND [*this was a slight distortion*] MIDDLE JULY UNTIL END AUG WRITE WOMAN'S ANGLE WAR STORIES AM STILL BRITISH SUBJECT AND BECAUSE OF THAT LONDON MINISTRY INFORMATION INFORMS CANNOT GUARANTEE PRIORITIES AIR TRAVEL LISBON LONDON AND BACK UNLESS PROVED IN NATIONAL INTEREST AND EVEN THEN EXIT PERMIT DOUBTFUL MY SOLE AIM TO SERVE ENGLAND AND OF COURSE MY EMPLOYERS PLEASE HELP PLEASE ADVISE.

I sent this cable April 10, 1941, and it cost me $8.60, a small price for the priorities and exit visa that miraculously materialized.

John Wheeler wrote me the good news. If I still wanted to go, although he was still strongly against it, I had his permission, and I would be assigned the credentials of a war correspondent for NANA. Having finally agreed, but waiting until the last possible day before informing the papers which took my Hollywood column, John Wheeler went to work to make the assignment a success. He had me meet the editor of the Newark *News*, who introduced me to Jack Bergen, now Admiral Bergen. "Jack knows some important people in England in the war effort, and I believe he is also going to England this summer." Jack, a bald, thin, pint-sized Irishman with an anticipatory smile and a blooming laugh, had a great idea. He was flying to England in a bomber and it would start me off with an exciting story if I went over in a bomber too. "How thrilling," I said, hoping I sounded enthusiastic. I was not sorry when, shortly before I was to leave, I learned this was impossible. There was only one toilet in the plane and they could not have one woman there, with all the men. Later, when the wife of the British Ambassador to Washington, Lady Halifax, flew over, a special toilet was built for her.

But now it was definite. I was going to England and I was too excited and busy to cry about the past. This was the future. Once again I was holding on to my hat with my face set forward into the wind.

✿ CHAPTER THREE

I WROTE to Johnny, "I have a reservation on the July 15 Clipper from New York for Lisbon, and the office is paying all expenses, as well as my salary. My headquarters will be London, but I can spend a couple of days with you, wherever you happen to be. [After trying for active service, Johnny had been accepted as an officer with the R.A.S.C. and was stationed in Birmingham.] I'm going to listen to Winston Churchill tomorrow, and I do hope he has something to say to relieve the gloom. Is it true there is a shortage of chocolates and sweets and silk stockings? I could bring some of these over and give them to people. I suppose now that you're in the Army, you don't need a torchlight. But how about a pair of field glasses and vitamin tablets? Has the Savoy Hotel in London a good air-raid shelter? It's near Fleet Street and I'm thinking of staying there if I can get accommodations."

In another letter to Johnny—"I can't believe that I am actually to be a war correspondent. What a strange up-and-down life I have had. If anyone had ever told me when I was a child what sort of life I was to lead, it would have seemed fantastic. I can hardly wait to finish my Hollywood contract. My mind is so full of the assignment that there is nothing else I can write today. Just think, by the time you get this letter, there'll be only a few weeks before I start."

The night before I left Hollywood, I had dinner with Eddie Mayer, whom I will always love for having introduced me to Scott Fitzgerald. Eddie was sorry to see me go, but he understood and was a little envious of me. As we drove to the restaurant in his big Buick, a moth flew into the car. I'm terrified of moths, and I was ducking and carrying on and I can still hear Eddie telling some people we saw later that evening, "She's going to the war in England tomorrow and she's frightened of a moth!" Everyone thought it was very, very funny.

I made a will, leaving everything I possessed to Scottie. In my letter to Judge Biggs, appointing him as executor—"The books in storage—most of them were brought me by Scott. In a lot of them Scott has written amusing or instructive things on the first or last pages. At the back of the Wells *Outline of History* there is a football tactic—if you want to know what the figures are.

"I'd like all the papers in storage, private or to do with my work, destroyed without reading them—WITH THE EXCEPTION OF THE RED FOLDER MARKED 'SCOTT' which Scottie might like to have for a glimpse into a part of her father's recent years. The big black diary cornered with RED and titled inside *The Book of Lillith*, I want destroyed UNREAD. It contains a few notes for a book I was planning. BUT PLEASE DESTROY THIS.

"The two children's pictures in similar frames—one of me as a little girl and the other of my ex-husband as a boy—perhaps they could be sent to him, Major John Gillam, care of Lloyd's Bank, Ltd., 399 Oxford Street, London—if it is possible to do so.

"Everything else that Scottie doesn't want can be destroyed or thrown away. The new typewriter might interest her.

"I hope this small sum of money will be of help to Scottie and make your task of administrating her affairs a little easier. It's a tiny thank you to Scott for having known him."

I saw Scottie in New York again. She was glad I was going to England, and delighted when I told her I'd had some cables from Donegall. Scottie thought it would solve everything if I married Donegall and she promised to come and stay with us in his ancestral castle. He didn't have one, but it was all very gay. Scottie, who was working for *Time* Magazine, told me, "I was going through Daddy's folder in the *Time* library the other day and came across a note by one of the reporters—'Contacted Sheilah Graham—she is very beautiful and charming.' There's a yellow slip about *me* which will amuse you. 'Born Frances Scott, etc. As yet shows no artistic leanings.' That's a hell of a classification!"

Edmund Wilson wrote me. He had read *The Last Tycoon* and thought it was excellent and would have been the very

best novel about Hollywood. And perhaps the best of all
Scott's writing. He told me that Scribner's had now decided
to publish the half-finished novel. "I have been asked to
edit it," he informed me, "with all of Scott's notes. I need
your help and perhaps you'll spare me some time. Would
you be able to come and stay with us in Wellfleet?" "Of
course I will come," I replied. "I'll tell you everything I
know about the book." I could not tell much about the un-
written part of the novel, however. Scott never discussed
what he was *going* to write. He believed it would weaken
his material. Hemingway once expressed the same view.

I learned from Max Perkins that Budd Schulberg had
offered to finish *The Last Tycoon*, which surprised Edmund
Wilson and me enormously, because how could Budd Schulberg finish Scott Fitzgerald's book?

The journey to the Wilson home in Massachusetts was
long and tiring. All journeys were getting difficult, although
America was not yet in the war. I followed his explicit
instructions. I had to change trains twice and the last part
was by bus. Mr. and Mrs. Wilson—he was married then to
Mary McCarthy—were waiting in their car and they drove
me to Wellfleet. They had rented a house, comfortable, but
not luxurious. We had a drink in a small study before dinner, then into the dining room, which was much larger. I
don't know who cooked the dinner, but it was not very good.
The potatoes were on the hard side, and I wondered, if I
had to choose between living with an intellectual and living
with a good cook, which would I really want? At that moment, when I was depressed and somewhat ill-at-ease, I
would have chosen a good cook. I have learned since that
Mary is an excellent cook, in fact a famous cook. Well,
unless someone else cooked the dinner, she wasn't then.

I had first met Mr. Wilson and his wife with Scott in
their Stamford home. Mary, then not long out of Vassar—
serious, brunette, attractive, slender, with chiseled features.
Wilson, pink, round face, not much hair, and sort of sup-
pressedly glad to see Scott again. Scott was happy to be
with the man he respected so much and eager to listen when
Wilson talked of Kafka. "But Mary is more enthusiastic
about him than I am," Mr. Wilson said. We all listened
respectfully to Mary, and Scott promised to read Kafka.

How delighted Scott would be, I thought, to know I was a

guest in the home of his "literary conscience"; that I was with his most intellectual friend.

At dinner we discussed Scott and *The Last Tycoon* and the British Empire, which Mr. Wilson deplored and I championed. He told me stories about Scott—one, that Scott had *not* been kicked out of Princeton as Wilson had thought all those years. He really did have T.B. I could vouch for that, I assured him, remembering the night sweats and the temperatures. And there were stories to laugh at—the pranks at Princeton. And Mary smiled gently when I told her that Scott had read all of Kafka and had agreed with her opinion of him. But mostly we talked of the unfinished book, and I learned for the first time that Scott had intended that his hero, Monroe Stahr, would die in a plane crash. I was fascinated by some of the notes, which I had never seen before. We talked at length about Scott's line, "There are no second acts in American lives." Scott's life had certainly lacked a second act.

"We should dedicate *The Last Tycoon* to you. I am sure that is what Scott would have wished," said Mr. Wilson. "Oh no, you can't do that," I replied. Zelda was alive and Scott would never hurt or embarrass her.

I told Mr. Wilson—I was shy and I hesitatingly called him Bunny as his friends did—that Scott had planned to eliminate Robinson from the book. He thought he was not leading anywhere. "As you know, Scott had written 60,000 words and the book itself was not to be much more than that, and he was not halfway through. He was going to cut about 10,000 words of what he had already written." But Mr. Wilson said, decisively, "I won't cut a word." And I thought, *How extraordinary, every single word Scott has written, mediocre as well as excellent, now that he is dead, is going to be preserved, and Scott is to live and take his place with the great American writers.* This was implicit in everything Bunny and Mary said that night, and there he had been living in Los Angeles all those years and only a handful of people had known he was alive, and few of his old friends had written him.

I had been surprised to find Scott's death a front-page story in the Los Angeles *Times. The New Yorker* had a long paragraph about him, chiding *The New York Times* for its error in the title of *The Beautiful and* [the] *Damned.* The writer was unhappy about Scott's absolute obscurity at the time of his death, and *The New Yorker* accolade ended with, "In a way, we are glad that he died when he did," comparing Scott, unknown and declining in popularity, with Dick Diver at the end of *Tender Is the Night.*

The following day, Mr. Wilson took me to Provincetown. He bought a little toy duck for his son that teetered drunkenly around the sidewalk when wound up. It was cold as we walked by the ocean, but we stopped frequently to test the waddling of the duck. I was surprised that this great brain found pleasure in such a simple thing. I'm not sure what I had expected—probably an absent-minded professor type, addicted to long words and impossible intellectual discussions. Nothing of the kind—in fact, he prodded me on Hollywood and seemed to enjoy my gossip about the stars.

Mary was not there when her husband and their son were playing with the duck, but later I heard her reading to the little boy from the classics. Mary read to the one-year-old boy every day for an hour. I realized that this was on the same principle as having a young child listen to good music; that it would sink in and become part of his intellectual fiber. Of course, any child of Mary McCarthy and Edmund Wilson would grow up with a liking for well-written sentences, since that would be all he would ever hear.

. Mr. Wilson showed me the many-windowed room he used for his writing. It was on a small hill near the house, quiet and serene. He gave me two letters of introduction, to Harold Laski and to George Orwell in London. I am not very good at presenting letters, but soon after I arrived I went through the motions of calling Laski. He was busy and I did not press him; I gave him Edmund Wilson's regards on the phone. I'm sorry I did not get to talk to George Orwell, because my son Robert is a great admirer of his, and a few years ago when he read *1984* and *Animal Farm* I would have liked to say that I had met him; I had tried to find him, but it was hard to find people in wartime England. There were no up-to-date telephone books, and I was to discover that except for a very few friends, almost everyone I had known had either left London, was on active service, or had been killed in the war.

❦ CHAPTER FOUR

JOHN WHEELER gave me my first assignment before I left.
It had nothing to do with the war, except perhaps in-
directly. I was to interview George Bernard Shaw on his
eighty-fifth birthday. I have always been a lucky reporter.
Shaw's close friend, Gabriel Pascal, was on the same Pan
American Clipper taking me to Lisbon. We were flying there
via Bermuda and the Azores, and a British Government
plane would take us from Lisbon to England. What a stroke
of luck to find Pascal on the plane. I asked the stewardess
to introduce us. He was a little man, with dark shoebutton
eyes, wide face, quite swarthy, rather dumpy without being
fat, and his black hair grew low on his forehead. I told
him of my assignment and asked, "Can you help me?" He
replied, "Mr. Shaw doesn't see newspaper people and he
hates to talk about his birthdays, but"—after an appraising
look—"I will see what I can do." He went back to his seat
for the takeoff.

An hour out of New York the big seaplane began to lurch
and roll. It was eleven in the morning but quite black outside the windows. We were in the worst kind of storm. I
was frightened and I found myself praying. I remember there
is a God when I am frightened. I had thought I didn't care
whether I lived or died, and here I was, praying fervently, my eyes closed tightly, hanging on to the seat belt
and mumbling "The Lord is my shepherd, I shall not
want" over and over, until the fearful turbulence subsided.

The skies were blue in Bermuda and the rest of the flight
was calm, but we had some trouble leaving the humid, hot
Azores. The water was extremely choppy and there was
some question as to whether the seaplane could take off.
We made three tries to get up and could not. I don't believe anyone considered the danger. Our only thought was
to get away from the Azores. The prospect of another day
in that godforsaken hole was worse than dying. The plane
managed to gain altitude on the fourth try.

Mr. Pascal took the vacant seat next to mine and I told
him of my plans to write about the war in England for my
syndicate. I must have talked a great deal because soon he

was yawning, and before I could shift my shoulder, he was asleep on it. He slept like an unconscious baby all the way across the South Atlantic. I didn't dare to move. He had promised to help me with Shaw and I never take chances. I had a bad cramp from my neck to my waist by the time our descent into Lisbon waters jolted Mr. Pascal awake.

I had been to Lisbon once before on a cruise with some friends during my "society" period in England. This time there was a different kind of reception committee: a large crowd of men, women, and children, some well-dressed, some shabby, and all with the same yearning expression, all looking at us well-dressed, well-nourished people from America. It seemed they looked at me in particular as if to say, "Why are you coming to Europe, which is so full of war and misery, when you have the wonderful freedom, the wonderful privileges and the wonderful money and everything that goes with it in America?" I was sorry for them, but also glad that I could go back to that wonderful America. Many people came to this place every day, hoping that by some miracle they could get on the plane and fly away from Europe and the heavy sound of war.

Mr. Pascal took charge of me in Lisbon. He was staying at the Ritz with some friends. It was hot and I remembered the nearby Estoril at the sea. Could he get me a room at the big hotel there? He could and we arranged to meet there for dinner. I swam in the ocean and felt fresh and renewed. I must have been the last tadpole to have left the sea. It has always washed me clean of unhappiness.

Lisbon and the Estoril were swarming with spies of all nationalities—German spies, Russian, Italian, American, English spies, and there was a tangible cloak-and-dagger atmosphere. After dinner, in the Casino, Pascal introduced to me the chief Italian spy, a youngish handsome elegantly dressed man who said, "Didn't we meet in Hollywood?" He had worked there as an actor. He was probably a bad actor and in any case, I had never heard of him. It all seemed totally unreal, not only the spies but the prosperous men and women with the same greedy look of gamblers all over the world, in war and peace. The fact of being with Italian and German spies who were at war with England did not frighten or disgust me. But when I was in Lisbon again, for the return journey, I would not have talked to a German or Italian if my life had been at stake. Having been in England and seen the very real suffering and deprivation of the war, Coventry, the dreadful bombing of the East End of London and the dock areas of all the big seaports, I too hated the Germans and the Italians.

After some roulette, Mr. Pascal took a group of us to a night club. While the rest of them danced I talked in an anteroom with Pascal, or rather, he was talking, telling me how great he was. "I am the greatest producer in the world. I am the most attractive man in the world." Then, still declaiming, he put his hand on my knee. After a few seconds of wary attention, I flung it off. He looked at me with great scorn and said, "You should be flattered that I touch you." I decided I would try for my interview with Shaw without troubling Mr. Pascal any further.

The takeoff to London was at midnight, in absolute darkness. The windows were covered with heavy black material, and no one spoke. It was like a spy film. In the darkness I tried to swallow two sleeping pills with my saliva, but they remained lodged in my throat and I slept badly. The other passengers were mostly British soldiers and officers coming home for rest or reorientation from the Egyptian campaign. We all more or less awoke at the same time. Those near the windows pushed the black curtains aside. It was morning and we could see land below. "We are over Dorsetshire," said a happy English voice. I was nauseated from the undigested sleeping pills and was horribly embarrassed, after landing, to throw up everything I had eaten for the past week, it seemed. Feeling weak, but much better, I allowed the pleasant officer who had sat next to me in the seaplane to put me on the train to London. We made a date to dine there that evening.

Waterloo Station was full of men and women in uniform. Very few children—most of them had been sent to the country when the heavy raids had started. There was one line of late starters getting into a train with some cheerful-looking teachers. Some of the children looked depressed; their small and big bundles seemed sad and defiant.

I had decided to stay at the International Sportsmen's Club, where I used to play squash rackets with Donegall and swim and ice-skate with Jack Mitford, Judith Hurt and her Etonian friends. Now there was no water in the pool and no ice in the rink. The large lounge and all the rooms had black curtains behind the heavy damask drapes, and notices everywhere urged great caution in keeping out every chink of light. A message in the bathroom advised, politely, to please use only six inches of water. It was comforting to find the same porters and the same ancient elevator men who had been there when I first joined the club in the early thirties. They smiled at me and seemed delighted to have me back. There was something new in their attitude— an equality with the members that was not there before the war. This must be true when officers and GIs go into battle together. The possibility of death makes all men equal. I wondered if there would be an air raid that night.

There was a note from my former fiancé, with a telephone number in the country. But I did not call him. I was exhilarated at being in London. It was summer and warm and the twilight was long. The young officer called for me at about nine o'clock. I remember how hard it was to get a taxi and the ghostly voices in the night calling "Taxi, taxi." All night long—"Taxi, taxi." There were few taxis because gasoline was strictly rationed.

We dined at the Berkeley, where I had gone with Judith and Jock and the Earl of this and that, and the gentle people of my happy years in London. There were no waiters, and some of the waitresses looked as if they'd been slapped together with spit. I asked our sloppy-looking girl for some lemon with the fish. She glared at me with great contempt and said, "Don'tcha know there's a war on?" I was properly reprimanded, although I did not know that you could not get a lemon for all the gold in the Bank of England.

After the meager meal, I walked down Piccadilly with the officer. It was a different world without cars or lights. The black darkness was soft and strangely familiar with the rustle of clothes and footsteps and the laughter of soldiers and their girls and the prostitutes with dimmed flashlights to show their faces. Glowworms in the dark night. It was an enchanted city which I did not want to leave because I would never find it again. I can still feel the magic of my first day and night in wartime London, with the strange covering of captive balloons in the sky, traps for low-flying German planes. Later the nights became less fascinating and the moon, lighting up London for German pilots with their mission to kill, even less so.

Johnny had asked to meet me. But I had written him, "There are no definite flight schedules and if you expect me and I don't arrive, you'll be in misery wondering what has happened." I had not seen Johnny since the summer of

1937, but we had written to each other several times a week, and when business went sour for him on occasion, I gladly helped him. But not once in the hundreds of letters did I mention Scott Fitzgerald or that I was in love with him. This would have distressed Johnny, would perhaps have made him feel lonely and abandoned. In a letter two months after Scott died, I wrote him, "There isn't much to report at my end. Life goes on just the same. Reading, work, tennis. I am getting very good at the latter. Rather bored with the middle, and with reading, still very excited and interested. I am reading Plutarch's 'Lives' and Gibbon's 'Rome' and I am fascinated with history and politics. I wish I'd had the sense to go in for this during my idle years in London, and had employed a tutor to give me a thorough groundwork in these subjects. Now I am getting it the harder way —reading alone, although until recently I had the help of an awfully nice man, but he died just before Christmas." That had been my only reference to Scott.

Johnny, happy to have me in England again, came to London every weekend. Now in his mid-fifties, he was graying but looked trim in his uniform. I was pleased when I saw soldiers of lesser rank saluting him. When we were married we used to walk all over London, and now we walked and walked. Chelsea—the house we had lived in before I had gone to America in 1933 was a bombed ruin. Wigmore Street—the apartment, our first home, furnished by Drage on the Hire Purchase Plan had also fallen to the German bombs. There was hardly a street without damage from bombs, and it seemed that all the churches and public houses were empty shells—perhaps because they were usually on corners. I was dazed by so much destruction and I hated the Germans and could not understand how I had ever liked any of them.

The Sunday after my arrival I telephoned Lord Donegall. He came in from the country and we had dinner that night. Don was kind as always, and sympathetic about Scott. The old dream of being a marchioness, of belonging to the British aristocracy, was again possible. "I have the chapel," Don continued, mentioning the private chapel on one of the big estates of England, owned by one of his friends. He was sure we would be happy. If we had waited a year, I would have agreed with him. But this was too soon after Scott's death, and he reminded me too much of Scott. He had the same gentle thoughtfulness and could put away a drink or two as well. I realized he was under great strain. Everyone I met in England was under terrible strain from lack of food and lack of sleep, owing to the continual air raids, although there was now some respite in the summer of 1941. The Russians were now under attack, reeling and falling back while the Luftwaffe polluted Soviet skies.

I wondered how it would be with my first air raid, and the raid was not long in coming. Niles Trammell, then head of NBC in America, knew of my job in London from John Wheeler and he sent a request to Fred Bates at NBC London for me to give my impressions of England at war on one of his daily radio reports. This was about a week after I had arrived. I talked of my lunch with my friends, the Paul Willerts. Someone from the country had sent them two small pigeons, and I was eating a whole one. While I was picking at it, I looked at their plates and to my complete embarrassment realized they had only *half* a pigeon each. And I don't even like pigeons. I talked about British matter-of-fact courage and my impressions of the incredibly hard work by the women in the factories I had visited. Donegall had come along to the broadcast and I was glad to have him with me. It was pleasant to be looked after.

It was about 11:30 and we were planning to have supper at the Dorchester. As we entered the foyer, the quietness was cut by the *whoo-ooo* wail of the sirens. An air raid! I was too stimulated for eating and remained in the lounge. Middle-aged and old people emerged in their dressing gowns and settled into armchairs. Don told me this was normal procedure when there was a raid. Some, not all, of the hotel guests would leave their rooms and come downstairs where there was less danger from the glass of shattered windows. Only a few went to the shelter in the basement, and these people were somewhat despised.

Don asked me, "How would you like to watch the raid from the roof?" "I'd rather not," I replied. I did not want to sound afraid, and strangely, I was not afraid. The idea that I was actually in an air raid I found quite thrilling. And besides, no one else seemed afraid—merely resigned. Nonetheless I was glad to be inside when I heard the loud drone of planes. "Theirs," said Don somberly. The thud of bombs. "Our planes." But what really frightened me was the crashingly loud *bang, banggg* of the antiaircraft guns in Hyde Park across the street.

When the All Clear siren sounded, I accompanied Don

to the roof. The darkness was punctured with many fires and I remembered Ed Murrow's broadcast and his strong beautiful voice saying, "London is burning." I had listened to that one with Scott and he had mimicked with awed excitement—"London is burning."

I was pleased when Don said, "You behaved very well for your first raid." I was less brave with my second. I was in Leeds, to visit some factories where women made parts for tanks. My room at the hotel was on the top floor. As I opened my door the air-raid warning sounded. Without waiting for the elevator, I ran, in absolute panic, down all seven flights of stairs, sure that unless I reached the bottom before the siren stopped its screeching I would be killed.

❧ CHAPTER FIVE

NOTHING has been so easy in my journalistic career as getting the interview with George Bernard Shaw on the occasion of his eighty-fifth birthday. I merely picked up the phone in my room at the International Sportsmen's Club and telephoned the Shaw residence in Ayot St. Lawrence, Hertfordshire. His secretary, Miss Patch, was most sympathetic. "Dear me, you've come all the way from America? Of course you will have your interview. Just put your questions in a letter. Mr. Shaw will answer them and I'll post them back to you." This was too easy. I made it more difficult. "I'm visiting some people in your neighborhood this afternoon," I told her. "I'll *bring* the questions." This was fine with Miss Patch, but I could not see Mr. Shaw. I understood. I did not trust the mails and I wanted to be sure.

I waited a few days and called Miss Patch. She sounded happy. "I was just going to post the interview." Still not trusting the erratic wartime mails, I told her, "I have to see my friends in your neighborhood again." Again I rented a car and drove to the rather ugly house in Ayot St. Lawrence.

Miss Patch was quite excited. "This is your lucky day. I told Mr. Shaw you were coming and he will see you." I was unprepared. *My God, what should I say to him?* I followed her into a sitting room lined with books and, hoping for some ideas, frantically read over my questions and his answers.

Q. Have you any suggestion as to what should be done with Hitler when England has defeated Germany?

A. The Germans may have settled that before the defeat is consummated. What is more, Hitler will be defeated, if at all, by the British Commonwealth, plus the U.S.A., plus the U.S.S.R.; and they will all have a say in the matter. If he falls into our hands we shall have to keep him in protective and perhaps preventive custody. We can do no worse to him because we declared war on him, not he on us; so he must be treated as a prisoner of war. But if the Poles or Czechs get hold of him first, heaven help him!

Q. How close to the line dividing them has the war brought the ruling (moneyed) class of England and the poor (working-man) class? And, if close to the line, will it last after the war?

A. There is no change. Nowadays England is like America: the division is between incomes; and the test is intermarriage. The daughter of a duke can seek a husband at a ball given by a millionaire shopkeeper; and her brother can seek a rich wife there. When I was a child, shopkeepers and dukes could not be on speaking terms except across the counter. But the class division is more insurmountable than ever because the extremes of income are farther apart. In my youth $50,000 a year was wealth beyond the dreams of avarice. Today its possessors are ranked by multimillionaires as poor devils.

Q. What sort of Socialism, if any, will there be after the war?

A. There is only one sort of genuine Socialism: the democratic sort, by which I mean the organization of society for the benefit of the whole people. There is a bastard Socialism which has arisen through the demonstration by the Socialists that the most productive system is the amalgamation of all the private capitals into single national trusts with State organization of labor and State provision of new capital. The profits are enormous; but they are distributed in the old way; the lion's share to the shareholders and landlord, and to the proletariat as little as it can live on. There will be plenty of that after the war. It will provide the industrial machinery for real Socialism, but also a greatly increased power to suppress it.

Q. How long do you think it will be before England and Russia are actually friendly with each other?

A. I suppose you mean how long will it be before the

capitalist newspapers stop lying about Russia; I don't know. There is no other obstacle to reciprocal friendliness.

If only I could think of something else to ask him. But my mind was a blank. "I can't wait," I told the astonished Miss Patch, and that was the cue, of course, for Mr. Shaw's entrance.

Walking very slowly, in came this tall feeble gaunt old man with his white beard and white hair. He gave me the same feeling I once had in Spain, when I saw hundreds of dropping wax candles in an old, very dark stone church—not of distaste, nor of fear, but a desire to be warmed by the sun. His face was so pale, so transparent, a translucent pink, you could almost see what was going on behind it. I thought he might die with a sigh. His eyes, underneath overhanging white, scattered eyebrows, regarded me severely. He looked so old, so feeble, and yet he lived another nine years.

While he waited for me to speak, I thought, For heaven's sake, what can I ask this man? Desperately, I repeated my first question in the written interview: What should be done to Hitler when we win the war? Shaw gestured impatiently, "No, no. Don't add anything to what I have written. You'll only spoil it." Good, I'm not supposed to ask any questions. I'll try to be politely social. I told him about my friend Eddie Mayer, who worshiped him. Eddie had written to Shaw, who had replied most graciously. But he did not remember Eddie at all, which made our brief interview even more ghastly. I got away as fast as I could, but not before Mr. Shaw, who must have felt sorry for me, and now seemed less annoyed, took me into the garden, pointing out the tomatoes, carrots, and lettuce he grew for his meatless diet.

I sent my story to NANA. I was glad I had not failed in my first assignment.

✞ CHAPTER SIX

LORD BEAVERBROOK invited me to lunch, just the two of us, in his suite of rooms in the big Shell Building off the Strand. He had recently left the Air Ministry to become Minister of Supply; his job was what it sounded like, to supply the various departments of war with the matériel needed for tanks, guns, planes, everything vital for the war effort.

Some officials were in his office, but Beaverbrook left them brusquely to shake my hand, and before telling me to wait, turned to a general, introduced me, and said, "She's an American journalist. This is how they turn 'em out in the States." When they had gone, lunch was served in the same room.

"You should stay in England, the country needs the tonic of pretty women," he told me, helping me to the Australian tongue, lettuce "from Cherkley" (his country home), cherries, and "wine from Alsace." Everything uneaten was put back in the icebox. His man came in from time to time: *Mr. Churchill wishes to speak to you . . . Lady Ashley . . . Sir Walter . . . Lady Castlerosse . . .* Beaverbrook subjected me to a barrage of questions and statements. "America will come into the war . . . I can tell America things. They will take it from me because I am a Canadian." And talking of his birthplace, New Brunswick: "I am without any question of doubt her most famous son. . . . Are you a serious reporter? . . . Do you go to night clubs? . . . Are you in love? . . . Are you an isolationist?" When he was Minister of Air, he once interrupted a serious discussion with a group of high officials to ask his number-one aide, "Ever had a woman, Westbrook?"

He told me that in his sixty-two years, the ladies whom he admired had cost him a lot of time. I added, "And trouble and money?" "I don't mind the time, I don't mind the money, but if I'd entered a monastery as a boy, I'd have saved myself a lot of trouble," he replied. After lunch we sat in the sun on the small circular terrace overlooking the river. "When the war is over," he said, "I'm going to retire." "But you like power," I reminded him. "I shall probably be Governor of Bermuda," he said, "or Nassau. The climate there is good for my asthma. The British climate is a great trial to me." I thought he looked remarkably well, still like a mischievous Kewpie doll, although somewhat more wizened. He saw me to the elevator and invited me to lunch at Cherkley on Sunday.

I was picked up at the International Sportsmen's Club in Lord Beaverbrook's large Rolls Royce. I sat between his Lordship and Billy Rootes of the car firm. Sir Walter Leyton was in front with the chauffeur. During the drive, Sir Walter pointed to some iron park railings and said, "We could use those." "Tear them all down," replied Beaverbrook. A few days later, I read that all park railings in London were to go to the Ministry of Supply—Berkeley Square, Grosvenor Square, Hyde Park, all the squares of London were to lose their iron railings. I liked them better open.

During lunch, Beaverbrook talked of his grandfather, a Scottish minister who preached the gospel and migrated to Canada. "He was a great preacher, a bad moneymaker." He told us that Cherkley was a meeting place for bygone Liberals. Gladstone had been a frequent visitor.

Herbert Morrison, the Laborite, who was then Home Secretary in Churchill's nonpartisan cabinet, sat at my left. He got into an argument over steel priorities with Beaverbrook. The Beaver wanted steel for tanks. Morrison needed it for air-raid shelters. The argument became heated and all of us, except Beaverbrook, were embarrassed and looked down at our plates. At the end of the rather tense meal, my host asked me, the only woman present, to leave them. They went out to one side of the large uncut lawn and I wandered away. I half expected a fistfight, and was relieved to hear laughter.

At another visit to Cherkley, for dinner, there was again an altercation at table. The guests included Aneurin Bevan and his attractive dark-eyed wife, Jennie Lee, both members of Parliament. Bevan accused Beaverbrook of unorthodox tactics in the running of his ministry. "As long as I produce figures, I will have the British public behind me," snapped Beaverbrook. "You won't have after I have finished with you," replied Bevan. The Beaver jumped to his feet angrily and said, "I won't be threatened at my own dinner table." They all calmed down. But the Beaver's stomach whistled—his asthma, he explained. He could make it whistle at will to force sympathy from his friends and foes.

To fill in the awkward silence, I said to Beaverbrook, "It's funny, I read so much about you in the American press, but practically nothing in the English papers." This apparently rankled, because after dinner he produced a stack of British press cuttings and said to me, "Weren't you the person who said there was nothing about me in the English press?" He turned to his guests. "This girl has been making fun of me for ten years." If I had, it was because I was really in tremendous awe of him, but I knew he despised Yes-men so I was perky and provocative, hoping to amuse him without making him angry. He was a kind man. He had helped a Jewish girl leave Austria when Hitler took over. She telephoned Cherkley that evening. She was ill and he gave instructions for her care. "You're sweet," I told him. He laughed and said, "No one's ever said I was sweet. I've been called a great man, but never a sweet man."

Lord Beaverbrook was very proud of his son, Max Aitken, an officer in the R.A.F. He showed me a big iron swastika "from a Messerschmitt brought down by my son." He referred to him continually as "my magnificent son . . . my glorious son." His pride was understandable. Flying Officer, later Group Captain, Aitken had defended England in the dark sky to the utmost of his endurance and beyond. He had accounted for dozens of German planes and was amazingly brave. It was told that one time he had taken off to Germany on an unauthorized daylight raid "to rest his eyes."

Beaverbrook was against the blackout. "The darkness makes no difference to the German flyers; they know exactly where everything is." When his beautiful home in London, Stornaway House, was reduced to rubble by the raiders, he believed it had been done deliberately to kill him. "I'm glad it was bombed," he related philosophically. "Now I don't have to pay taxes on it, or ground rent."

It was getting a little embarrassing with my ex-fiancé. He had camped on my doorstep, so to speak, from the time of my arrival. I liked him but I wanted to see other people and in fact had to because of my job. There was the Sunday he wanted to drive me to the country to visit some friends. I put him off with the excuse that I had a luncheon date with Lord Beaverbrook. Actually I had promised Alec Waugh to spend the afternoon with the Countess of Jersey, formerly Virginia Cherill and once married to Cary Grant. She was having a luncheon at her home in Hampton Court for some Polish flyers—she was godmother of their squadron —and Alec thought this would make an interesting story for me. The Poles in exile were the most reckless of all the flyers. They went on the most dangerous missions, flying so low they almost brushed the roofs of the factories they were bombing. They had an all-consuming hatred of the Germans for the shambles they had made of Poland.

Afterwards, Alec took me on the Thames in a small boat and punted with a long pole while I trailed my hand in the sun-warmed rippling water. In spite of the uniforms everywhere, including Alec's, it was hard for me to realize that England was at war.

Quentin Reynolds invited me to a dinner party he gave in the big restaurant at the Savoy. My ex-fiancé happened to be there, spotted us, and Quentin asked him over. He had had a few drinks and he quarreled with me. He had heard of my lunch at Hampton Court—"Beaverbrook," he said to me angrily, "you said you were going to Beaverbrook's. Why did you lie?" Why did I lie? Why do most women lie when they do not wish to hurt a man's feelings?

I had been surprised to find that Quentin, whom I had seen quite frequently when I first came to New York, was, next to Winston Churchill, the most popular man in England. Quentin had been invited to speak on the nine o'clock Sunday broadcast on B.B.C. to which everyone listened, and on the advice of Arthur Christiansen, the editor of the *Daily Express*, he started his radio talk with, "Dear Mr. Schicklegruber," Hitler's real name. All of England was laughing. For Hitler to be really Schicklegruber was somehow ridiculous. It broke the tension.

Quentin had received congratulations from Churchill himself and was a guest at 10 Downing Street and at Chartwell, Churchill's country home in Kent. He was quoted frequently in the English papers and with great affection. Quentin was living at the Savoy, where the American correspondents gathered every evening in the bar. I dropped by most evenings to learn the latest news of the German drive which was penetrating ever deeper into Russia.

Important Americans were always coming to London. Dorothy Thompson had arrived the same day I had. She was treated like royalty. The British needed American help, and they gave the molders of American opinion, newspaper publishers and political columnists, the best they had—and when the British treat you well, no one in the world treats you so well. This was reflected in the stories the Americans wrote or told when they went back home.

Albert Victor Alexander, the First Lord of the Admiralty, and Brendan Bracken, the Minister of Information, gave the Baltimore *Sun* publisher, Paul Patterson, a dinner at the Savoy in a private room downstairs. The *Sun* used my column and I was invited. I wore my gray dress with the deep crimson jacket that I had worn when I first talked with Scott at the Writer's Dinner in July 1937.

We made speeches and toasted one another. Walter Monkton, an important British Government official, toasted me for wearing a gay red jacket in the midst of such a drab war. The First Lord of the Admiralty had a piano wheeled in, and we stood around it, my arm entwined in Mr. Monkton's, and sang "A Bicycle Built for Two," "Tipperary," and "Knees Up, Mother Brown." It was a wonderful party and I admired the British more than ever that they could forget the war and have simple fun, as they were having in that basement room in the Savoy Hotel.

I was very busy. Among many others, I interviewed Lady Asquith, widow of the man who had been Prime Minister at the beginning of the First World War. At that time, I had been a child in an orphanage, and it gave me satisfaction to be Lady Asquith's luncheon hostess that day. Frail, gray-haired, she seemed to have shrunk to almost nothing. But she had a healthy appetite. She lived in a top-floor flat in Bloomsbury and when I asked, "Do you come downstairs during the raids?" she snorted, "I do not. I would never allow that dreadful man [meaning Hitler] to make me leave my home."

Lady Astor, in her drawing room in St. James Square, went off on a tangent about the percentage of babies that died in childbirth in America. This annoyed her very much, as of course it would anyone. I asked her how she found time to do so many things and she told me something I have found to be true: "If you want something done, ask a busy person." But there was an unpleasant repercussion to the Lady Astor interview. I was having dinner with Alec Waugh at Grosvenor House—grouse, a fine change from the dull rations—when I was paged. Lady Astor was on the phone.

She had been sent our interview and was absolutely furious and denied everything about the stillborn babies. I was worried when she said, "I don't believe you should be allowed to go back to America. I shall have your exit visa revoked." I knew then that I did want to go back to America.

At the beginning in London I had thought that perhaps I would stay, but now I knew I would not. I wanted to return to New York, but not as soon as John Wheeler was demanding.

Quentin Reynolds and several of the American correspondents were leaving for the battlefront in Russia and I wanted to go with them. I discussed this with Drew Middleton

who was then with the Associated Press. He told me whom
to contact at the Russian Embassy. If it were a *fait ac-
compli*, I was sure John Wheeler would approve. But he
cabled me to return to New York at once. The Duke and
Duchess of Windsor were expected in Washington for their
first visit to America since their marriage. This was a big
story. He wanted me to cover it. And then I had a telephone
call that was to change my whole life.

❦ CHAPTER SEVEN

I'M giving a cocktail party," said Jack Bergen, with his
normal buoyant urgency. "Be sure to come, there's a man
I want you to meet." It was early September and Jack had
arrived from America that day—via bomber. As president
of Grumman Aircraft, he had frequent business with the
British Government during the war. He was staying at
Claridge's Hotel, with other important American businessmen, rich refugees from Hitler's Europe, well-to-do Brit-
ishers who had been bombed out of their homes or who
could not cope with rationed, servantless, heatless, uncomfortable wartime England. Also Captain Clark Gable and
several throneless kings. The story went that if you ate in
your room at Claridge's you might get an ounce more meat.
And if you were very lucky, an occasional egg for breakfast.
And if you were *really* lucky, the egg would be fresh.

Jack's sitting room was bright with flowers. There weren't
many flowers being grown, and Jack must have had most of
them. On a side table was a goodly display of liquor, very
expensive during the war—most of the whiskey was exported
to America for precious dollars. Jack introduced me to his
other guests—two middle-aged British businessmen, an
American girl in uniform, a tall thin American from the
Embassy. Jack was gay, telling us of the bouncy trip by
bomber. I told him of the air-raids and of my interviews
and experiences throughout the country. Then the telephone
rang, and it was Trevor Westbrook. "Come over right away,"
Jack boomed enthusiastically. It seemed only minutes later
that Mr. Westbrook arrived, and he was eager to meet this
girl whom Jack had written him about. He sat next to me
and took stock. He obviously liked my blond hair and green

eyes. He was also aware of my silk print dress, nylon stockings and smartly styled shoes. It was not being fair to clothes-rationed Englishwomen, but I enjoyed the advantage. Four hours later he said I had the prettiest teeth and the nicest smile he had ever seen and he nicknamed me "Smiler."

Trevor Westbrook was fairly tall, slim, black-haired, dark-eyed, with very high cheekbones. He looked Spanish. He had been right-hand man at the Air Ministry to Lord Beaverbrook, who once told him, "This war will be won by three Brooks—Tobruk [the North Africa campaign], Westbrook, and Beaverbrook." Trevor had just returned from a special mission to the Middle East for Churchill. His report had castigated several army officials, one of whom had to pass on the accusations for censorship. This was Trevor Westbrook, solid citizen, blunt, honest, truthful to the verge of tactlessness. His family had lived in Clapham, the home of Harriet Westbrook who, more than a hundred years earlier, had married Percy Bysshe Shelley. On his mother's side there was Portuguese ancestry. He was sixteen when his father, a well-known doctor, had died. There was no money for further education, and Trevor worked as an apprentice in the aircraft section at Vickers-Armstrong. By the age of twenty-eight he had climbed to the position of manager of all aircraft production. Trevor never wasted time on pleasantries, and the true story was told that when the Vickers chairman, Sir Charles Craven, had wanted to visit his busy manager, he had found his entry barred on several occasions by an electric gadget Trevor worked from his desk to keep his door closed, thereby infuriating Sir Charles. When Trevor refused to accept an executive he considered incompetent, he was fired. An unprecedented situation arose. The men went on strike, demanding Trevor's reinstatement. The publicity of the strike brought Trevor and his fine record to Beaverbrook's attention. Trevor had produced the Spitfire over top echelon opposition; the maneuverability of the Spitfire was credited with saving England in the Battle of Britain. Trevor was Beaverbrook's kind of man. He got things done, he did not ever accept "No" for an answer. I liked Trevor immediately. He was the antithesis of Scott. There was nothing about him to remind me of the past four years.

The others left, and there was Jack Bergen, Trevor and me, and Jack took us to dinner, downstairs, at the 400 Club. The upper part had been destroyed, Donegall had told me

—"I was going upstairs and met the gentlemen's cloakroom coming down."

Afterwards Trevor drove me in his Bentley car to the International Sportsmen's Club. He parked opposite the club and we talked for about an hour, and I thought, This man would never get drunk. A girl could lean on a man like this.

I had only two weeks left in London and I saw Trevor every day. I enjoyed being called "Smiler," although I didn't realize I was smiling. He said once, "I don't have time to read books," and even that had charm for me. It was so different from Scott, whom I had to forget. It was pleasant having Trevor drive me to my assignments when they were in the neighborhood of factories where he had business, and he seemed to have business wherever I did.

A few days before I was to leave England, we lunched at Claridge's. While I was sipping my coffee, Trevor took out a small jewel box from his pocket. It contained a diamond ring. I put my coffee cup down and stared at the ring and at Trevor. "I want you to have it," he said casually. I was surprised, it *was* so sudden. Recovering, I smiled flirtatiously and asked, "Which finger do you want me to put it on?"

"You can put it on any finger you like."

"Is this a proposal?"

"If you like." I put it on my engagement finger. It was a nice ring and glittered expensively. "If I don't marry you," I promised archly, "I'll give it to you back."

"I don't want it back."

I liked him enormously and was very much intrigued with the unexpected situation. But I did not know whether I was in love with him. Perhaps that would develop.

On the way out of the restaurant I stopped to talk to C. B. Cochran, the producer of my musical-comedy days. What a change had taken place. There was still the ruddy intelligent smiling face, but he was crippled with arthritis and was walking slowly with the aid of two canes. He seemed delighted to see me. He told me he was living with his wife, Evelyn, at the Hinds Head Inn near Maidenhead, just outside of London. "You will telephone me?" he asked wistfully. I did not because I had no time, but I wished I had later when I heard of his tragic death. He was scalded by boiling water in his bathtub; he was too stiff with arthritis to move up to turn off the tap.

I was going to Bristol by train, then by seaplane to Lisbon. I had a last lunch with Donegall. I was sorry to say good-bye to him. He had helped me with my assignments and he had been extremely kind. I knew he would always be a good friend. Trevor drove me to the station. We walked up and down the platform awaiting the train. He held my hand and said, "I shouldn't let you go. I should keep you here." If he had said, "I *won't* let you go," I would not have gone. We'd have been married in England and perhaps we might still be together today. But he wasn't sure and I wasn't sure.

I had arranged to meet Johnny *on* the train. That was the only way I could see him on that last day. He got off at the next stop, but I had a half hour with him to listen to his plans and problems. Johnny mentioned that he had won a thousand pounds in the Irish Sweepstake and I was de-lighted. His pre-war business had evaporated when he joined the Army.

Bristol was a shock. The entire center of the city had disappeared into flat rubble. It was most depressing. I was lonely and glad to leave the next day. From Lisbon I flew back to New York in the same Pan American Clipper, and the same envious people were at the quay, wishing they could go with us.

I had had some worthwhile experiences in England. I had added to my reputation as a journalist. I was semi-engaged to Trevor Westbrook. I was not sure we would marry, but I smiled often in the plane thinking of him, and looked fre-quently at his ring on my engagement finger. I wondered what I would find in the new life awaiting me in New York.

❧ CHAPTER EIGHT

I RENTED a furnished apartment at the Shoreham Hotel on West 55th Street. It had a kitchen in a cupboard, a bedroom and a small living room, and I started life again. I saw a great deal of Margaret Brainard, my first woman friend in America. Eddie Mayer was now living in the East. Also Buff Cobb, who had looked after me in California when Scott died. Roland Young, whom I had met with Robert Benchley at the Garden of Allah in Hollywood, came in frequently at cocktail time.

I met Abel Green of *Variety*—he lived in the apartment house next door with his wife, Grace. I wrote articles for him about my experiences in England. And I worked as a roving reporter for the North American Newspaper Alliance. I went to Montreal and wrote about the pilots who ferried war planes to Britain, and met Madeline Carroll's French ferry-pilot husband for whom she had divorced Sterling Hayden. I went to Baltimore and wrote a story on Glenn Martin and his aviation plant. I went to Washington to cover the visit of the Duke and Duchess of Windsor. And I was very bored, and very lonely. I missed England and I missed Trevor. I felt that I was foolish not to have stayed there and married him. He was writing to me all the time, sending me cables, and I thought, I *am* in love with him. I talked interminably about Trevor to Abel Green, extolling his virtues, and one day Abel said, "Why don't you marry him?" I thought perhaps he doesn't believe there *is* a Trevor. And *is* there a Trevor? Everything seemed dreary in New York. I was back where I had started in 1933, and I was miserable.

In late November, John Wheeler took me to the Ritz-Carlton on Madison Avenue to meet Harold Ross, the editor of *The New Yorker*, and his wife, Ariane. She was a beautiful, blue-eyed blonde in a lovely white dress, and I thought, How lucky she is to be loved and cherished. I felt like Gertrude Stein's Melanctha, blue, awfully blue. It was while I was feeling so sorry for myself that John Wheeler said, "That's a god-awful hat you're wearing." I burst into tears, rushed into the street, crossing and recrossing Madison Avenue, not watching the traffic, not caring what happened to me. Who cared whether I lived or died? I went back to the Shoreham and sobbed. My world was a mess—what should I do?

The next morning I came to a decision. I am always more optimistic in the morning. I realized I needed a rest. John Wheeler was angry when I called him. "I'm going to Florida for three weeks," I announced. "You don't have to pay for this vacation"—although I had not had any vacation that year. He took me at my word, and unsalaried for the first time in eight years, I flew to Florida. It was warm there and a little rain was falling and there was the sea.

My large comfortably furnished room at the Cromwell Hotel overlooked the ocean, and I was happy. The next day, a beautiful day, I swam and lay in the sun. The season had not yet begun and Miami was uncrowded and quiet. I played tennis every day with the Pro at the Roney-Plaza Hotel. In the evening the hotel was full of officers who came over from the Navy base, among them Al Wright, whom I had known in Hollywood when he worked for *Time* Magazine. Al was an admirer of Scott Fitzgerald's writings, and he now included me in his worship of Scott. I would have liked to stay in Florida forever, but my three weeks were up and I went back to New York and to reality.

It was the beginning of December, and I was desperate about the approaching first anniversary of Scott's death. New York was freezing and I caught a severe cold. Everything seemed to be falling apart again and I was like a trapped animal as the December 21st date came nearer. I simply did not know what to do about it.

America was now at war with Japan, Germany and their assorted allies. I heard the news at a concert in Carnegie Hall, Sunday, December 7th. At the end of the concert, a man came on stage and said, "Ladies and gentlemen. The Japanese have bombed Pearl Harbor. We are at war." I was having dinner that night with Al Wright, who was on Navy leave, and the John O'Haras. Instead of dinner with Al and the O'Haras, I took Al to the airport to fly to his base in California to report for active duty.

The clock tolled the days to the anniversary of Scott's death. My colored maid from Jamaica did not understand why I was weeping, but she wanted me to feel better. "Don't worry," she said. "It can't be that bad. Everything will be all right, you'll see." "I don't know what to do," I said to her stranger's face, and as I walked aimlessly from the bedroom to the living room and back, I cried soundlessly, "Dear God, help me." And God, who always listens to me although I don't always deserve it, heard my despair and immediately took care of the matter.

"You must go to Washington at once," John Wheeler said on the phone. "Churchill and Beaverbrook are in Washington for conferences with President Roosevelt. You should be able to get some good interviews. You must leave immediately." Trevor Westbrook was one of the government officials who had come to Washington with Winston Churchill and Lord Beaverbrook.

I stayed at the Mayflower Hotel, where Beaverbrook, Trevor Westbrook and most of the English visitors were staying. (Churchill was at the British Embassy.) They had all come over in a secret new battleship, H.M.S. *George the Fifth*, and they would return to England on the same ship. Trevor gave me a front-page news story to use after they had returned. The battleship had been protected by a string of destroyers all along the route to America, but in one area, off Egypt, the convoys had confused their instructions. For 24 hours, Winston Churchill and all the top members of the British Government had been unconvoyed and completely unprotected, except for the ship's own guns. What a target they would have made for a U-boat. How fortunate that the Germans did not know this.

Trevor asked me to marry him and I said yes. "I don't know how long I will be in Washington," he told me. We decided to marry immediately, in Arlington, Virginia, just over the bridge from Washington. "When I'm back in England I'll arrange for you to fly over," Trevor promised. I was in a pleasant haze and stifled the small voice that asked, *Am I marrying Trevor because I cannot face the anniversary of Scott's death?* Trevor was aware of my doubts and we almost called it off. But we had the license, the ring, and the blood tests. And we were both desperately anxious to belong to each other. The next day, with God knows what witnesses, we were married by a very inebriated justice of the peace. After the rambling ceremony, the judge said he must make an important telephone call. We caught one sentence: "Yes, a case." For years I wasn't sure whether we were really legally married.

I was the only passenger on the plane back to New York. The captain sent me a note signed by the crew members: *We understand that you have had the ship to yourself. We hope you are enjoying your flight.* I was. I looked at my slim platinum wedding ring, and I thought, I will make a success of this marriage. I will be a good wife to Trevor Westbrook. Trevor is a good man. I will make him happy. I could be a better wife to Trevor for having known Scott.

Trevor called me from Washington two days after our marriage, using our code signal to explain he would be leaving in a few days. No movements of battleships could be mentioned on the telephone. He came to New York for a day and a night before he left, and stayed with me at the Shoreham. We attended a party at the Pierre Hotel with the Jack Bergens, and I was in a strange cocoon of unreality. I was married to a man I hardly knew. I respected him, and he gave me a wonderfully warm feeling of protection. I was not on the outside anymore. I too was cherished and loved, and it was legal. I would give up my job and fly to England as soon as Trevor had cleared the red tape and made the arrangements. I cabled him: I AM LONGING TO BE WITH YOU. And then the miracle happened.

❦ CHAPTER NINE

I was feeling rather strange, a lassitude, a floating vaguely through space. I was not functioning on all my cylinders. One morning I had to sit suddenly, I felt so dizzy. Of course I knew all about babies and how women were dizzy and fainted—but I was sterile. I had seen this on Dr. Rubin's note pad one time when he had left the room. I turned it around and read: PRIMARY STERILITY.

I had met Dr. Rubin in 1933, soon after my arrival in New York from London. Mrs. Donald Stralem, a wealthy society woman, convinced that she could not have children, had adopted a girl on the advice of Dr. Rubin. Then, as frequently happens, Mrs. Stralem became pregnant. She told me that Dr. Rubin had safely delivered Alice Roosevelt Longworth of a baby after many years of a childless marriage. I was married to Johnny then and we had hoped to have children.

Now I visited Dr. Rubin again and said, "Something seems to be the matter with me. It can't be a baby because I'm sterile." He replied, "Perhaps we'd better find out." He took the usual test—if the rabbit died you were pregnant—and it would take several days to know the answer. I was certain I was not pregnant, but I was still feeling most peculiar. I thought, Good Lord! Perhaps there's something really serious the matter with me. I tried to forget the whole thing, but I could not dismiss the growing suspicion that I was with child.

"You'd better come in," said Dr. Rubin gravely when I called for news of the report. "Am I pregnant?" I asked, my heart pounding. "You'd better come in," he repeated. Obviously not, I thought, and there *is* something the matter.

Dr. Rubin was out, but his nurse was there. She was glum and seemed to avoid looking at me. I'd better learn the bad news. Very casually, "Well, I suppose the test was nega-

tive." In a dull, unemotional voice, she replied, "No, it was
positive." I jumped so high I almost hit the ceiling. Positive!
I was pregnant. The miracle of miracles had happened.
Primary sterility—who cared what that meant now? This
was the most exciting, fantastic miracle. I almost said aloud,
"Wouldn't Scott be pleased." I had told him once how much
I wanted a child. Obviously, he had talked to the big-shots
in heaven and said, "Give her a baby." I had felt so incomplete when my friends in London and America had
babies. Charwomen had babies, everybody had babies, it
seemed, and now I too would undergo this tremendous experience. Sound the trumpets, and Hallelujah, and thank
you, God—and Trevor.

Dr. Rubin cautioned me, "You must be very careful,
you're not twenty, you know."

"Don't worry," I promised fervently, "every step I take will
be a careful one. Do you think I should cancel my flight to
England?"

He considered for a moment, then said, "The first three
months you could lose a baby with traveling and too much
excitement."

"Then I won't travel. I'm not taking *any* chances of losing
this baby."

I wanted a boy who would look like Scott, which certainly
was not fair to Trevor. I knew that some women who have
longed for children often lose interest in the father as soon
as they become pregnant or as soon as they have the child.
This did not happen with me. I was full of gratitude toward
Trevor for his part in this miracle. But I had been to England and I knew the possibilities of invasion and bombing,
and I was not going to lose my baby. I cabled the wonderful news to Trevor and I metaphorically sat down to hatch
my egg and I took no chances.

Trevor had concluded arrangements with the British Government for me to fly to London, but I was firm. "No, the
doctor has advised me not to travel at this time."

I continued with my job, which was now mostly reviewing
plays for NANA and interviewing celebrities in New York
City. It was impossible for Trevor to send money out of
England because of the strict regulations. It was a difficult
time. I became nauseated easily, especially in the morning.
The smell of coffee was unbearable. Dr. Rubin chided me,
"When a woman wants a baby as much as you have, there

is usually no nausea. I can't understand it." I smiled sickeningly.

I was interested in every aspect of having a baby. I wrote to the Department of Health in Washington for all the pamphlets. I bought every book I could find on expectant motherhood. I was the only woman in the world who was ever having a baby. I think I had an idiotic grin on my face for all of the nine months.

All the time, I was getting letters and phone calls from friends of Trevor's who were in New York, urging me to come back to England. He wanted me with him. He wanted to take care of me. He wanted me to rest.

Lord Beaverbrook came to New York in May and invited me to his suite at the Waldorf. "Trevor asked me to use my 'considerable powers of persuasion' to have you come back."

"I just cannot take a chance of losing this baby," I told him. "The one doctor I trust in all the world is Dr. Rubin. I know he won't let anything happen to me or the baby. Please tell Trevor I will come after the baby is born."

He relayed my message, and Trevor accepted it with good grace.

"How long can you keep working?" Trevor wrote. He had managed to borrow two thousand dollars from a New York friend, to see me through when the time came. He repaid this after the war. The baby was due in September. I could work until the end of June. I might have gone on longer, but I almost fainted while interviewing the principal of a charm school. I looked forward to the rest.

I began to read again. I reread the books Scott had given me. To give them a home—there were about 300 books—I moved from the Shoreham to an apartment at 1045 Park Avenue. It was a happy time, but lonely. I did not know many people in New York and I've always been a loner. Bing Crosby had a hit that year—something about St. Jo . . . and wherever the four winds blow. I still feel lonely and nauseated when I hear this song. I went to the movies a great deal and there were times when I wished I was like most women who had a husband with them at this time. But I had chosen to carry the happy burden alone.

At the end of June I went to the Sea-Spray Inn by the ocean at Easthampton. I met some attractive women there, women whose husbands worked in faraway cities while their wives and children vacationed in the sun. They wondered about me. They thought it was strange that here I was, expecting a baby (I was quite large) and my husband was in England. But it was wartime and these things happened in the war. They were kind and they made a fuss over me—one especially, a Mrs. Richardson, who asked me all about Los Angeles because she was going there to live in the fall. In the afternoons, I walked slowly into the town of Easthampton with its attractive little shops. People eyed me curiously, such a pregnant woman—and alone. But my chief thought was, Be careful of the baby, make it strong. In the evenings I sometimes went to the movies with Mrs. Richardson, but mostly I took slow walks along the tree-shaded streets, with the honeysuckle strong on the night air. And I was content.

❦ CHAPTER TEN

SCOTTIE FITZGERALD came to Easthampton for two week-ends. We had an exquisite dinner with the Gerald Murphys in their charming house on a cliff overlooking the ocean. Scottie was in love, she told me, with "Jack" Samuel Lanahan, and they wanted to marry, but the immediate outlook was not hopeful. He was in the Navy and had shipped out somewhere from San Francisco. Young Lanahan could have been hand-picked by Scott for a son-in-law. He was very good-looking, an ex-Princetonian, and from an old, wealthy family in Baltimore. It occurred to me that had Scott been around, he might have hampered the romance. Scott always wanted to make every situation more enchanting. But he was unable to cope when things went wrong. Scottie was handling her life very capably. She was now working for *The New Yorker*, writing the "Tables for Two" column and signing it F.S. for Frances Scott. She took me back to New York early in August and we laughed when some college boys at the Easthampton station, regarding my size, sang the popular song, "Jingle, Jangle, Jingle, I'm Glad that I Am Single." Scottie was as happy as I was about the baby.

"It's such good news," she had said when I first told her. "Really, I am *so* happy about the baby and I know it will be simply adorable. I've got my knitting needles out of mothballs and I'm madly making tiny garments." Scottie at once appointed herself godmother to the expected infant.

The following spring she became Mrs. Samuel Lanahan

the Third, while Jack was home on leave. It gave me enormous pleasure to buy her wedding gown and some other things I thought she might need. In a letter she wrote soon after:

> I want to thank you again for your superb wedding present—all this and the wedding dress too? Of course I used the charming little suitcase on what I laughingly call my honeymoon [two days]. . . . I have just read *Tender Is the Night*, having been sick in bed for a week with grippe. I found it a most remarkable work of art giving one much on which to think, although I am not entirely convinced of its validity. . . . Lately I have been doing much thinking about Daddy because I've had to go through reams and reams of correspondence before turning the impersonal part over to the Princeton Library. It has been absorbing, especially the letters from Hemingway, the Murphys, and Bunny Wilson, but has left me so confused I doubt whether I shall ever completely know him. I can't figure out whether he was wise or foolish, rational or irrational, etc., etc. and would like very much to talk to you about him some more very soon. The further away from me it gets the more curious I become to really understand him as a person, not as a father I didn't get along with.

On September 10, 1942, I was dining with some Easthampton friends in my apartment when a rhythmic contraction in the top center of my abdomen began to interest me. I thought, Of course, this has to happen when I'm eating. It's the same on planes. As soon as they serve the food, the weather invariably gets bumpy. I surreptitiously glanced at my watch and timed these fairly strong upheavals. They were coming at intervals of five minutes. But I was not panicky. "You will know the baby is coming when your back feels like it's breaking," Margaret Brainard had replied to my incessant questioning during one of our gin rummy sessions.

One of my guests said, rather nervously, "Don't you think you should call your doctor?" I reassured her with a smile and a stiff British upper lip, "Oh, no. It isn't time yet; my back doesn't feel like it's breaking." When the interval between the contractions was reduced to three minutes, I was persuaded to call Dr. Rubin. Terrifyingly, he was unreach-

ble. He had been lecturing in Virginia and was on a train
returning overnight to New York. I talked with his associate.
I described what was happening, adding, "But I don't
think this is it. My back feels fine." He replied, casually,
"Well, I have to go to the hospital right now; why don't
you meet me there, in let's say, one minute?"

I had a problem. While I have done some dangerous
things in my life—looping the loop in an open plane, speeding down the Bob Run at St. Moritz sandwiched between the
Lanfranci Brothers, which facts I never fail to tell my children when they accuse me of cowardice—the fact is that I
am horribly allergic to physical pain. I am known among
my friends as a Grade-A sissy.

I had already caused enough smiles with my ultra-careful-
ness during the pregnancy, and the one thing I wished to
avoid was going into the hospital too soon. I promised to
meet the doctor there on condition that this was merely a
consultation, that he would not keep me there unless absolutely necessary.

My bag was packed—I had read those pamphlets—and my
dinner guests and I walked the ten blocks to the Lenox Hill
Hospital. After a brief inspection, I was rushed to the ante-
chamber next to the delivery room, where the nurse gave me
a sedative and laughed when I said, "You're sure I won't
sleep through it all?" "Don't worry, you won't," she promised
grimly and left me. There was a telephone at hand and I
immediately called Margaret. She shrieked when I explained
where I was. "My God, the baby must be coming any
minute." "But my back isn't breaking," I reminded her.
"Never mind your back," she spat out. "Relax, be calm,
don't worry." "I'm not," said I, dropping off to sleep almost
at once.

When I awakened, it was light. I looked at my watch as
I always do. Eight o'clock. Then I remembered. The baby.
Did I sleep through it all? No. I was just as big as ever.
And I was in a different room. The doctor had played a
trick on me. He had kept me in the hospital overnight
and Margaret and the others would laugh. I called Doctor
Rubin, who had now arrived at his home. He was surprised to find me in the hospital and he was there almost
before I put the phone down.

Was I having any pain? No. Contractions? Not now. He
was kind, but skeptical. "Why don't you get dressed," he
suggested, "and go to a movie." "And have all my friends

laugh at me? Never!" I wailed. "Then what do you want me to do?" he asked, gentle as always. "Operate," I said in a wavering voice.

A few months previously, after an examination, Dr. Rubin had told me that because of an earlier operation I might have to have a Caesarian. I reminded him of this. "It's always better to have a natural birth," he replied. "But why did you mention a Caesarian?" I persisted. "Is that what you want?" He was holding my agitated hands. I hesitated, then thought of the laughter. I nodded. He turned to the nurse. "We'll operate at three." If they had not, my daughter Wendy would have been stillborn, and I might have died. The cord was wrapped twice around her neck and she had just about stopped breathing. They never did find the placenta. It was a tense moment after the birth, I was told later, the pediatrician breathing into the baby's mouth while Dr. Rubin sewed me up, asking all the time, "Is she breathing, is she breathing?" Lord, I have thought of other women who do not have a Dr. Rubin, a doctor flexible enough to be swayed by the whim of a patient; other women who wake up from that long nine months to learn there is no baby. Some women love their psychiatrist. I will always love Dr. Rubin, who, with a stroke of his surgeon's scalpel, gave me a life in depth, a second and deeper savoring of all the satisfactions and all the gradations of giving and receiving.

❦ CHAPTER ELEVEN

WHEN the children were small, I had a dream that Satan or God or some unearthly spirit gave me a choice—I could have Scott Fitzgerald back in return for my children. No, no, I shouted, and woke up, terrified, and rushed to see if Wendy and Rob were still there. I could imagine Scott smiling reassuringly and saying, "Sheilo, there is no contest."

He was right. These children were mine. They would belong to me for all time. So many people I had loved had left me. My mother had died before I was eighteen. My father took to his grave when I was eleven months old. Even Scott had left me. I had been quite angry about that. It had been cruel of him to die after teaching me how to love without reservation, without thought of tomorrow. He had been so fiercely possessive, greedy for my every thought, my every possibility as a human being. And when he died, he took it all with him, leaving me utterly destitute. No, there was no contest. All the love and devotion for Scott, all the anxiety, the fear, the obsessive concern over him, all the energy that had been consumed in my grief over his death, now belonged to my children—poor things.

I was terrified of my firstborn, Wendy, the most beautiful girl ever to yell her heart out in the maternity ward at the Lenox Hill Hospital on Park Avenue, New York City. She is definitely the Park Avenue type. I have taught her to like the good things of life, materially and intellectually. I was poor as a child and I have tried to give her everything I did not have.

When Wendy was born, I expected a surge of mother love to flood my heart and I would know at once the proper way to behave. Nothing of the kind. When the German nurse placed her for the first time in my tautened arms, Wendy opened her eyes and for a six-pound, seventeen-and-a-half-inch bundle let out a shriek that Zsa Zsa Gabor being attacked by a poor man would have been proud of. "Take her," I begged the nurse. I didn't hate her. But I didn't like her. Was I going to be an unnatural mother? I felt absolutely no relationship between the baby and myself. Had they switched infants? The nurse, a florid, blond middle-aged woman, assured me that the baby was mine—hadn't I noticed the necklace of beads around her wrist with WEST-BROOK spelled out? "Yes, yes," I said hastily, but to make sure the strange package would go away, I said, "I'm tired, I'll try to sleep." They departed, leaving me to ponder this unexpected anticlimax. Were other women lying when they talked of their children? Was this nature's supreme trick, to make you want children, then to welch on the built-in love that was supposed to come with it? Who, where, and what was Wendy Westbrook? Why didn't I love her? I had planned to call her Penelope—Mrs. Ulysses had all those suitors. But a Penelope should be tall and blond. Wendy was tiny and brunette.

The next day, we tried again. Wendy was wide-awake and yelling again. But I was feeling a bit stronger and with detachment I studied the volcano in my arms. It was cute, with a black Japanese haircut and quite clearly de-

fined eyebrows. But not my type, I decided. After a few
softer sobs, the mouth closed, and if it had had any teeth,
they would have been clenched. The face was suddenly
quite red, there was the tiniest grunt, the eyes closed and
it was sleeping. The nurse found me smiling and I smiled
every time I awakened that night, thinking of her red face
and the little grunt. How funny it had been. She was human!
She was my baby, and I smiled and laughed and loved her
more than I had loved anyone before. I would kill anyone
who hurt one hair on her Japanese head.

I hired a nurse, a stocky, grizzled woman, and she loved
new babies and New York. She visited me twice in the
hospital and bought a woolly gift for Wendy—she loved her
at sight because, of all new babies, this one looked the
newest and the smallest. She called her "Mousie" right away
and it was a long time before we could rub that out.

Wendy, the nurse and I were ensconced in a suite at
the Surrey Hotel; my lease at 1045 Park Avenue had expired.
The nurse slept on a folding bed in the living room, near
Wendy in her small basket. I spent most of my time in
bed. I would remain in New York for six weeks and then we
would fly to California. It would be better for Wendy to be
in a warm climate until the spring. England was still at
war, and the prospect of the dark heatless winter was unthinkable for this beautiful bundle I had produced so miracu-
lously. I had used up the dollars Trevor had borrowed.
Money could still not be exported from England, and it was
necessary for me to resume my column. Trevor was disappointed but, always trying to please me, conceded that
perhaps I was right.

I never tired of watching the nurse dress and undress
the baby, and oil her like a precious machine. I breathed
over her shoulder when she sterilized the bottles and made
the formula. I took notes on everything she did, even the
simplest preparation, such as—*Put clean towel on table.*
I wrote down everything just in case the nurse had a heart
attack and I would be left all alone with the baby. This
was the most sterilized baby. The nurse would not allow
my friends to come within two feet of her, and even then
they had to wear a mask.

The nurse loved candy. I could put her in a good humor
any time of the day or night by feeding her candy. She'd
had all her teeth removed so she would not have to bother
with cavities caused by candy. With her false molars, she

could chomp away at chocolate and cake all day without interrupting visits to the dentist.

There was a glorious pastry shop on Madison Avenue, about a half a block from the Surrey Hotel. It was a nice day and I was taking a brief walk. I was not wearing my glasses, and without them I'm quite blind, but I thought the baby carriage outside the pastry shop was familiar. I went closer and there was my daughter, all alone on Madison Avenue where anyone could have snatched her or the carriage, or both. I was still weak from the operation, and I fainted dead away.

The noise and the crowd caused the nurse inside the shop—she enjoyed disasters—to hold up her candy and cake spree and come out to investigate. Have you noticed that nurses always love accidents? This one would tell me the most gory stories of cooks who fought with butlers while they chased them with knives in the kitchen. When I revived on that pavement, as white as her uniform, I gasped, "Don't ever do that to us again." "But I was looking at Mousie all the time," she protested. "From now on," I promised her, "*I* will buy all your cake and candy." I was so angry I had to close my mouth tight or I would have fired her there and then.

John Wheeler warned me against flying to California. "People in the war effort have top priorities—you'll be thrown off the plane." "Pessimist," I jeered. "I'm always lucky." But at 4 A.M. in the morning, when we landed at Fort Worth, the nurse, the baby and I—with a large laundry bag on each wrist, one for used diapers, one for fresh, and holding the enamel sterilizing pan with both hands—were put off the plane. We did not know when, if ever, we would get out of Fort Worth. We were five days getting to Los Angeles. The strain of it gave me a stiff neck for weeks.

Until I could find a house for us, I took a bungalow at the Garden of Allah, where I had first seen Scott Fitzgerald. We did not stay there very long. It was too noisy. The nurse complained continually about the loud, sometimes tipsy writers who clattered around the pool in the late afternoon and at night. She was also quite worried about Errol Flynn in a nearby bungalow. She did not trust his being so close to my six-week-old daughter. And it was altogether too expensive.

I rented a house in the 200 block on South Palm Drive,

on the wrong side of the tracks in Beverly Hills—everything below Santa Monica Boulevard in Beverly Hills is the wrong side of the tracks. My landlord was Mr. Tutwiler, a short, rotund, eager-to-please retired businessman who lived with his wife in the other house he owned, across the road. Our new home, built at the height of the imitation-Spanish era in Hollywood, featured wooden grill bars, busy archways all over the place, and a painted peacock on my bathroom tiles. In the living room, the heavy beams hung like a ponderous dark forest from the ceiling.

Mr. Tutwiler was delighted to have a minor celebrity and her baby daughter for his tenants. But his joy was of short duration. I cannot blame my nurse for all the torture we inflicted on poor Tut—I did my share and more. I was surely the most apprehensive mother in all recorded history.

Early in the war all the Japanese gardeners in Los Angeles had been interned. We had a small plot of grass in the backyard and a few bits of shrubbery in the front patio. In the goodness of his unsuspecting heart, Mr. Tutwiler offered to do the gardening. My nurse at once geared for battle. The first time he came to do the watering, she hissed in his hearing, "The dampness will kill Mousie." Naturally alarmed, I said to the startled Tutwiler, "Perhaps you could water after lunch, while Wendy is asleep?" "Oh no," the nurse said funereally, "the dampness will still be in the atmosphere and Mousie will catch cold." Mr. Tutwiler, quite bewildered, suggested, "Perhaps I should water at night when your daughter is asleep?" we grudgingly consented, and Tut would come over stealthily, sometimes near midnight, to do his watering.

My nurse decided to dislike the oranges I bought at the market. She sniffed and sneered. "All the best California oranges go to New York City. These oranges do not have vitamins." To me, an orange is an orange is an orange, but it was unthinkable for Wendy to be robbed of her vitamins. I had a happy inspiration. Hedda Hopper's radio show was sponsored by Sunkist oranges. I called her and when I gave my name, she asked briskly, "What can I do for you?" Rather hesitantly, I began, "I have a baby, and my nurse says the oranges in California lack vitamins." I sounded ridiculous even to myself. "Could your sponsors send me a case of the oranges that usually go to New York, which, of course—" in a rush—"I will pay for?" Taken aback by this unexpected request, she answered briefly, "I'll see what I can do." I never heard from her again on the subject.

Sleep, said the nurse, was more important for a baby than food or even breathing. She convinced me something terrible would happen to Wendy if she did not get her right amount of sleep—about 22 hours a day in those early weeks. It was a major catastrophe when noise in the neighborhood awakened the baby.

On our first afternoon in the new home, shortly after Wendy was put to sleep for her long nap, the merry clang of the Good Humor Man's bells awakened her and she at once went into her favorite sport—screaming. The nurse emitted a stream of dire prophecies through the candy she was munching, and stated, "You've got to stop those bells." "I will," I promised grimly.

The next afternoon, I was on the mark like a sprinter for a race. As soon as I heard the first faint sound of bells blocks away, I raced up the street, caught up with the Good Humor Man, and shouted dramatically, "Stop." He seemed surprised that I needed ice cream in such a hurry, and even more so when I explained, "I have a baby and your bells wake her up. Please turn them off before you pass my house." He regarded me as though I were some kind of nut. "I can't do that," he said severely, "I have to sell my ice cream." "Then," I replied, "I will make sure that everyone in this neighborhood boycotts your ice cream." I was going to save my daughter from whatever it was she would catch even if I had to ruin the Good Humor man.

After a few days of all sorts of threats, the vendor of ice cream compromised. About a block away, he would turn his bells down. Sometimes there was a new man who did not know about the crazy woman who lived on his route, but pretty soon all the Good Humor Men knew about me and most were as good-humored as their product and diminished the bells.

I must have been the joke and certainly I was the pest of the neighborhood. The houses were very close together, and Wendy's bedroom was on the side of the house where my next-door neighbors had their living room. Every Tuesday night at .7:30, they tuned in on the Bob Hope Radio Show and they made sure they could hear it in every room *and* their backyard. Obviously, something had to be done. And I did it.

I have always prided myself on my letters and my understanding of the mentality of the person to whom I am writing. I wrote my neighbors a charming letter. I told them about my daughter, how old she was and that she wasn't getting her sleep. I ended with, "Bob Hope is a friend of mine, and while I'm sure he would appreciate your enjoyment of his program, the fact that it is keeping my daughter awake would upset him very much." I mailed the letter, certain that everything would now be all right— and received back a real stinker. The gist of it: I should either move my daughter's room, or I should go back to England where I came from. The next Tuesday, the Bob Hope Show *really* blared, and not only was Wendy awake until 8:30 P.M., but my impotent anger prevented *me* from sleeping until quite late, not until I had tiptoed into Wendy's room and she was sleeping as sweetly as a madonna, despite the shattering racket from the snoring of the nurse.

❦ CHAPTER TWELVE

THERE had been many changes in my year and a half away from Hollywood. Directors of top caliber—John Ford, Willie Wyler, George Stevens—were in the Army or Navy making war documentaries for the government. Laurence Olivier and his wife, Vivien Leigh, had been among the first of the British colony to return to England. Olivier had taken flying instruction in California to be ready to enlist in the R.A.F. as soon as he landed. David Niven had preceded him in '39, impatiently finishing his *Raffles* film for Sam Goldwyn. Scott had told me how David had pleaded with Goldwyn at the outbreak of war between England and Germany, "For God's sake, let me go now." Sam had insisted, "You must finish *Raffles* first." Richard Greene was rushed to England by some of the older English actors. They felt guilty at not going themselves, and I believed, as did Richard, that they were sending him as a sop to their conscience.

Some of the top stars were gone. Jimmy Stewart had enlisted as a private in the Air Force. He told me later, when he was an officer, "What I hated most about being a private was the lack of privacy." Clark Gable had joined up soon after Carole Lombard's tragic plane crash. Robert

Montgomery was in a high-ranking position in the Navy, as was Douglas Fairbanks, Jr. Lew Ayres was in disgrace and seemingly ruined for his stand as a conscientious objector. In the war in the Pacific, Lew was to prove his courage in the front-line medical corps. Bob Hope, Eddie Cantor, Jack Benny, and Jimmy Durante were entertaining the GIs in camps. And Cary Grant gave most of his picture salary to war charities.

Some new stars had emerged while I had been in England and New York—Robert Mitchum and Alan Ladd. I had interviewed Alan in New York in the spring of 1942 after his hit in *This Gun for Hire*. Mitchum, with his unlikely face for a movie star, was to make stardom in *The Story of GI Joe* for Lester Cowan, who had given Scott his last job—the movie script of *Babylon Revisited*. A blond bombshell, Betty Hutton, had exploded in the Hollywood heavens. And all the mothers of America were sighing soulfully over a freckled redhead with an engaging smile, Van Johnson. Newcomer Gene Kelly was dancing up a storm in *Me and My Gal*. Dan Dailey had left a promising film career for the Army. Victor Mature had said good-bye to Rita Hayworth and was guarding America in the Coast Guard. William Holden's promising start in *Golden Boy* had been interrupted by the Army, which had taken him and another promising young man, Glenn Ford. They were quite sure the war would prove fatal to their careers in Hollywood. Gray hair among the men became quite fashionable. It was easier than explaining why they were civilians.

The beach homes at Santa Monica and Malibu were sold for a song. They were too far away for the limited gasoline ration. The prices of houses in town spiraled to the skies. My housekeeper, more courageous in these matters than I, bought houses and sold them for a profit without moving in. One house I vaguely considered buying was $25,000 one week, $47,000 the next. It was a time of great prosperity in Hollywood. Every picture was a hit, and the studios vibrated with activity.

My column was printed seven days a week and I visited the studios every working day. Claude Rains, on a sound stage at Universal, asked about Wendy and said, "My wife is jealous of you for having known Scott Fitzgerald." He saw the tears and said, with great kindness, "There are all sorts of compensations, aren't there?" But my chief recollections of that time are of leaving the film studios in the late afternoon, speeding to Wendy in our small house on South Palm Drive. I remember the thought, I am so anxious to get back to her, and she doesn't know who I am.

It was Mrs. Richardson's idea that I should return to England to be with my husband. "You owe it to him," she insisted. "You're out of your mind," I replied. "How could I leave Wendy?"

The rich, fashionable Helene Richardson had come to Los Angeles as she had promised when I was expecting Wendy at Easthampton. She was petite, slender, a beautiful brunette and the wife of an Eastern industrialist. She called on us with a silver drinking cup "from John," her six-month-old son. She had one other child, a boy of fifteen at school in the East. A girl of two had died. This elegant woman had rented a big modern house in Bel Air. She visited us frequently and was eager to help at all times. I liked her very much.

At Easter, Mrs. Richardson invited me to Palm Springs. She was taking her son and nurse. "It will do you good to get away from Wendy for a few days. She's an obsession with you." Wendy was now six months old. For the first time since she was born, I left her. I was more and more miserable with every mile on the drive to Palm Springs, with Mrs. Richardson at the wheel of her white Cadillac convertible. I tried to be gay at dinner at the Racket Club that night. I joked with host Charlie Farrell, chatted with William Powell, who called me "Gams" Graham, but my heart was heavy.

The next day I told Helene that I simply must return home. I could not stand another night away from Wendy. What if there had been a fire? What if Wendy were ill? I had left the nurse my number, but she might have lost it. "Why don't you call her?" she suggested. I did, but it seemed to me that the nurse was evasive. "I have to go back," I told Mrs. Richardson. She was exasperated, but I was adamant.

It was a long, tedious trip by train, and my heart was thudding as the taxi stopped at the house on Palm Drive. I raced inside. Wendy was sniffling. She had a cold. I glared at the nurse. I thought, the first time I leave her, she neglects the baby. I was not being fair. The nurse had taken tremendous care of Wendy—too much, perhaps, but that was better than too little.

A month later I thanked the nurse for her care of Miss Mousie. "I know you don't like California. I'm sure the housekeeper and I between us can manage." She was glad to go home.

When the nurse actually left I was somewhat apprehensive. Was it a mistake? No, we could manage. A few weeks previously I had hired Stella, a housekeeper who had worked for Frank McHugh for nine years. She was a good cook, patient, and she loved Wendy. Stella prepared the first nurseless meal for me. I cradled Wendy in my arms and she was a heavenly bundle. No nonsense now, this child is going to eat. The cruel infant knew I was worried, and she simply would not eat.

I tried everything. I wore a bright belt, and tied all sorts of things on to it—a rattle, a bell, and Wendy's favorite toy, a small wooden "little man." I gyrated around and around (this is a good stomach exercise), and craftily, as soon as her mouth opened, I plunged the spoon in, and she swallowed the food while watching the cast of characters on the belt and all the delightful noises they were making. When that palled, I made all kinds of silly faces, or laughed and sang. I did anything and everything to make her eat. The nurse had merely taken two hours for four ounces of milk. I seemed to be feeding her all day.

There was the dreadful morning when Wendy, after whimpering most of the night, awakened with a temperature of 103, and the milk and food came up as soon as it went in. Oh, why had I let the nurse go! The doctor arrived soon after my frantic call. There was a virus epidemic, he told me. High temperature, vomiting, diarrhea. It was Saturday and Stella was off. In the evening when the diaper service had not come, I called—there had been a fire. "All of the diapers were destroyed." At ten that night, with not a clean diaper in the house, and with no washing machine, and sobbing with exhaustion and rage, I washed, by hand, 50 very soiled diapers.

It was getting harder to find eggs, bacon, vegetables and fruit in the markets. On the few occasions that I dined in restaurants I ordered oranges and raw eggs and took them home for Wendy. Mrs. Richardson had no shortages. Her basement bulged with canned foods, sides of bacon, cereals —everything for the well-nourished child. She introduced me to her adoring butcher and I was able to get some meat.

But there, as everywhere, there were long queues. Life was getting inconvenient on the home front. And we did our share of grumbling.

I drifted through the days, looking after Wendy, writing my column, sending Trevor our news and promising to come soon to England. But summer was almost over and Wendy would be a year old September 11th, and I was still in Beverly Hills. Jack Bergen was in California visiting Walter Pidgeon. They both brought presents for Wendy, and Jack asked, "When will you go back to England?"

"You *should* go back," Mrs. Richardson persisted. She was vehement about my not taking Wendy. "Why, anything could happen to her over there. *I* will take care of her while you are away." One day in late September I capitulated. I wrote Trevor that I would come to England alone, that I was leaving Wendy with Mrs. Richardson. He replied, advising me to bring Wendy: "I am sure you will be miserable without her." No, Mrs. Richardson was right. I could not bring Wendy to England. I had been there. I knew how difficult it was.

I returned to England in October 1943—I would stay for the winter and learn the worst of the air raids, of conditions, of food and heating, and if it was at all tolerable, I would return to California in the spring and bring Wendy to England. I would go by plane and return by boat to decide which was the best way for my daughter.

No one, especially Stella, believed I would actually go. They knew how my entire life revolved around Wendy and they thought I would not have the courage to leave her. But Trevor had been so patient. I had to give our marriage a chance. We had had so little time together.

✿ CHAPTER THIRTEEN

ENGLAND was different in the winter of 1943. The war had entered a more victorious phase for the Allies. There would be a tomorrow after all. So no more living it up. Let's save today because tomorrow we will live. People were angry, depressed and unspeakably bored with the war.

I had flown courtesy of the British Government from Baltimore to Newfoundland, to Shannon in Ireland, then somewhere to the south of England where Trevor was waiting for me when we landed, waving and smiling behind the wire fence when I passed him on the way to customs. It was good to see this solid sincere man again after an interval of nearly two years. I would try not to miss Wendy too much. I would devote myself to this virtual stranger I had married.

We rented a small Mayfair apartment on Hill Street. I cooked, shopped, and waited patiently in long queues, turning in my ration stamps for the ever-decreasing portions of food—two pints of milk per person a week, about six ounces of meat a week, theoretically two eggs a week, but there weren't any. The fish, when you could get it, was often smelly and inedible. The seas around England were mined —it was dangerous for fishermen, and transportation was uncertain. We were all dedicated to one shop—the butcher, the baker, the candlestick-maker. Large families were better off than small. Several six ounces of meat per person added up to a small roast for Sunday. To fill up, we ate quantities of spaghetti, potatoes, and the gray bread, and we all gained weight.

Johnny was now out of the Army. As younger men were trained and recruited, older men were released, and Johnny was back in London trying to get his business going again. When, after four tries, I finally succeeded in making a cake, I sent half of it to Johnny.

I did not telephone or see Beaverbrook this time. I was on leave-of-absence from NANA. I wanted to be the complete wife, only concerned with Trevor—who left home early, while it was still dark, and returned for dinner sometimes as late as nine o'clock. Dinner was mostly macaroni, with a thin grating of cheese, which I baked in the small British gas cooker.

I hoped that Trevor and I would have another baby. To help matters along, soon after I arrived I visited a doctor on Harley Street, explained I was anxious to have another child and could he do something to speed things up? He gave me some instructions and some hormone pills. It occurred to me that if these pills were potent enough to hasten having a baby, perhaps Trevor should take them as well. Trevor is always open to new ideas, and on my assurances, he took the pills. One night not long after, he awakened in great pain. His chest was hurting and I could see his breasts were swollen. "Could it be those pills you gave me?" he asked. "Perhaps—Oh, dear!" I replied. I called the doctor in the morning and he said, "My God, you didn't give him the pills? These are *female* hormone pills. What are you trying to do to him? Turn your husband into a woman?"

Donegall was living in an apartment on Mount Street with his wife, Jean Coombe, a pretty brunette. They had married a few months after my marriage to Trevor. The Donegalls had us to dinner. Don discussed airplanes with Trevor, but we were somewhat constrained and it did not lessen the awkwardness when I was suddenly nauseated. They thought I was pregnant, but in spite of all the pills and instructions, I was not.

I had little to do in the daytime and I volunteered as a nurse's aide at the Great Ormond Street Hospital for Children. My job was to feed some of the small patients who were so ill with rheumatic fever they were not allowed to move even a finger.

I also worked in a day nursery. The mothers brought the children in the morning and left them while they worked in war factories. There was one tiny girl, pale and terribly thin. I think she was three years old, but she weighed only 20 pounds. She became my pet. I used all my clothes coupons to buy her a red velvet dress with matching coat, leggings and bonnet. The assistant head nurse complained that I was spoiling her. But the fragment of a girl reminded me of Wendy, who had been so tiny when she was born. It was heartbreaking, the thinness of this mite who, when she saw me, always stretched out her arms for me to hold her.

Jack Mitford and his sister, Iris, were living in London in a flat near Marble Arch. They invited us for dinner, and, just as we were leaving, an air raid started. It seemed that every night, whenever we were about to go out, the siren would shriek its mournful message. I took as long as I possibly could getting ready. I was afraid, as I am sure everyone else was, but only cowards admitted this and as far as I could see, there were no English cowards except me. Trevor was impatient at my delaying tactics and snapped, "Come on. Hurry up." We weren't getting along too well.

The raid was in full blast as we went out, and the noise from the guns in Hyde Park was deafening. It was hard to find Jack's flat in the blackout. "Wait here while I look," said Trevor. I cowered in a doorway, shaking in rhythm to the *bang, bang, bannnggg* of the guns. No one could see me and I allowed myself to tremble uncontrollably. When Trevor returned to say he had found the flat, I stopped shaking and tried to sound casual.

Dinner with Jack and his sister was more of a success than with the Donegalls. I was simply more at ease with the Mitfords, as was Trevor. I was touched at their sharing of their rationed food—some lamb cutlets. It was their entire meat ration for the week. Jack told me that their niece Unity Mitford, who had been so devoted to Hitler, was ill and living in Oxfordshire with her parents. Tom, dear handsome Tom, the only son and heir of Jack's brother, Lord Redesdale, was in the Army. He was to be killed on the last day of the war, blown to kingdom come by a land mine in Burma, I was told years later in Hollywood by his close friend and cousin, Randolph Churchill.

Trevor showed me a letter from a friend, the editor of an aviation magazine. It was a belated congratulation on our marriage. He had heard I was in England, and he would like to meet me. The letter ended with a half-serious suggestion: "Remember she is not an aeroplane, she is a woman, and no woman is perfect." I smiled because sometimes I felt that Trevor regarded me as a faulty plane and would have liked to send me back to the factory for a repair job.

Trevor was unused to having a wife, and I was not used to Trevor. He had worked hard all his life and had always demanded capacity performance from the people around him. He was now supervising production at the important De Havilland Aircraft factories. He was unhappy there, but he gave every ounce of his remarkable energy and dedication to the job. The long hours and the disagreements with some of the De Havilland executives made Trevor irritable sometimes. He was a controlled person and never gave in, but sometimes the strain was too much.

One evening we had a violent quarrel. We were getting on each other's nerves more and more. We simply did not understand one another. I was worrying about Wendy and Trevor was working too hard. The quarrel was about a lecture we were to attend at the British Museum. Trevor was tired after his long day at De Havilland's. He didn't really want to go. The phone rang. It was the friend who had informed us of the lecture. "Ask him what time it starts," I demanded of Trevor. When he did not, I repeated, "Ask him about the time." Trevor put the receiver down, shook his finger at me angrily, and said, "Look here, you must learn to behave." The waving finger seemed enormous and I wanted to bite it. Instead, I dropped the big Dickens book I had been reading with a loud thud on the floor, and rushed downstairs into the night. There was a raid on, as usual, and it was dark and noisy. I bumped into Irving Reis, a director I had known in Hollywood. I was crying, but he was too amazed at seeing me to notice. He was now in the Army making training films, he told me. He could not get over finding me like this, during an air raid in London. "Let's go to the 400 Club," he begged. I was tempted, but I thought of Trevor, alone in the flat. I knew he would be calmly washing the dishes and I said, "No, I must go back to my husband." I went upstairs and said I was sorry.

Trevor, like most Englishmen, remained friendly with girls he had courted before his marriage. One Sunday, he drove me to the country where, after visiting the manager of a plane factory, we had an early dinner with a former girl friend, a beautiful model now married to a doctor. Good-byes always take too long, but the long good-bye this particular evening saved our lives. If we had left just five seconds earlier, we should both have been killed.

❦ CHAPTER FOURTEEN

DRIVING toward London, Trevor told me that the Germans had attempted an invasion after Dunkirk. "All roads at danger points in Dover and Scotland were mined. Drums of petrol in tanks of water were set afire." I interrupted Trevor. "We seem to be going away from London." He explained that all road signs were purposely misleading so that German paratroopers dropping into the country would lose their way. He laughed and said that English people were also losing their way.

We saw red flares in the distance and heard the faint thud of guns. Trevor looked at the discolored sky with a practiced eye and said, "Hmmm, they're trying to get the Battersea Power Station. I'll take you home through Putney." But this night the Germans were trying to get Putney. Bombs were dropping all over the place as we raced across the bridge.

Suddenly the world rocked. A hundred feet in front of us, smoke and dust were rising from a large crater. Trevor neatly swerved the car. The noise was awful—explosions all around us, and the shudder and clatter of antiaircraft guns. This was no time to be brave. I crouched in the bottom of the car, which suddenly halted. Had we been hit? In a muffled, strangled voice, I said, "Why did you stop, Trevor? Go on, go on." He answered calmly, "There's a red light." What could I do? I sat up and took my place next to Trevor Westbrook, who has always epitomized to me the courage of his countrymen and the calmness of the British during danger.

The weeks of winter dragged on. It was cold, uncomfortable and exhausting from the continual air raids at night—as soon as one stopped, another began. I must admit when the sirens wailed, I put the covers over my head, stuffed my fingers in my ears and tried not to hear the awful Armageddon outside.

I loathed the blackout. It had been enchanting in the summer of 1941, but now in the dark winter, it was unbearably dreary. I have never been able to see well in the dark. Trevor had a flashlight but used it sparingly to save his batteries, which were in very short supply, and many times he had to save me from falling.

I knew I was not the good wife I had promised I would be to Trevor. I was moody and did not put myself out for his friends. I have always been shy with strangers and when they came, they would find me knitting, with my head down, absorbed in the clacking needles. It was my way of coping with the situation—knitting all the time. Trevor had wanted to show his friends the glamorous girl he had seen when he met me in England, and here I was, a sad homebody with a passion for knitting, not caring too much about how I looked.

After a few months of ill-concealed unhappiness, Trevor urged me to return to California. "Get Wendy," he said. "You'll never be happy in England without her." I was dubious. Could I ever be happy in England with Trevor? He had tried hard to please me, but the harder he tried, the more depressed I became. "I'll give you breakfast in bed," he said helpfully one morning. "No," I replied, "I like to make my own breakfast." And this is true, but I should have accepted the gracious gesture from a busy man.

I hated asking Trevor for money. I had been independent too long. I have worked all my life and have always spent the money I have earned, easily and without worrying. I *am* extravagant. I take taxis everywhere. I buy fruit out of season. I like expensive clothes. "But I gave you ten pounds last week," Trevor would protest when I asked for more money. "Where did it go?" I would try to explain, then give up with an irritated shake of the head. Oh, for a weekly paycheck again, which I could spend with no questions asked.

And all the time I worried about Wendy. Was she well? Was she happy? I was frantic when Stella wrote me she had visited Wendy at Mrs. Richardson's house, "And she has a bad cold and cries all the time. I am sure she misses you." I must get back to her somehow.

Trevor supplied the impetus. He came home one evening at about 9:30, and after manfully swallowing the tough stew I had spent the afternoon preparing, he revealed, "The Germans have a new kind of bomb. They will fire it from launching pads in France and it will hit London and a radius of eighteen miles. We will have no warning and no protection —there's nothing we can do except watch them drop. We would have had them before, but we've been bombing their launching sites."

I must go back to America. I must go back to Wendy, I can't stand this any longer. I wrote John Wheeler that I was returning and would he send me the letter I needed to obtain my exit visa. He replied, advising I could not have my column back, and in that case, "Shouldn't you remain in England?"

When I had left for London this second time during the war, Mr. Wheeler had hired Inga Arvad, a blond Scandinavian writer, to take my place, "only while you are gone," he had said reassuringly. As far as I had been concerned, she could have the job forever. I was a wife and a mother and that would be my career. He wanted to pay Inga a ridiculously low salary, which I told him was impossible. "She must have at least $100 a week or she won't be able to live in Hollywood." Inga had met Hitler in Germany before the war when he had tagged her the perfect Aryan type. She was popular in Hollywood. And popular with Mr. Wheeler because of the low salary he was paying her.

Without a letter from NANA, I could not return to America as I was still a British subject. Day after day I walked around the long Serpentine Lake in Hyde Park, or studied the big map of the world covering one wall in the apartment, trying to find a way out of my dilemma. I had to get back to Wendy, who seemed a million miles away. I wrote to Henry Snevily, Mr. Wheeler's associate, and explained as clearly as I could without sounding too frantic (all incoming and outgoing letters were opened and read by the censors) that he *had* to send for me. Dear Snev, who died not too long afterwards, wrote to the British Ministry of Information and requested an exit permit for me to return to America because I was needed back for my job.

I had kept to my plan and flown to England. I would return to New York by ship—testing both media to learn which was best for bringing Wendy to England. Despite the quarrels with Trevor, I still hoped that with Wendy in London we could be happy, the three of us. Trevor began negotiations to buy a lovely Tudor House near London. I asked, "Is it beyond the danger zone?" He assured me it was.

The R.M.S. *Queen Elizabeth*, the largest luxury liner in the world, had been almost ready for service when war was declared in 1939. Before completion, it had been transformed into a transport for troops. The huge ship was hidden from German reconnaissance planes in the heavy mists of a harbor in Scotland. Trevor came with me on the train to Glasgow. It was a long, cold daytime journey, and we had to bring our own food. Our conversation was strained. I tried to hide my joy at the prospect of seeing Wendy soon, and I tried to listen to Trevor's talk about his work. But as the wheels went 'round and 'round, they seemed to say, Will you ever come back? Will you ever come back?

A day out at sea, the ship's news broadcast told of the new bomb that was hitting London and the towns close by —the Buzz Bomb. I knew that Trevor would accept this new hardship with a fatalistic shrug, but I confess I was thankful to have escaped this latest horror of the war.

The voyage was rough. We took a course toward the North Pole to avoid the ever-waiting German submarines. Snow, sleet, and violent winds shook, rattled and rolled the R.M.S. *Queen Elizabeth*. There were no beds in the staterooms or any furniture, just army cots. The few women aboard, tweedy-type lecturers, were given various army ranks. They were mostly majors. I was a captain, and should have saluted them. But this was difficult, as I was in a prone position most of the time. The other passengers were wounded soldiers and sailors or men going back to Canada for rehabilitation and rest. The ship was a floating hospital and I was one of the patients. I have never been so seasick in my life. If I lifted my head an inch from the small, hard pillow, it was disastrous. There were no dining rooms as we know them on luxury liners, and no food served in the cabins. To stay alive, I would dash down to the large eating area in the very bottom of the ship when the loudspeaker announced the number of my particular mealtime, grab a ham sandwich or a roll and run back to my cabin, lie flat, eat, and then lose it again.

I heard the guns on the top deck booming in the frequent practice drills. The daily and very necessary lifeboat drills I could never attend, and I prayed we would not be engaged in mortal battle.

Near the end of our ten days at sea, I managed to get up on deck and saw what I had been missing—literally thousands of young and slightly older men who whistled as I staggered around. I looked curiously at the German names carved on the handrail by prisoners of war who had been transported on previous voyages to camps in Canada.

The officers gave a cocktail party on the last evening aboard and invited the five or six women. We had drinks and canapes and the officers sang a song they had composed: "There Ain't No Toilet Paper on the Largest Ship in the World." It was too true.

Our boat docked at 3 A.M. There were Red Cross workers with hot coffee and doughnuts and sandwiches for the soldiers and sailors, and I have never been so glad to see a country in my life. I actually did kiss the ground, and I promised myself I would never leave this wonderful America again. Or my daughter.

❦ CHAPTER FIFTEEN

I THOUGHT Mrs. Richardson would never pick up the phone. Ah, there she was. "Helene," my words tumbled out eagerly, "how is Wendy and how are you and isn't it wonderful that I'm back?" I had expected "How marvelous" or at the least a happy "How are you?" Instead, a cool "So you're back." What was the matter?

"I would never have taken Wendy for such a short time," she continued in the coldest of voices. It had been five months, an agonizingly long time for me to have been away from my daughter. "John has become used to her." Now there was unmistakable irritation—"It will upset him. How soon are you coming?" "As soon as I can," I promised, almost in tears.

There was the unexpected problem of getting space on the train to California. Everything was booked for weeks and months ahead—war priorities. A civilian had very little chance. I called my friends at the various studios, but they could do nothing. "Try the Army or the Navy," someone suggested. "They have all the seats." Finally Dave Lipton, then with Columbia Studios, told me he had managed a roomette for me on the Super Chief—in two weeks. This was after Bob Gilham at Paramount had told me, "You don't have a Chinaman's chance." Bob was going west on the same train, and when I saw him on the platform I could not forbear jeering, "Not a Chinaman's chance, hey?"

While waiting for my departure to Los Angeles, I managed a dozen lessons at the Cordon Bleu, the famed French cooking school in New York. I was determined to be the best cook for babies in America, if not the world. They were somewhat surprised when I told them, "I only want to learn how to cook baby food." "But we are French cooking," the woman said almost angrily. "Then I will be the best *French* cook for babies," I replied.

The tapioca pudding was my supreme achievement. It was quite difficult to make, putting in the right amount of tapioca to the right amount of water, stirring all the time, and at the very end folding in very gently, with a sideways movement, a stiff white-of-egg. I smiled, thinking, Won't Wendy be surprised when Momma comes home and is a marvelous cook with no nonsense about eating.

I believed I was a better woman for my experiences in England. I was confident I would be a better mother. I had fed and looked after desperately sick children, I had taken care of well children. I felt that I would never again be afraid of my daughter Wendy. In the London hospital, when children refused food, it was taken away from them immediately. This is what I will do with Wendy, I vowed. Stella, my housekeeper, had married again, and with everyone, it seemed, working in war factories, help in California was almost nonexistent. But with my new skill as a cook, I would manage.

Los Angeles. I looked eagerly for Mrs. Richardson. I was sure she would meet the train with Wendy, whom I was in a fever of anticipation to see. She was late—that Los Angeles traffic. The porter waited impatiently with my baggage—porters were few and in big demand. They weren't coming. Ah well, no matter. The taxi took me to the house in Bel Air. Frances, the seventeen-year-old maid imported from Pittsburgh, opened the door, backed away, then shouted inside, "It's Mrs. Westbrook." What was going on? A visitor from outer space would not have been less welcome. But behind one of those doors, or upstairs, was my daughter and it would take a hundred strong men to keep me out. "Please put my bags in the hall," I told the driver and paid him.

Jane, the Scottish nurse, came into the den where Frances had told me to wait. She was carrying a small precious bundle, my daughter Wendy. I hastened toward her, aching to hold the sweet little girl, her now blond hair adorned with a pink ribbon, wearing a short white dress and regarding me so seriously. Wendy turned sharply away and gave out that well-remembered yell. She had not recognized me at all. I was a complete stranger to her. She had always feared unfamiliar people, and I thought my heart would break.

"Stop it," Jane said sternly and attempted to put Wendy into my arms. She struggled and I said hurriedly, "Don't force her."

Jane had a message for me, an open note from Mrs. Richardson. She had made arrangements for me to stay at a hotel I had never heard of. I had expected to stay with Mrs. Richardson until I found somewhere to live with Wendy, who was still regarding me with great suspicion although the nurse had quieted her down. There was no option but to retreat. "I'll go now," I said to Jane, and to myself, "I must plan what to do."

The "hotel" was a cheap boardinghouse, drab and dark. I had no toilet, no bathroom, no telephone, and there were no facilities for food. "Stop crying," I commanded, sniffing back the tears. The first thing to do was to see Mrs. Richardson. The next, to find a place for my daughter and me.

Mrs. Richardson would be home in midafternoon. "She will see you between four and five," Frances had incredibly told me, avoiding my eyes. It was a fantastic, unlooked-for situation. But promptly at 4 o'clock, I rang Mrs. Richardson's doorbell.

After admitting me, Frances dashed upstairs and I heard her loud whisper, "She's here." Then more whispering, and the maid called me to come upstairs to the room where

Wendy and John had been sleeping in their cribs, but were now dressed to go out. Mrs. Richardson shook my hand without affection, asked me to sit down, then turned back to the children with whom she had been playing. "Come to Mama, Wendy," she called. I rose expectantly. But Wendy ran into *her* outstretched arms. She was Wendy's mother. I was an interloper, and I just stood by, helplessly, trying to fight back the tears and not quite knowing what to do.

Mrs. Richardson then told me they had been planning to go to Mexico, they were leaving in a week, and had, of course, intended taking Wendy with them. Now that I was back she assumed this was not possible, that I would naturally want Wendy with me.

All my waking hours were spent searching for an apartment or a house. There was nothing. It seemed that the whole world and his wife had settled in Los Angeles for the duration of the war, the poor to work in the labor-short factories, the rich refugees of Europe and the frivolous millionaires of the United States crowding the hotels—prisoners of pleasure in the sun.

Sir Cedric Hardwicke, British gentleman and actor, was living at the Beverly Wilshire Hotel. He invited me for breakfast sometimes, was most sympathetic and tried hard to get me into the hotel. I had no column, I had no pull, and there was no room for me at any hotel in Los Angeles. I was desperate as the day neared for Mrs. Richardson, her nurse and John to leave for Mexico. Every afternoon I went to her house—this was no time for pride—and Wendy gradually stopped crying when she saw me. But I had a long way to go to win my daughter back.

Charlie Einfeld, head of publicity at Warners, heard of my plight. We had always been good friends. He instructed his staff, "Find Sheilah Graham a home," and I will always be grateful to him for this. They had access to newspapers before they were sold; from an advertisement in the *Valley Times*, they found a small white clapboard house in North Hollywood, with real roses trailing around the door. I thanked Mrs. Richardson for her care of Wendy, rented a small truck, and packed her blue and pink striped highchair, her white crib, all her small possessions, and settled with great relief into our new home, for which I had to sign a one-year lease.

When I left Wendy for married life with Trevor in London, she had been a baby. Now, at eighteen months, she could walk and run, and the wonder of it when she spoke a few words! Everything she ate or drank she called "jui"—for juice. I marveled at how much she had changed in five months. There was a scar on her leg and I wondered how it had happened. How could I have left her? I regretted my broken friendship with Mrs. Richardson, and tried to understand her explanation, "I do not believe in two mothers in the same house."

Wendy and I were alone for two months in our North Hollywood home. I did not have a job. I could not afford help. I dipped into my savings to buy an old car from a hard-up movie cowboy for $400. Most afternoons I drove Wendy to the park in North Hollywood and we played peekaboo and I threw a ball and Wendy would run to pick it up. In an amazingly short time she accepted me as a person who loved her, and, with fast disloyalty to Mrs. Richardson, called me "Mama." It was as though I had never left her.

An early adventure in the feeding department—the tapioca pudding. I smiled with anticipatory pleasure, measuring the right quantity of water and stirring carefully while the water in the lower part of the two-tiered saucepan boiled. I fiercely whipped up the white of an egg until it was like crisp snow, then folded it in sideways as I had been taught at the Cordon Bleu. I tasted it—delicious. Happily, I lifted Wendy into the pink and blue high-chair and adjusted her best white bib with the blue duck. Now to serve my *chef d'oeuvre*—tapioca pudding *à la française*. I smiled; Wendy smiled, cautiously, and I popped a teaspoonful of the foaming stuff into her mouth. She rolled it around her pink cat's tongue, thought a bit about this new delicacy, and swallowed it. Success! When the dish was a third empty, without warning, Wendy closed her mouth. "Just a little more?" I coaxed. That did it. She threw the whole thing up in my face. Defiantly, I ate the rest of the tapioca. See if I care. But she did get used to having me around, and she did not starve.

I cooked and I cleaned. At night, after Wendy was asleep, I listened to the radio, and sewed, and knitted a sweater for her. Something went wrong with the instructions for the sleeves. They were so long. Wendy was still able to wear the sweater when she was eight years old. I wrote affectionate letters to Trevor. Wendy and I would come to England in the spring, I promised him.

The house was quiet—too quiet. I missed the excitement of my newspaper career, and the salary. I asked John Wheeler for my column back; he gave an unequivocal no. I suggested I write a weekly Sunday piece, interviews with the stars, for NANA. He thought this was a good idea. He would pay me $40 for each interview. I called Stella, my former housekeeper whose marriage had failed. "I will pay you forty dollars a week to work for me again," I told her. This was a big salary for a maid in those days. She came back. Now I could go to the studios and even go out sometimes at night.

Trevor was transferred on a temporary basis to Toronto, to oversee De Havilland aircraft production in Canada. There was no immediate reason to return to England. I needed to earn more than $40 a week, and I needed to get the brain working again. It had almost atrophied among the pots and pans.

Inga Arvad inadvertently gave me the push I needed. Perhaps she considered my presence in Hollywood a potential threat. Perhaps she just didn't like me. At any rate, she cold-shouldered me at the few industry functions to which I was invited. She was popular and pretty and Walter Pidgeon had arranged a screen test for her. I was at Metro to interview Greer Garson for my weekly story. Inga was in the Publicity Department, and I went in to say hello. She was looking at the photographs of her test, and some were passed to me. Without intending to be rude or annoy her, I said flippantly,

"You look like a younger Gloria DeHaven." She turned on me in a fury and said, "Everybody told me you were a bitch, and now I know you are." I was embarrassed and on the verge of tears and very angry. In that instant I decided I would get my column back.

In the past, when I had wanted to maneuver John Wheeler, I found it helped if the request also came from some of the editors of my column. In 1941, when I had wanted to work as a war correspondent in England, I had written to some of the editors, asked what they thought of the idea, and if they liked it to please write to John Wheeler. Now I wrote to Lloyd Lewis of the Chicago *Daily News*, John Rosenfield, the drama editor of the Dallas *News*, Jay Carmody of the Washington *Star,* and Roy Roberts of the Kansas City *Star.* I told them I wanted my column back, and could they help? Fortunately for me, they had not cared for the columns by Inga Arvad. I had only seen the first. She had a dream about Hollywood, she had written, and I had cautioned her, "You cannot have a dream about a dream. You must make Hollywood seem real to your readers." She had been grateful and rewritten the column. I heard, mostly from the editors, that her column was too nice. She was as sharp as I was in real life—sharper—but in print she was all sugar. Unless you are a brilliant writer, you cannot adore everyone so much. It makes for dull reading.

To my dismay, the letters from the editors had no effect on John Wheeler. He wrote me, "Inga Arvad will continue to do the column." My savings were dwindling rapidly. I must get a job with another syndicate. I asked my friends in the studios, "Is any syndicate in the market for a Hollywood columnist?" After a few days, Johnny Campbell, in the Publicity Department at 20th Century-Fox, told me he had heard that the McNaught Syndicate was looking for another Hollywood columnist. He was not certain of this; in fact, he thought it unlikely since they already had Jimmy Fidler. But it was enough for me.

I left Wendy with Stella and flew to New York to see Charles McAdam of the McNaught Syndicate. "Yes," he said, "I think we can use you." And how much salary did I want? "Two hundred dollars a week," I replied. John Wheeler had been paying me $160 a week. Seem confident, ask for more. You can always come down. The price seemed right. "There is only one thing." Oh, Lord, I groaned silently. "The syndicates have an unwritten agreement," he continued, "that we will not raid each other's talent. I thought you worked for John Wheeler and the North American Newspaper Alliance?" "Oh, no," I said eagerly. "John has Inga Arvad—he hired her when I left for England—I'm absolutely free." And impatient to clinch the deal, "Why don't you telephone him—now?" John was somewhat taken aback, but after some hesitation told McAdam, "Sure, sure, that's all right if you hire her. She does one column a week for us, but we'll release her."

I practically danced all the way back to the hotel. I would rather have worked for NANA, but the McNaught Syndicate was among the best and it was more money.

There was a telephone message at the hotel requesting

me to call Mr. McAdam. My joy evaporated. What now? John Wheeler had discussed the matter with his editor, Joe Agnelli, who told him, "We need her, I recommend that you do not let her go." John had called McAdam and threatened a lawsuit. I called John. "Well, *am* I working for you —do I get my column back?" John Wheeler gave me back my column and agreed to raise my salary to $200 a week. Pushing my advantage, I said, "I think NANA should buy me a car and pay the expenses for it. You know I only use it for my job." John was anxious lest I still might sign with the McNaught Syndicate and he agreed.

Trevor spent Christmas with his daughter and his wife in North Hollywood. Wendy was two years old and this was their first meeting. He was quietly pleased when she kissed him and called him daddy, as though he had been there always.

"Remember that house I was going to buy?" he said. "The one that was safe?" I replied. "Yes. It was bought by a lady-in-waiting to Queen Wilhelmina of Holland. A buzz bomb scored a direct hit when she was having a bath, which made it rather awkward." How glad I was that Wendy was in Southern California. But I had had enough of North Hollywood with the hot sun by day and the freeze at night. Trevor had been so cold during his brief visit, he had put the heavy bedroom rug on his twin bed to keep warm.

I decided to move to Beverly hills. With $200 a week and a new car, I could afford it. A week after Trevor returned to Canada, an agent I had contacted found a rent-controlled English-style one-story house at 522 North Palm Drive in Beverly Hills—on the right side of the tracks. I signed the one-year lease.

I loved the house, I loved having my job back. I loved Stella. I loved Trevor's almost nightly calls from Canada. In the spring of 1945, he told me he would come to Los Angeles for the weekend. "That's such a long trip for you, just for the weekend," I said. "I'll meet you halfway—in New York." It meant going by train and returning by train, but I had not been in New York for more than a year. And Lo and Behold, the miracle happened again. A few weeks after returning to California, I lost my breakfast. I was pregnant.

✠ CHAPTER SIXTEEN

I ALMOST died having Robert. And it was partly my own fault. Doctor Rubin was in New York, but I decided that since I was working in Hollywood, I would have a good local doctor. Doctor X was uninterested, and I was uncomfortable with him from the start. I cannot function unless I am loved. My cook has to love me. My secretary has to love me. My friends have to love me. And above all, my doctor has to love me. There are only two people who do not have to love me—my children. They are *In,* no matter what. Dr. X did not hate or even dislike me. I was merely a mural on the wall of his Hollywood office— a rather large mural.

I was enormous while I was carrying Rob, and it must have been embarrassing sometimes for the people I interviewed. Van Johnson, then at the height of his popularity, would rush to give me a chair when I visited him at M.G.M. When I interviewed Charlie Brackett, the producer, an old friend of Scott's, at Lucy's Restaurant near Paramount, he insisted on my drinking a whole quart of milk. I was so big, it seemed a foregone conclusion I would have twins, if not triplets. But my size did not interfere with my work. I squeezed into my small Studebaker and drove to the studios and attended some of the parties. I was not as careful as I had been with Wendy. I did not rest as much, and Cecil B. De Mille was quite concerned about me. It was nice to have so much attention. I visualized my hospital room at St. John's filled with flowers from every studio and every star, and even though again Trevor was not to be with me, I felt pampered and loved. Of course, when I had time to think, I knew it was all quite superficial, and sometimes I was quite frightened. But Stella was with me and I prayed that God would be.

Trevor visited us in the late summer, after Wendy, Stella and I returned to North Palm Drive from the apartment I had rented at Malibu Beach. The war in Europe had ended, and Trevor talked of my returning with Wendy to London, to have the new baby there. With the war over in Europe, Trevor was out of a job. An ungrateful industry had quickly forgotten his enormous contribution to wartime aviation. And to make the situation worse, he had lost a great deal of his savings in bad investments.

"*I* have a good job," I told him. "Why don't you live in America with us? They need planes for the war with Japan. I'm sure you could get a good job here. I know Howard Hughes. I could talk to him about you. In America your drive and the results you always get will be appreciated." With Trevor out of work and two children, I was fearful of giving up my job. The old specter of financial insecurity was on my back.

Poor Trevor, he would have been better off if he had married any one of the pretty girls to whom he had introduced me in England. When he realized I would not return to England to have our second child, Trevor, never one to do anything by halves, stopped all communication with me, and I did not hear from him again until after Robert was born, when he asked me for a divorce.

The baby was due about the middle of January. It was now the middle of December, and in the chill that is always underneath the sun in Hollywood, I caught a bad cold. It was time for my weekly check-up and remembering how careful Dr. Rubin had been with expectant mothers with colds—he always made them stay in bed—I called the nurse and said, "I have a cold. I'd better not come." "It won't hurt you to come," she replied. I kept the appointment, but I was disturbed.

It was time to talk of my fears. "The Caesarean was almost too late the last time," I told the doctor. "You won't wait too long to operate?" He replied, "I don't like Caesareans. We'll wait until you are in labor, then if an operation is necessary, that will be time enough." Then— "When labor begins, you will get in touch with Miss Robertson, my nurse. She will take care of everything." "The nurse—not you?" He smiled aloofly and said, "You won't need me at the beginning." He left me for the next expectant mother.

On arriving home, I telephoned Dr. Rubin in New York. "Is it too late for me to come east?" I asked him. "Not if you leave by the next train," his comforting voice replied. Civilian plane travel was out for the duration of the war, but in any case, airlines in that era of slower flights did not accept very pregnant women. No one wanted a baby to be born in the sky.

I had a premonition that I might not survive this baby and I sold the jewelry Trevor had given me to the head-mistress of a fashionable Los Angeles girls' school for $1500 and bought Savings Bonds for Wendy, just in case.

I was sneezing and wheezing from my cold, and Johnny Campbell, my good friend at 20th Century-Fox, tipped the porter on the Super Chief $20 to take care of me; but I rarely saw him during the uncomfortable three days and two nights of coughing my way across the country as the speeding train rocked on the tracks.

In Chicago, another 20th Century-Fox publicist drove me to the Ambassador East Hotel to rest between trains. "You look ill," he said in a concerned voice. "Why don't you wait over in Chicago until you feel better?" But I had to get to Dr. Rubin. I had to get to him if it meant crawling to New York on my knees, and I practically did.

Another rough night and then, blessed Grand Central Station, a racing taxi, the Gotham Hotel and the comfort of a non-rocking bed. The doctor was there in minutes. He was sure I would have an enormous baby. "But we don't want it to come too soon." He did not like my cold and gave me some pills and admonished, "Stay in bed." He would keep in touch with me.

A good night's sleep and I'm always ready to conquer the world again. Feeling much better, I telephoned Scottie, who was living in New York with her husband, Jack Lana-han. "There's a cocktail party this afternoon at '21,'" I told her. "Would you both like to come with me?" She consulted Jack. They would love to come.

The private room upstairs at '21' was stiflingly hot, blind-ing with cigarette smoke, and all the people seemed to be shouting. It hit me like a physical slap. I wished fervently that I had stayed in bed at the Gotham. All these people laughing and unpregnant. What had I to do with them?

It had been cold outside and I had liked that, but now I was sweating profusely. I saw some Hollywood people I knew, and the owners of '21' were there, the aquiline Jack and rotund Charlie, and we talked and I tried to sound very gay. But I had to get out of there. I intercepted a glance between Scottie and her husband. "Let's go, Sheilah." Scottie slipped her arm through mine.

The cold air made me feel somewhat better, but I was shivering and then I was hot. I was obviously quite ill. It was a short walk to the Gotham, just three blocks on Fifth

Avenue, but we took a taxi, and I promised Scottie I would call the doctor immediately. She wanted to stay with me, but I have never allowed my friends to see me ill. I have always tried to create an impression of strength—perhaps because I have so many weaknesses.

While I waited for Dr. Rubin, I sprawled, shivering and sweating, on the suddenly narrow twin bed. "Of course you shouldn't have gone out," Dr. Rubin told me sternly. My temperature was 101°. "I'm putting you into the hospital right away," he said. "Not yet," I begged him. "I promise I'll stay in bed." I ached all over and I felt awful. But I was sure I would be all right in the morning. Dr. Rubin believed in humoring his patients if possible. But he insisted on getting a nurse for me. He stayed with me until she arrived. She was instructed to give him constant reports. If I took a turn for the worse she was to call him, no matter what time it was, and he would put me into the hospital immediately.

The nurse took my temperature every hour and gave me some hot tea, but I could not drink or eat. It was one of the worst nights of my life. I had this huge bundle on my stomach, any movement was a tremendous effort, and I was hot and cold and full of fever. The nurse was worried and wanted to call the doctor, but I said, "No, let him sleep." At 6 in the morning she contacted Dr. Rubin. He ordered an ambulance to take me to the hospital. The attendants came to my room and put me on a stretcher in my nightclothes. I was too weak to dress, and they covered me with the mink coat that Trevor had bought me. I was glad it was early and not many people were in the lobby of the Gotham Hotel to see this strange procession—me in my nightgown, covered with my fur coat, the two attendants carrying me on a stretcher, with the nurse bringing up the rear. The clerks and the elevator attendants were smiling. No one had been able to miss the fact that I was expecting a baby and they thought my time had come.

It was my first ride in an ambulance, and, I hope, the last. It felt vague and unreal, rushing through the New York streets, the sirens screaming. At the Lenox Hill Hospital, I learned something about private ambulances. You cannot, no matter how ill you are, even if you are dying, you cannot get into bed until you have paid for the ambulance. It was $25, and even though I was so ill, I had to write out a check while swaying on my feet. I suppose they are afraid you will die and they will never get paid.

Dr. Rubin was worried. Should he perform the Caesarean immediately or wait in the hope that my temperature would go down? An operation with a high temperature, I gathered from his concern, would be extremely dangerous.

I received some messages. Scottie had called the Gotham to find I had gone into the hospital. Alec Waugh, now in New York to sell some stories, called every day. But I could see no one. I just lay there, coughing and breathing raspingly through my mouth. Dr. Rubin visited me three times a day. One morning I was coughing so violently that the water protecting the baby flooded the bed. The doctor on duty called Dr. Rubin, and with my temperature going up instead of down, he decided they would have to operate at once.

Was I afraid? Not until I reached the operating room. Then I was terrified. Would I be alive when I came back from behind that door? "I don't want to go in there. I'm afraid," I said to the stretcher orderlies. They avoided looking at me. They could do nothing, there was no escape. I had to go through the door. I had to have the operation or I would die anyway.

When you are pregnant, after the first few months you are committed. You have to go through the allotted nine months. And are all women, when the time comes, afraid? But it is pointless to be afraid. There is no escape. You have to go through the door. My case was more serious because I was very ill, with a high temperature, and no one was betting on the outcome—except Dr. Rubin. He had never lost a mother and he was not aiming to begin.

Dr. Rubin had decided on a spinal even before I had become ill. This was the new look in operations. No violent unconsciousness via ether. I would be awake and I would know what was going on.

They wheeled me in, and immediately put me into an oxygen tent. I dared not look at the nurses and doctors in their masks or at Dr. Rubin. I felt the sharp long pinprick into the spine and sensed that the operation was in progress. I had been worried that I would feel the knife. All I felt was a void. It was a strange sensation when I coughed, with nothing to push against.

Then I heard, as though coming from a great distance, a hushed chorus, "It's a boy." I had a boy. But I did not care what I had. I did not care if I lived or died. I was

coughing and that was my main preoccupation. I heard a
cry and whispered to Dr. Rubin, "How long has it been?"
"Six minutes," he replied. And I thought, Now my troubles really begin. The three days after a major operation
are very difficult and full of pain. "Would you like to see
the baby?" he asked. I was faintly curious, but not much.
A nurse was holding my son. Wendy had looked Japanese.
Robert resembled a small Chinaman, with his legs crossed
and his brown hair greased to a point.

No more children, Dr. Rubin had decided. Two difficult
Caesarians were enough. To prevent future pregnancy, he
was tying up the Fallopian tubes. I heard him say, "Now
where is that other tube?" I was irritable, and whispered
hoarsely, "Don't you remember? I told you one tube was
removed when my appendix was taken out in England."
"Oh yes, of course."

"You're sure you *are* tying up my remaining tube? I
wouldn't want to be half safe." I tried to laugh, but it was
a poor attempt. Then it was all shadows and pain and
penicillin and blood transfusions and coughing.

John Wheeler came to see me, and it was he who made
me realize how desperately ill I was. He sat near the door
because John is always careful not to catch things. I didn't
think he would catch this baby. He hesitated, then said,
"If it's any comfort to you, if anything happens, I will adopt
Wendy." I thought, My God, I must be dying! I could not
die. No one could adopt Wendy. She was mine. I decided,
I will not die. I took hold. I fanned the small spark.

Two weeks later, I actually walked a mile to the Algon-
quin Hotel to have lunch with Alec Waugh.

Rob was an enormous baby. He weighed in at 8 pounds
4 ounces. If he had gone the full term, Dr. Rubin told me,
he might have been a 12-pounder. I hired the same baby
nurse, which was incredible after all the irritation she had
caused me. But she had brought Wendy safely to California,
and in spite of her hatred for the Golden State, she was
willing to take another chance.

We stayed a month in a suite at the Warwick Hotel in
New York. There was still no possibility of civilian flying
to Los Angeles in January of 1946, and I booked a drawing
room on the Super Chief. I was anxious to get back to
Wendy at 522 North Palm Drive. Stella had put her on
the telephone to me and she had sent her precious gift,

"I love you," winging from coast to coast. New York was terribly cold. There had been a fierce snowstorm on December 24, the day Rob had been born, and I was impatient to return to the warm sun in California.

The nurse had not changed. She grumbled all the way across country, and it was difficult for her, sterilizing the bottles in the small kitchen on the train. She got in everybody's way and she glared at them and they glared back at her. She always had disagreeable stories to tell when she returned to our compartment. I lay quietly and watched the snow-covered scenery rush past and tried to conserve my strength.

I must get well in a hurry because of my column. I had typed the last one the night before the operation, on a portable typewriter on the hospital table across my bed. It had not been easy, but I had managed to get a week ahead and with a three-week vacation, there had been a month in which to have the baby and recuperate from the Caesarian. Now I must resume the column, and I worked on the train. I can't remember where I got my news from, but in New York, at the Warwick Hotel, I had been in touch with Hollywood. I don't want to sound like a superwoman, but looking back, I don't know how I did it.

Wendy remembered me this time; she was almost three and a half years old and I had only been away five weeks. She was delighted to see me and the baby. Stella wept, and her niece Josephine wept, and I wept. But Wendy smiled and danced around me and the nurse and wanted to give her ball to Robert and asked to hold him. I was happy to be back in California.

While I had been at the Warwick Hotel, I had tried to have a reconciliation with Trevor. I had believed he would be so delighted to have a son that perhaps we could get together again. I had not heard from him from the time he had decided the situation was hopeless, that I would never come back to England. I wrote him, explaining how ill I had been and what a lovely son he had. And I said once again, "If you do not have a job, why not stay with us in California until you decide what to do?" His answer was a request for a divorce. Trevor had made up his mind, and when Trevor makes up his mind, there isn't much you can do about it. I wrote back saying if he wanted a divorce, I could not blame him.

II

✌ CHAPTER SEVENTEEN

WITH two children and out in the wide open sea, I must navigate a good course for them and for me. I could not expect support from Trevor. This is when I decided, as deliberately as deciding to cross a street, that I would be what we call a success. I would give these children everything I had not had when I was a child. The best home, the best food, the best clothes, the best schools, the best love, the best care, the best everything. I tacked on my wings and flew to the heights and surveyed the statistics of success.

The successful people in Hollywood all seemed to earn $5,000 a week. Lana Turner's salary was $5,000 a week. Van Johnson was earning $5,000 a week. Robert Taylor was making $5,000 a week. Clark Gable, who was an enormous star at Metro, was making a little more—$7,500 a week.

In those days, with few independent producers, no percentages, no $1,000,000 a picture for Elizabeth Taylor, it was the golden era for the major studios. It was the day of the long-term contract. The studio bosses were kings. The word of Louis B. Mayer at Metro, or of Darryl F. Zanuck at 20th Century-Fox, Jack Warner at Warner Brothers, or Howard Hughes at RKO, was law. When Greer Garson refused to star as Mrs. Miniver, Mr. Mayer called her a son-of-a-bitch and screamed obscenities until she capitulated. The old tycoon had been right. Greer won an Oscar for "Mrs. Miniver"—and a husband, Richard Ney, who had portrayed her son.

The sun has set for the major studios but they were thriving in 1946, and happily giving out contracts of $5,000 a week to the stars. I decided to aim for this figure. If they can do it, I thought, I can do it. They are no brainier than I am. They are not creatures from outer space. What they did was not so miraculous. I have believed all my life that you can have anything you want if you want it desperately enough. You must want it with an inner exuberance that erupts through the skin and joins the energy that created the world. I have nearly always had what I have wanted. It has not always made me happy, but I have usually had it. And be careful what you want, for you will get it.

At that time, for a columnist to be successful the column must be read in Los Angeles and New York, and one must have a radio show. A few months after Robert was born I went to New York to see Jack Lait, who was editor of the New York *Mirror*. Ahead of me I sent some of my columns. He told John Wheeler he liked them. He singled out an item about Lauren Bacall. She had sung a song in *To Have and Have Not* with Humphrey Bogart, but a boy had actually done the singing for the low-voiced actress. Mr. Lait thought this behind-the-scenes truth unexpected and interesting. He bought the column from John Wheeler. I was read in New York.

I studied the Hollywood situation. Where could I squeeze in? The Los Angeles *Examiner* had Louella Parsons, also Harry Crocker doing a pleasant, innocuous gossip column. Harry Crocker was a friend of Mr. Hearst's. I liked him. He had helped me get my first interview in Hollywood with Charlie Chaplin and I was not going to try to push him out. Besides, I knew I didn't have a prayer with Louella Parsons.

There was the Los Angeles *Times*. Ed Shallert wrote the news and Hedda Hopper had been doing the column for some years. In the afternoon papers, the *News* bulged with established syndicated and local columns. The *Herald Express* had Harrison Carroll and Jimmy Starr. There was the Hollywood *Citizen News*. Of all the newspapers in Los Angeles, I preferred this newspaper. It was dignified. It had more foreign news than any of the other papers. The print looked clean. The film columnists were Sidney Skolsky, Florabelle Muir and Lowell Redelings. They seemed to like lots of film columns and perhaps I'd have a chance. Armed with some of my best efforts, I called on Harlan Palmer Jr., the dark-haired, brown-eyed managing editor and son of Judge Harlan Palmer, the publisher, who had founded the paper. Mr. Palmer was polite, but he did not see how he could buy my column because they already had so many. I suggested, "Why not try mine once or twice a week?" He pondered the idea while I "willed" him to take my column. He said he would think it over and let me know. He called the next day and said, "You can tell Mr. Wheeler I'll use your column twice a week." In about a month, with good reaction from readers, he used it three times a week. Soon it was every day. My son is eighteen years old now, and I am still with the *Citizen News*, although it has since changed hands.

The *Citizen News* under the Palmers was so conservative and non-scandalous they would not use my scoop that Mrs. Gable, Lady Sylvia Ashley, would divorce Clark at 2 o'clock one afternoon in 1952 at the Santa Monica court.

I had called the *Citizen* with my Gable-Ashley divorce scoop. Usually I gave the New York *Mirror* my exclusive scoops, but this time I thought: I'll be a heroine in my own town. Let them see how good I am. After I gave Mr. Palmer the story he said, "Well, it hasn't happened yet, has it?" I said, "No, but it will in three hours." He replied, "We'd rather let the other papers publish it first."

Two of my objectives were accomplished. My column was appearing in New York where the film executives could read it and my column was seen in Hollywood, where the Hollywood studio officials and stars could see what I had written about them. This is enormously important, especially in Hollywood. They only believe what they see. They only rate you as important if they see what you are writing. You can be published in every other paper in the country, but if you are not in New York or Hollywood, you don't exist as an important columnist.

Now for radio. My first attempt to be a radio star, in October 1937, had been disastrous. Scott Fitzgerald had attacked my sponsor and they had paid me off. Since then I had done little in this field. I had been too nervous. I was still too nervous, but it must be done. I must forget my nerves and think of the objective—to be a success. Louella Parsons had a radio show; Jimmy Fidler had a radio show; Hedda Hopper had a radio show. I must join this exalted group and also have a radio show. I opened my energy valve at full strength. Within a week I was ON THE AIR.

How to get a radio show? Where to start? I did not tell my closest friend in Hollywood—in fact, no one has a closest friend in Hollywood—that I was trying for a radio show. I have learned that part of the formula for success is to keep quiet about your objective until you get it. Just as the universe is filled with positive energy waiting to join your own, there is also destructive energy emanating from people who do not like you. I am always surprised at how many jealous people there are and alas, I am one of them.

I called on Bob Hussey who had been in the Publicity Department at Columbia and had recently joined the Young & Rubicam advertising agency. After congratulating him on his new job, I said, "Bob, how do I get a radio show?" He considered my request, then replied, "First you must get an agent."

"Whom would you recommend?"

"I think Ken Dolan would be good for you." I nodded. Ken was a husky, genial Irishman I had seen at industry functions.

"Perhaps," I suggested, "you could call him." Young & Rubicam were big advertisers, and it was good business for Mr. Dolan to please Mr. Hussey. "Could you call him now?" I added. I always do things immediately. This is part of the formula. You never put off until tomorrow or even this afternoon what you can do this morning. Attack the objective when your desire is strongest.

He called Ken and made an appointment for me to see him that afternoon at his office in Hollywood. I wore my navy blue silk suit and a white straw boater with a jaunty blue ribbon bow. I looked trim and I felt confident.

Mr. Dolan listened politely, then smiled. "You know, it's the strangest coincidence, but this morning Hal Kemp of the Kemp, Roche, and Cleary Agency was in. He asked if I knew someone like Jimmy Fidler, only not as expensive." The sponsor was dissatisfied with a fifteen-minute weekly song medley and had already canceled the singer, Ken told me. "He wants to change to a movie gossip show," he continued. "We'll make a recording tomorrow morning." Even before he ushered me out of his office, my mind was grappling with the format for a fifteen-minute radio show.

I made the record, and he called me the same day—Friday afternoon—to tell me I would be on the air "this Sunday." That's how fast it was. The same thing had happened when I had wanted to go on the stage. I was interviewed on a Friday and was leading a chorus line in a London West End theatre on Monday. And I couldn't even dance. Now, could I do a radio show?

The product was Rayve Creme Shampoo. Just before going on the air at the Don Lee Mutual Studio, I met the sponsor—Ray Lee. He was good-looking, in his very early thirties, and extremely pleasant. "We'll all have dinner—if you are free—after the show. There's nothing to be nervous about." He smiled. I met Hal Kemp, who looked a bit worried. Ken

Dolan nodded encouragingly. It was like the time I went on for the star at the London Pavilion. I was in that golden haze where nothing could go wrong, where everyone loved me and I loved everyone. I smiled at my announcer, Don McCall, waited for the signal from him, and plunged. They were very pleased.

The original plan had been for me to finish the singer's remaining five weeks, at $200 a show. I did not quibble about the price—$200 added to my $200 from NANA and the $400 I was receiving from my monthly piece for *Photoplay* came to $500 a week, a good start toward my ambition to earn $5,000 a week.

Almost immediately, Ray Lee decided to continue for another 13 weeks, and after six months, Ken Dolan managed a raise to $300 a week. Jack Hellman, in *Daily Variety*, informed Hollywood: "The doubled rating has the Rayve bosses planning a coast-to-coast whirl for Graham." They were not, but it was nice to read it.

After an early show, Mr. Lee told me, "I'd like to buy you a present. What would you like?" Yes, there *was* one thing I needed. It was June 1946 and I could not get a washing machine for love or money or influence, and with two children, I really needed one. The very next day, a used machine, in good order, arrived at my house from the sponsor.

My Regimen for a Good Radio Performance: I cut out the cookies and candy, although I like sweet things, and I cut down on the bread and potatoes; James Melton, the opera star, told me that singers avoid foods with starches because it creates phlegm in the throat. For the column, it was necessary to visit the five major studios each week, but now I saved the exciting and controversial news nuggets for the all-important show. These tidbits were then used in my Monday column.

I wrote the show on Friday and polished it on Saturday. I have always done the hard work and the agonizing *before* the day of performance. On The Day, I must be serene and confident. No rushing around and no getting exhausted. Of course, there were sometimes last-minute scoops, such as the nearly fatal plane crash of Howard Hughes right in Beverly Hills a minute before air time.

On Sunday, I slept as late as possible, remaining in bed until noon, making a few phone calls in the morning on such up-to-the-minute stories as the Ingrid Bergman-Dr. Lindstrom-Rossellini situation. At 12 o'clock, I turned on my bedside radio and listened to the news. At 1 o'clock, lunch, which was always a small broiled steak with no fat, string beans, half a grapefruit, and a cup of tea without milk. Eddie Cantor had told me after my first show that the tannic acid in the tea was very good for the throat. At 4 o'clock, I might go for a walk, a very short walk. All my strength, if not my sweetness, must be rolled up and hurled into the show. At 4:30, another cup of sugarless tea with lemon. Then I slowly dressed. At 5 o'clock I drove my car calmly and carefully to the Don Lee Broadcasting Company below Sunset Boulevard on Vine Street, picking up the morning Los Angeles *Times* and Los Angeles *Examiner* on the way. If Louella Parsons had anything interesting in her column for Monday, I would check it out. Her radio show was a half hour before mine. When I knew an item was incorrect, I gave the true story.

At the station, the director would run through the show with Don McCall, a slight man with a sweet smile and a limp. We listened to the playback. My voice was clear and beautiful. Five minutes before showtime, I would go to the ladies' room, because you cannot do your best if you have to go to the bathroom. I had my microphone and Don had his. Thirty seconds to go, and then invariably, having told myself I would not do it, I would clear my throat. And this was fatal. Invariably, I rasped the vocal cords and most Sundays I had one or two bad "frogs" in my throat. After all that training. And while no one else, including the sponsor, seemed to care, I felt I spoiled the show with this nervous frantic clearing of the throat.

This never happened to me in television. There was always too much confusion for me to worry about my voice. I never prepared for a television show as I prepared for my radio show and I have rarely had a frog in television. I have never felt the necessity to clear my throat just before the two small red eyes on the camera materialize me for the viewing audience. In radio, all they had to judge me by was my voice. In television they can see me, and a frog, if it comes, is unimportant.

Ray Lee sponsored me for two and a half years, during which time I established myself in the top ranks of radio commentators from Hollywood. A few weeks after Ray sold his product to Charlie Luckman of Lever Bros., I landed a coast-to-coast show with Conte Castile Shampoo.

Then a year for the Mutual Network, always on prime

early Sunday evening time. Walter Winchell was ahead of me on ABC, and as soon as he signed off, the people in Hollywood switched to me. My voice, with its distinctive British accent, was as good as a credit card. It was recognized by storekeepers when I wanted to pay by check. It was not quite as English as when I had first arrived in America and I was careful to use the short "a" and American expressions, especially after I auditioned for Mars Bars and they stated flatly they could not understand a word I said. This was in 1947 and the sponsor hated everything British because of the situation in Palestine.

But I remember 1947 mostly as the year when the earth disappeared under my feet, when everything I had built up for myself and my children was about to crash into a terrifying void. It was the year that an anonymous vicious enemy used my own newspaper (the Hollywood *Citizen News*) to accuse me—at the height of the Communist witch hunt in Hollywood—of being a Communist.

❦ CHAPTER EIGHTEEN

IT began soon after my American citizenship. On the morning of August 11, 1947, in the Los Angeles courtroom of the very old Judge "Jefty" O'Connor, I, (with about 50 other immigrants of all nationalities) had foresworn allegiance to the land of my birth. Henceforth, I would be a loyal citizen of the United States, I would bear arms if necessary. I had memorized all the facts of federal and civil government; I knew every line of all the 22 Amendments. I had passed the final examination with ease. I was happy and proud when I kept my appointment for lunch with Henry Rogers, press agent for Lucille Ball, Kathryn Grayson, June Allyson, Dick Powell and a host of other stars.

Mr. Rogers, tall, stylish, with a smooth boyish face, had a fine news story for me. Nineteen Hollywood personalities, including Danny Kaye, Humphrey Bogart, and Lauren Bacall, had chartered a plane to Washington to plead the right of the First Amendment on behalf of "The Hollywood Ten," among them Dalton Trumbo, Jules Dassin, Ring Lardner Jr., and actress Anne Revere, who had refused, under the First Amendment, to state before the Senate Sub-Committee on

Un-American Activities whether they now or ever had been members of the Communist Party.

"We have formed a group—'Committee for the First Amendment.'" Henry showed me a typewritten list with names of the members of the new group—Archibald Mac-Leish, Leonard Bernstein, Walter Wanger, Henry Hatha-way, Arthur Hornblow, dozens of top stars including Burt Lancaster, Gene Kelly, Myrna Loy and Deanna Durbin, and four U.S. Senators. Also, a heavy sprinkling of well-known Hollywood Democrats: Melvyn Douglas, John Garfield, William Wyler, Danny Kaye and Edward G. Robinson.

I was full of the privileges of Americans under the Constitution, and in a burst of Justice for All, I said, "Put my name down too." I knew very little about practical politics and nothing of the Communist movement in Hollywood. I had studied Capitalism and Communism with Scott Fitz-gerald in 1940. As he did, I considered Stalin a monstrous tyrant and Communism a blight on individual liberty. I could not imagine any American preferring the Russian way of life. I had stated this at a party in Beverly Hills, and a gravel-voiced actor had called me a dumb blonde. I had thought Chaplin was wrong when he demanded a Second Front during the war. He was not a citizen and it was none of his business.

And politics was not my business. My column was only concerned with motion pictures, film personalities and the film industry. But now, as an American citizen, I had be-come deeply concerned with freedom of worship, freedom of speech, freedom to assemble and to petition the government for a redress of grievances. So I said, "Put my name down too."

I regretted the gesture almost immediately. The next morn-ing, I called Henry and said, "I don't know a thing about politics and as a columnist, I should not belong to any group. Please take my name off the list." "Of course," he reassured me. "I'll call Bill Blowitz [another Hollywood press agent]. He's in charge. Your name will be removed. You have nothing to worry about." I was not unduly worried. The Committee for the First Amendment had not yet been dubbed a Com-munist front by the FBI: But why meddle with something I really did not understand?

When "The Committee for the Defense of the Hollywood Ten" flew back to Hollywood in their chartered plane, some of them were not as friendly to "The Hollywood Ten." They had learned a thing or two in Washington—chiefly that an actor who sympathized with possible Communists might find himself acting to smaller and smaller audiences. Humphrey Bogart gave an interview at the Los Angeles airport stating he had been misled. He assured the press he was sorry he had made the flight to Washington, that an actor should not meddle with matters that belonged to the FBI and the United States Government.

Every day, Hollywood stars suspected of being Communists were ordered to appear before the House Un-American Activities Committee. I was quite astonished when I read that Larry Parks had confessed to being a card-carrying member of the Communist Party. How amazing and how foolish, I thought. I had never discussed politics with him and this was a tremendous surprise. But there was another surprise in store for me.

To impress Hollywood with the strength of "The Committee for the First Amendment," Bill Blowitz took a full-page advertisement in *Daily Variety,* listing the names of the members. And lo, there was Graham, Sheilah. I was more annoyed than alarmed. I called Mr. Blowitz, who was later interrogated by the H.U.A.C., and said, "Bill, didn't Henry Rogers tell you to take my name off?" Bill promised pleasantly and deceptively that he would see to it. He never did. The ad appeared several times with my name. Oh well, I thought, there can't be anything too wrong if Archibald MacLeish and Deanna Durbin are members.

And then the letter appeared in the Hollywood *Citizen News.* The anonymous writer demanded of my newspaper, "How can you, who denounce Communism on your editorial pages, use the column of Sheilah Graham on your entertainment page?" I read the letter and reread it and reread it. How could this be? To be accused of being a Communist in that period of frightening hysteria was a one-way ticket to oblivion. For *me* to be tagged Communist was not only erroneous but ridiculous. Why, some of my best friends in Hollywood were fascists! I even called a couple of them and discussed the letter, and they laughed and said, "Don't worry —*we'll* write a letter to the *Citizen.*"

I called on Harlan Palmer at the *Citizen News* and asked, "Why was the letter published? Surely you don't believe I am a Communist?" "Of course not," he replied slowly. "But I do believe that some of them have been using you. For instance, you have written quite a lot about Larry Parks."

"But Larry Parks has been a top star since *The Jolson Story*," I protested. "If you look back in the column, you will see that I have written just as much about Adolphe Menjou and much more about John Wayne and Gary Cooper"—three stars who were very active in groups that fought Communism.

But the letters continued. I became horribly fascinated by that section of the *Citizen News*. Every day I looked for letters from my studio friends who had been shocked at the unfounded charge against me. But only one favorable letter appeared in that week of dreadful nightmare.

Then came an amazing epistle. The writer had actual proof that I was a Communist. "If you will refer to Sheilah Graham's column of November 11 . . ." I almost fell upon my files and extracted the column for November 11. Ah yes, I had been visiting Metro. In the early part I mentioned meeting Peter Lawford, who, I noted, was wearing bright red socks. Later in the column I had chatted with Elizabeth Taylor, whose adolescent figure was blooming "'neath a flaming red sweater." With no thought beyond tying the two fashion items together, I had added, "Red is obviously the color to wear this season."

This was too much. I would withdraw my column from the Hollywood *Citizen News*. I called on Mr. Palmer with blood in my eye and anger in my voice. "I can't write for your paper," I informed him. He pacified me—they liked my column. They knew I was not a Communist. He was sorry. He promised the letters would stop. I have never known why they were printed. But I have always had a strong suspicion of the political fanatic, female gender, who wrote them. The earth stopped rocking and the terror and anger left me. But I still shudder when I read or hear of "The First Amendment." In my dictionary, they are frightening words.

❦ CHAPTER NINETEEN

EARLY in December of 1947 I bought a house in Beverly Hills. Wendy was five years old and Robert would be two on Christmas Eve. It was time for a gamble and time for a change. I had learned that with the expected demise of the Rent Control Act, my Irish landlady, Mrs. Murphy, was planning to raise the rent from $180 to $300 a month.

There was a beautiful house for sale in the next street, North Maple Drive at 607, and it was Open House every Sunday afternoon. To pass the time and to get my mind off the coming radio show, I would walk over, inspect the large rooms and imagine us all living there, happily ever after. The Spanish-style house was on two floors, with a red tile roof, a big fireplace in the huge living room, and a beautiful black wrought-iron staircase at the back of the double entrance halls. I could visualize Wendy coming down the steps as a bride. In front of the house, fringing the lawn, were sweet-smelling magnolia trees. In the back, a walled garden of grass with a drooping weeping willow, lemon, orange, apricot and fig trees. It would be good to have roots as strong as the trees', to stay here for the rest of my life, to raise my children here, and give them a fine home.

The price had been reduced, the real estate man said, from $55,000 to $52,000. It was a bargain, he assured me. I simply could not afford it. Ah well, it was only a daydream, and I enjoyed it every Sunday.

One Monday afternoon, the man from 607 North Maple Drive called at 522 North Palm Drive. I was glad to see him, but I told him at once, "I cannot afford $52,000." "What *can* you pay for it?" It was fun to play for a few seconds with the idea of owning a beautiful house in a beautiful neighborhood. "What *can* you afford?" he persisted. It sounded as though I had him, but I dared not get too excited. I would make an impossible offer. "I cannot pay more than $40,000, and I can only give a down payment of $15,000," I told him. It was all the money I had. He shook his head regretfully and replied, "Dr. Witter will never accept that."

The next day, there he was again, beaming. "You can have it for $40,000, with a $15,000 down payment, the rest at $250 a month." Without hesitation I signed the papers. And of course, the week after we moved in, with no furniture beyond Rob's crib, Ray Lee sold his shampoo to Lever Bros. and they dropped my show. This is infallible. If you buy a house or if you have a baby, you invariably lose your show. Mrs. Don McCall, my announcer's wife, was expecting a baby, and this made it doubly sure.

Here we were, with my income chopped in half, in an empty enormous house with only the barest essentials. I bought us each a bed, an unpainted chair, table and chest of drawers. The rest would have to wait.

George Delacorte, the very successful publisher and New York philanthropist, called on us soon after we moved in. With the unsmiling face of the very rich, he shook his head mournfully and said, "You shouldn't have put all your eggs into one basket." I knew that George was a pessimist. Nonetheless, his words depressed me very much. His wealth has dazzled, but it has never warmed me. Fortunately, I have an optimistic friend, Jimmy O'Toole. He came to see me about the same time. He admired the house and said, "You have done wisely." Jimmy was right. Eleven years later when I sold the house for which I had given $40,000, I was paid $65,000.

Except for one brief period, the years at 607 North Maple Drive were very satisfactory. I realized my ambition to earn $5,000 a week. I gave my children a spacious home, a secure bastion in which to inch upward, to become good people, to develop proper values while the great glamorous, synthetic world of Hollywood swirled outside our door and sometimes seeped inside. They met most of the big beautiful people. Marilyn Monroe attended a party at our house when Robert was seven and Wendy ten. But Robert remembers it better, because Marilyn kissed him.

He was four when I took him with me to visit Elizabeth Taylor at her mother's home, two streets away. She had interrupted her honeymoon with Nicky Hilton to have some photographs taken in her wedding gown. She started to undress, realized that my son was in the room, hastily covered her bosom and said, "Little boy, will you please leave the room?" Rob was playing with a piece of string and couldn't have cared less that Elizabeth Taylor, the most beautiful girl in the world, was about to strip. This was almost the last time he was to be oblivious to feminine charms.

There was the lovely time of outwitting Louella Parsons over Hopalong Cassidy. It was 1950 and Hoppy was on the crest of his fabulous fame. Every child in America was wearing Hopalong outfits, complete with guns, boots and hats, and my children were loyal members in good standing. As soon as they came home from school, they changed into their "Hoppy" uniforms and rode their "Hoppy" bikes. He was their hero. They never failed to watch his weekly television show. I wrote about him a great deal, but I had not met him. These were old films that had been sold to television, and his early fame was over before I came to Hollywood.

Louella Parsons, never one to overlook good exploitation, had a fine idea. It was the Christmas week, and with "my neighbor," Dorothy Lamour, as co-hostess, she would have a children's party at her home to be used for her radio show, with Hopalong Cassidy as the big attraction. She lived six doors from my house on North Maple Drive, and when I read of the impending party in the trade papers, I waited for her to invite Wendy and Robert. She knew I had two children—they were regular trick-and-treaters at her door on Halloween. The previous Christmas, she had sent them each a gift. She had even referred to herself as their Aunt Lolly. Of course she would invite them. But she did not.

It was embarrassing, the more so because Dorothy Lamour's son, Ridgeley, was a close friend of Robert's and all he talked about was the coming party with Hoppy. Obviously, something had to be done at a high level. Should I call Louella and ask her to invite my children? I could hardly do that, but there would be no harm in chatting with her on the phone. I called her, talked about the party and talked about my children, whom I had sent to whoop it up outside her door in their Hoppy clothes and on their Hoppy bicycles. But she resolutely did not invite my kids.

Okay, sister, this is war.

I telephoned Hoppy at his home in the Hollywood Hills and introduced myself. He seemed pleased to hear from me. After a sentence or two about "your wonderful success," I said very casually, "Oh, Hoppy, I believe you will be at the Louella Parsons radio party tomorrow." "That's right," he replied. "How nice," I purred. And then, as though suddenly hit with a great idea, "You know, I live on the same street, just six doors away. Why don't you stop at my house on the way? I'd love to meet you—so would my children." He reckoned he could come. "What time would you-all like to see me?" The Parsons party was at 4 P.M. "How about 3:30?" I asked brightly. Well, he thought that was all right. It didn't occur to him that perhaps it was a breach of faith with Parsons, who wanted to swallow him exclusively for her show. "You will wear your Hoppy clothes?" He sure would.

I called my newspaper in Hollywood. Such an event had to be recorded for the friends of my children, and their children. Yea, even unto the fourth generation. Also for Lolly.

I had the photographer come at three, in case Hoppy was early. The doorbell rang at 3:29, and there was Hopalong, looking larger than life in his Hoppy outfit and guns. He smiled approvingly when he saw Wendy and Robbie in *their* Hoppy outfits and guns. They gravely saluted each other with, "Howdy, Pardner." Then the photographer and I took over. We posed the trio in front of the Christmas tree, in front of the TV set, and in the backyard with the kids on their Hoppy bikes. The *Citizen* published the photograph with six guns at the draw in front of the tree. My children were regarded very highly in their circle. And to hell with Louella.

Actually, they had been somewhat disappointed in Hoppy. Wendy, who always says what she thinks, asked me, "Why is he so old?" "It's the films that are old," I explained. Hoppy was now white-haired and not quite the same man. But I was jubilant. I had scored a coup. I was a superwoman to my children.

I found it a delicious thing having children. It was a re-birth, a reliving; it was making a childhood for myself that I had never had, and in a very luxurious style.

The movie stars were always giving parties for their young children and Wendy and Rob were frequently invited. I had to be on the alert to protect their egos. Judy Garland gave a birthday party at Santa Monica for her daughter Liza. She was the tiniest little girl, three years old at the time. Many offspring of movie stars had been invited, and the photographers descended in full force. The main attraction was a donkey. The photographers, about twenty of them, grabbed the famous children and plopped them on the donkey, one after another, while the cameras flashed and clicked. The donkey was supposed to provide pleasure for the children, but it was used blatantly as a prop for the photographs.

The minute Miss Minelli was getting the most rides and the most photographs. Judy was there and they had her holding the bridle, with Liza smiling into the camera and her mother smiling. The Paul Henreids and their daughter were there, and Claire Trevor and her young son Charlie, whom we regarded as Wendy's beau. They all had rides. But each time I tried to put one of my children on the donkey, the photographers brushed them aside and grabbed a movie star's tot.

This irked me. My kids were as good as anybody else's, if not better. Their egos were taking a beating. I determined they would ride the donkey if I had to carry it home. Whether they were photographed did not concern me. But they were going to ride that donkey. I picked a strategic spot where the placid beast started to slow down, after making a halfhearted circle. "Whoa, Neddy," I hissed, grabbed the bridle with all my strength, yanked the movie star's progeny off with a smile and a pat and put my child on.

The photographers put their cameras down and looked disgusted. I did not care. When the round was over, I put my other child on the donkey, and then we left. I detested the falsely gay atmosphere, the *clickety-clack* of the cameras. The famous offspring ate ice cream—"Hold it"—*clickety-clack*. They kicked and screamed—*clickety-clack*. It was a ghastly experience. I said aloud, "This is the last time." There was no fun. It wasn't a party, it was a publicity stunt.

But like everyone else in Hollywood, or elsewhere, I entertained for my children on their birthdays. When Wendy was five, I hired Bozo the Clown, and invited about 15 of her acquaintances—Claire Trevor's Charlie, Ralph Edwards' son and two daughters, songwriter Sam Coslow's five-year-old Christine, who wore a long evening gown, and three of writer Frank Scully's children. Also, Stella's two nephews, Irvin and Leslie. There were a couple of little boys visiting next door, and when they looked over the fence I invited them over for good luck. Bozo in his clown's makeup and outfit frightened Rob, who was not yet two, and most of the time I had to hold him on my lap.

One advantage of being a Hollywood columnist was that I could have any movie shown for me at any time. For Wendy's sixth birthday, I asked Joe Reddy, Walt Disney's publicity chief, "Could we see some Disney shorts at the studio and have a cake for Wendy's birthday party?" At six, I felt that Wendy needed entertainment more adult than Bozo the Clown. "It would be a pleasure," said Joe. We decided *The Three Little Pigs* would be fine.

Producer Joe Pasternak's six-year-old Michael came with us in the car; also Kent Smith's Stacey. She was a quiet little girl, blond, with straight bangs in front of her short hair. On the drive back, Mike Pasternak told a faintly off-color story, something about a man who lost his pants. Stacey, who had not spoken one word coming or going to the party, suddenly burst into uncontrollable laughter. I am sure she did not understand the joke.

I had been careful of the few films Wendy had seen because I did not want her ever to be frightened or disturbed. But incredibly I had forgotten about the big bad wolf in *The Three Little Pigs*, and when Disney does a wolf, he makes him ferocious and frightening. Wendy was terrified and held my hand tightly when the wolf huffed and puffed and blew the house down. That night, I had a difficult time getting her to sleep and I could have hit myself for not realizing that Disney's films for children are more frightening than Hitchcock's for adults.

Later, in 1950, when we saw *Snow White and the Seven Dwarfs* at the Pantages Theatre in Hollywood, there was a long queue outside and Rob said, "I'm glad *we* don't have to line up." I told him, "When you grow up you will have to earn the privilege of not having to wait in line."

They do not always care for the privileges that go with my job. At any airport in the world, especially in the United States, the passenger manager will usually take care of my baggage and we are put on the plane first. This embarrasses my children, and Wendy has often complained, "Why can't we be like ordinary people?"

On one occasion, she had good cause to grumble. We were going to Europe, the three of us, with my secretary, Adele Roy. Everyone in the TWA Hollywood office was informed that Sheilah Graham, her two children and secretary were flying to New York and then to Europe. So many people had been alerted that each thought someone else had made the reservations. At the Los Angeles airport, it was discovered we did not have seats to New York. Fortunately the plane was not full. Walter Slezak gallantly turned over his seat to me so that Wendy and I could sit together in front. Rob and Adele had seats at the back. My daughter could not resist reminding me, "Mommy, if you had booked us as ordinary passengers, this would not have happened."

But worse was to come.

In New York we stayed at the Warwick Hotel. Europe is always cooler than New York in the summer and we were glad we would not be long in the hot city. The day after our arrival, a TWA official called and informed me a car would take us to the airport. We had a great deal of luggage among the four of us and I was pleased about the car. At 7:30 P.M., on a humid evening in June, we checked out of the Warwick and pointed happily toward Europe.

At the airport, the passenger agent was nowhere in sight and each counter in the old non-air-conditioned building had a long line of perspiring passengers. Tut-tutting with impatience, I led our group to the end of one line. This was the time of the great ingress of Puerto Ricans. They were coming in by the thousands, looking for jobs in New York, and the airport was a milling mass of bewildered dark brown humanity. Which made it all seem hotter.

After an unbearably long wait in line, it was our turn at the desk. I showed our four tickets and the official made the customary call to find out which seats we had. We did not have any seats. This was the busy season. There was no possible chance of getting on the plane. It was the same story. So many people at TWA had known we were going that everyone had assumed someone else was booking the seats. We had the mortification while we were in the passenger agent's office of hearing our plane take off. He had suddenly materialized in anwer to my wail, "Get me Howard Hughes."

I do not often use the column as a stick, but this time I threatened, "I shall write about this in my column. It's disgraceful. I shudder to think of what goes on upstairs [pointing to the sky] with such inefficiency downstairs." The children were crying and I was crying and Adele was crying. This was her first trip to Europe and she had saved for two years. To make matters worse I had arranged with the children's father, Trevor Westbrook to meet us in London the next morning. He has always believed I am not as truthful as I think I am. I knew he would not believe my story and this added to my fury.

"Get me Howard Hughes," I hissed. They were trying to pacify me and trying to get the Hughes office in California, and Bill Gaye, his man, was on the phone, and I wept, "I have my children with me and I have these appointments in London tomorrow and there are no reservations whatsoever and we checked out of the Warwick and what in damnation are you going to do about it?" "We can put you on the flight tomorrow night," said Mr. Gaye soothingly. My answer was a sarcastic snort. "I will never travel TWA again and you can tell this to Howard Hughes."

The passenger agent made some calls while I stomped up and down his office, huffing and puffing much more furiously than Disney's wolf. Finally, "We have managed to get you the suite at the Waldorf Towers which is used by the Duke and Duchess of Windsor when they're in New York." Still fuming and still vowing I would never again fly

TWA, I accepted the beautiful air-conditioned three-bed-room suite at the Waldorf Towers. The children cheered up somewhat when they saw it, rushing from room to room. After a magnificent dinner, I suggested we all go to bed. I knew the Hughes office would be calling early in the morning, but I left word we would take no calls until noon.

At 10 A.M., I ordered a large breakfast for us all, called BOAC and explained what had happened. A charming girl with an English voice did some checking. Alas, everything for the night flight was booked (there were only night flights in those days), but she promised to perform a miracle and soon called back. "I have two tickets and just hold on, we still have some time." An hour and a half later she called to say brightly, "I have three seats, but I'm afraid everyone else has confirmed." Adele offered to stay behind. I wouldn't hear of it.

At noon I took the call from the Hughes office—they had been trying to get me all morning. "I shall never travel TWA again," I told the Hughes official. "That this should happen in Los Angeles *and* New York is inexcusable." He tried to interrupt me but I continued, "Nothing you say can make the slightest difference." When I paused for breath, he shouted, "We have four seats for tonight and Mr. Hughes wants all of you to fly to England as his guests." The silence was deafening.

I thought of Adele. It had taken her a long time to save for the trip. She would have extra money to spend. I thought of the fact that BOAC had only come up with three seats. I thought of the stifling sweaty city. "I'll call you back," I replied. I would make one more try at BOAC. Still only three seats. I called Hollywood. We would be the guests of Mr. Hughes.

It did not compensate for the upset and delay. I would have rather used our own tickets and traveled on schedule. I was sorry that Wendy and Rob had seen me so angry and were aware that my anger had caused a powerful airline to tremble. It was absurd and out of focus with the sense of values I wanted them to have. This was a herculean task in Hollywood—and all but impossible in glittering, rich Beverly Hills, where even the public school they attended was full of great names and glamour.

✿ CHAPTER TWENTY

THE Hawthorne School in Beverly Hills is in the 600 block on North Rexford Drive. The buildings are low, Spanish in style, with red tiled roofs, and there are three enormous playgrounds. It is in the heart of the most prosperous area in the world. The parents of the students are among the richest and most famous. At 8:30 in the morning and when school is over in the afternoon, a continuous stream of Lincolns, Cadillacs and Rolls Royces fetch and carry the well-nourished children.

Among the parents during the time of Wendy and Rob at Hawthorne were Ingrid Bergman and Dr. Peter Lindstrom, the Fred Astaires, Ralph Edwards, Robert Cummings, the Gene Kellys, Jimmy Stewarts, Van Johnsons, Dorothy Lamour, and innumerable producers, directors, high-priced writers and lawyers.

On the Father's Day shows, Jack Benny's top writer wrote the skits, Jerry Wald produced, and Ralph Edwards directed. On one occasion, Dorothy Lamour was to have starred in a sketch with a famed lawyer, Norman Tyre, director Norman Taurog and Ralph Edwards. At the last minute, Dorothy was ill, and Ralph called on me to substitute. "Wear your prettiest evening gown," he advised. "What do I have to do?" I asked. "You just have to walk seductively across the stage, with us in pursuit." I drove to 20th Century-Fox, where Marilyn Monroe was making *How to Marry a Millionaire*, and asked her to teach me to wiggle seductively. She really tried, but I have never been able to wiggle as I walk. I wore my pale pink taffeta bouffant Don Loper gown and a pearl-embroidered tiara and they said I looked pretty and did very well. I was elated. With that audience in front, it was like a Broadway first night.

There were the usual carols at Christmas. Gene Kelly's daughter, Kerry, was in Wendy's class and one year as Kerry walked onstage, she stumbled. I caught a glimpse of Gene's eyes, suffering beneath his shiny bald pate. Unlike Ralph Edwards, who always wears a toupee in public, Gene prefers to be *au naturel*.

One May Day, Ingrid Bergman was in the audience with

her husband, Dr. Lindstrom. Their daughter, Pia, was in the sixth grade. The next May Day, only the tall, thin, reserved Dr. Lindstrom was there. Ingrid had eloped to Roberto Rossellini in Rome. I tried, as everyone else did, to refrain from staring at the solemn girl. I was angry with Dr. Lindstrom for not taking her out of the school. It was all very well to be brave, but this was not her mess. My daughter told me she had heard a group of older children tormenting Jenny Ann, as she was rechristened as soon as Ingrid had left. "Why did your mother leave you?" "Why did she run away from your father?" "Will your father divorce her?" Why should she suffer more than she had from the devastating departure of her mother? It was many years before Pia forgave her.

I had the scoop of Ingrid's premarital baby with Rossellini. A friend had written me the startling news from Rome. I called Ingrid's press agent confidant, Joe Steele, in Hollywood. He had recently returned from visiting Ingrid and Rossellini. "Is it true?" I asked Joe. "It could be," he admitted. When a Hollywood press agent says "Could be," it means "Yes, it's true." "Well, what do you know!" I gasped. It was Sunday. Before I left for my radio show, Mr. Steele telephoned me. "I'm worried over what you will say about Ingrid and the baby," he said. "For heaven's sake," I replied, "I wouldn't dream of using an item like that." But the cat was out of the bag. Joe, alarmed, called Louella Parsons. The next morning, her headline, INGRID BERGMAN EXPECTS BABY, shook the world—and Miss Bergman. My daughter Wendy heard so much talk in our house about the baby and Louella Parsons that she came to her own conclusions. When we drove past the Parsons house at 619 North Maple, she asked, "Mama, is Louella Parsons expecting a baby?"

Wendy almost landed in the movies when she was six. I had a call from the Sam Goldwyn office. They needed a small girl for Teresa Wright's daughter in a film. Teresa was playing an Englishwoman, the child must have an English accent. "How about Wendy? Does she have your accent?" I was asked. I hoped so. It would be a good memento for Wendy later, to see how she had looked and sounded as a little girl.

That night, while she was in the tub, I tested her accent. "Wendy, what am I giving you?" She replied, rather surprised at my stupidity, "A bath." "Not bath, Wendy; a bahth." "No, it's a bath." Heaven help the director, I thought, who tried to make Wendy say what *he* wanted, not what *she* wanted. I tried again. I showed her a picture and pointed to a path in a wood. "What is this, Wendy?" "A path," she replied promptly. She was proud of her early prowess at reading. It was hopeless. Her *a*'s were all short, her accent was American, although her voice has always had a soft English quality. Next day, I called the studio and said, "My daughter is an American."

Rob was an imaginative little boy. At the beach he would flap his arms and skim along the sand, pretending to be a bird. Sometimes he was a radio and gave out all sorts of little songs and conversations and commercials. Then suddenly, great discord. "The radio has broken down," he would explain. And he would fix it with an imaginary screwdriver at his head and the radio show would continue. Rob's puppet shows were quite clever. He would pretend to be different animals and people, including Bob Hope. He invented a soap with an awful smell, and I gave him a slogan—"This soap not only kills body odor, it kills *you*."

Wendy was a bright student. She has had practically straight A's from kindergarten. She won almost every prize when she graduated from Rosemary Hall. Wendy's scholastic excellence was a shadow on Rob's early school career. Wendy, three years older, had set a high standard. Rob knew it was hopeless to try to compete. As Wendy's grades soared, Rob's diminished. There is no allowance made for a slower tempo, or for imagination that has nothing to do with two and two make four.

We were at the beach. Rob was three. He had been fretful and crying a great deal. He was usually happy and intent on his make-believe, and I thought, He is coming down with a cold. He had a slight temperature and he wept long and loudly when I put him to bed. The next day, his left leg was completely stiff, also his left arm. I assumed this was part of a game or a bid for attention. "All right, if it's attention you want," I said, and rocked him in my arms. "There now." But he would not walk. "Perhaps it's a chill," I said to Stella. This pretend game was lasting too long. Stella put hot packs on his leg and arm and we kept him in bed and told Wendy, "Stay away from him." He cried a great deal during the night. In the morning he still would not use his leg and arm, and a great terror filled me.

I called Dr. Verne Mason, who had the reputation of being

the best diagnostician in Los Angeles. He made an appointment for us with Dr. Samuel Mathewson, a top orthopedist and bone specialist.

Leaving Wendy with a neighbor, and with Stella holding Rob on her lap, I raced the car to Dr. Mathewson's office in Beverly Hills. The doctor tried to trick Rob into walking normally. He tried to get him to use his left arm. He gave him a lengthy examination. And then he turned to me and said, "Mrs. Westbrook, your son has poliomyelitis."

Rob had polio. I felt nauseated and dizzy. The doctor continued, "I must report it to the health authorities. You can expect a visit from them and they may decide he must go into the isolation ward at the General Hospital."

Wendy had played with Rob the day before, pretending he was her doll and breathing close to his mouth. I asked Dr. Mathewson, "Is it contagious?" He spread his hands helplessly. "We don't know. We know nothing about polio. But it has happened that someone in contact with a mild case of polio has come down with a bad case." I thought of iron lungs and total paralysis. "You must watch your daughter," said the doctor. "Make sure she rests. Call me at the first sign of anything unusual." Dear God, help us now. Don't let Rob get worse. Keep Wendy safe. Don't let harm come to Stella. The doctor put Rob's leg in a cast up to the hip. I carried him to the car, with Stella alongside saying cheerful things. Rob enjoyed the attention.

How did they know at the beach? I did not tell them, nor did Stella. But everyone knew there was a child with polio in the house where we lived and all the children were told by their parents to stay away. Wendy was miserable when the other children ran away when she wanted to play with them. We returned to town. It was more convenient for visits to the doctor in any case. The health officer paid us a call and debated whether to put Rob in the hospital. I pleaded, "Why put the boy in with very bad cases?" Dr. Mathewson was sure he was no longer contagious, that the worst that would happen to Rob would be a bad limp and a stiff arm. He could stay home, and I thanked God.

My radio producer, Helen Mack, called me on Sunday. She had heard about Rob's polio. She was upset. "Why didn't you contact me? What are friends for? I will gladly do your radio show tonight." I burst into tears. It had not occurred to me to ask Helen or anyone to relieve me of the show. She explained on the air why she was substituting for me. I received many, many letters of sympathy.

Rob's was the first case of polio that year in Southern California, and where it came from nobody knew. Was it in the air? Was someone a carrier of polio? What had made it happen? Why should polio suddenly strike Rob or any child? They have some answers now, and thank God for Dr. Jonas Salk. But it was the Dark Age of Polio when Rob was stricken in the early summer of 1949.

The doctor periodically removed the cast and I was alarmed when Rob's leg seemed to be shriveling. I called Dr. Mason to the house. He examined Rob's leg and when I asked, "How did he get it and why?" he replied quietly, "I don't know. My son died of polio."

It was a good day when, after six long months, Dr. Mathewson took the cast off. Then began an intensive course of gentle exercising and massage. What a relief it was to see him walking. His arm and hand had become normal almost from the beginning.

I had conclusive proof that there were no ill effects. Rob came home one afternoon from the Harvard School in North Hollywood, rather flushed. During dinner I said, "Well, what did you do today?" He replied, "Oh, Harvard had a relay race against St. John's." "Did *your* class participate?" "Yes." "Who won for your class?" "Oh, I did." In fact, Rob had had to run two of the relays; the boy who was to take over had not appeared, and Rob had continued the race. If there had been anything the matter with his leg, he certainly could not have run two relays to win the race for his class at the Harvard Military School.

♥ CHAPTER TWENTY-ONE

SHORTLY before I started my Hollywood column in 1936, "Deac" Aylesworth, a friend of John Wheeler's and then head of the National Broadcasting Company, gave me some advice. "Stay close to Louella Parsons," he told me. "One day she will retire and you will be in a strategic position to take her place." I did not follow this advice for one important reason. I had never wanted to occupy the Parsons throne in

Hollywood and actually, there is no throne today. With films in production all over the world and with so many stars preferring to live in Switzerland, London, Paris and Rome, the kingdom has shrunk to a principality.

I have always had two careers—as a columnist and as a private citizen. I believe there are more things in life than writing a gossip column. A story has to be very good for me to be interested after 8 P.M., although I can write gossip as well, and sometimes better, than either Miss Parsons or Hedda Hopper.

Louella and I only became friendly after her first severe illness, in 1946, ten years after my arrival in Hollywood. She was in the hospital and she listened to my Sunday night broadcasts. It was the first time the Queen of the Columnists was aware that I not only existed but that I functioned rather well. After Louella came out of the hospital, we met at a party and she told me, "I like your radio show. It's very good." She sighed elaborately and said, "You're so young. I'm getting so old. Ah, I'd better retire." Retire my eye. When she returned to her radio show, she snitched my format, so that when I went coast-to-coast I had to do something completely different or I would have been accused of copying *her*.

One summer, Louella decided to take a semi-vacation in Europe for eight weeks. She never ever completely vacationed. She always sent back tidbits for her substitute, Dorothy Manners, to put in the column. But now she needed people to fill in for her radio show. I hoped I could be one of them. I invited her to lunch at Romanoff's and was amazed at how everybody, all the film big-shots, stopped by and genuflected. I felt the power this woman wielded in Hollywood.

Between the meat and the dessert, I suggested, rather diffidently, that I believed she was getting several people to do her radio show while she was away. No one would do it more than once—Louella has never taken chances of being pushed out by a rival. "If I can do your show," I said stupidly, "perhaps I can get my sponsor to put me coast-to-coast." Louella's eyes took on her well-known I-cannot-hear look. As long as there was no encroachment she could be very generous, but this was her territory, and nothing doing.

When I had become her neighbor on North Maple Drive, she had sent me a big basket of flowers, with a note, "If I ever need to borrow some sugar, I shall send for your children." It was meant well. She liked me because sometimes, meeting on a walk around the block, I would slip her a story I could not use. And what really cemented our friendship was giving her a big casting item for her Sunday show that I knew Hopper was using as the lead in her Monday column. At the time, I was between radio shows and it was too late for me to use it myself. If you gave Louella a scoop, she was your friend for life. When my story *Beloved Infidel* was bought by 20th Century-Fox, she gave me two headlines, and I know I would not have been as generous to her. The only time Hedda Hopper mentioned *Beloved Infidel* was to laugh at Gregory Peck for playing Scott Fitzgerald. How funny, she fanged, that Greg was playing the man I had loved and he would not even allow me on his set, which was news to me—and to Mr. Peck.

Hedda and I are polite to each other, but never friendly. I feel uncomfortable with her. I dislike her raucous laugh. She sounds so tough and I don't like people who are hard. In my opinion, The Truth and Nothing But about Miss Hopper is that she is a most opinionated person.

She is always telling people what to do and what not to do. She is not as good a reporter as Louella, who, in her heyday, had all the scoops. Hedda is always so sure she is right. And she belabors the people she believes to be wrong. She has a God complex. But in playing God, she has forgotten that God has compassion.

She is the most unabashed person I know. When Bette Davis refused to see her after the birth of her daughter, Hedda simply went to her home, rang the bell, and put her foot in the door. Bette found it simpler to invite her in. The maneuver was successful, and they became good friends.

At a party a few years ago, I watched Judy Garland glaring at Hedda. She had resented something in her column. A glare like that would have sent me to another part of the room. Hedda just stood there glaring back.

When the James Masons came to live in Hollywood, Hedda was their closest friend. Pamela Mason told me recently what had happened to the friendship. "Sybil and Richard Burton were staying with us. Hedda called to ask me what I knew of the rumor that Richard was having an affair with his leading lady. I told her I knew absolutely nothing, and even if I did, the Burtons were our guests and I couldn't give any information. 'You obviously don't know which side your bread is buttered on,' she snapped at me and hung up. She hated us in her column from then on."

When Claire Trevor married Milton Bren without telling Miss Hopper, the columnist telephoned her and called her several nasty names and ended with, "You'll regret this to your dying day!" Hopper refused to speak to Joan Crawford for years, although God knows Joan tried to speak to her, all because Joan neglected to call her with a correction on a previously given story.

As happens to us all now and then, Hedda had her come-uppance. It was at a party in London. Vivien Leigh was there, and the unsuspecting Hedda said to her, "I hear you've been ill." "Only when I read your column," said Miss Leigh and walked away.

And yet Hedda has her good points. She is very courageous, and some very discerning people like her—among them Bernard Baruch and Arthur Sulzberger of *The New York Times*. I saw Mr. Sulzberger actually get out of his wheelchair to greet her at the annual *Times* party for the publisher members of the Associated Press, the only person I saw him do this for.

Perhaps the very thing she is so proud of, that her life has been so blameless, that she has had only one romance, her brief marriage to the elderly actor, De Wolfe Hopper —she was his fifth wife—is what has made her so unyielding. Hedda was a beautiful woman, and is still, in her seventies, very elegant. Perhaps in her subconscious, she would have preferred a more interesting private life, and gets this out of her system by sitting in judgment on others.

And what of me? How do I operate as a columnist? Can I be objective and honest about myself? Probably not. Let's see. I, too, am playing God, making people happy or unhappy. Sitting at my typewriter banging out the items, I sometimes laugh as I stir my witch's brew, putting in the onions and the herbs to give indigestion to people I don't like or to those I think have slighted me, the great me. It all seems quite absurd and unreal, like the eternal sunshine of Hollywood which is sometimes gilded with large gobs of smog.

In conversation, I try to register a forthright friendliness that is sometimes deceptive. While I'm smiling and talking, I'm thinking, What would be the best question? What will make the best story? I'm absolutely cold on the matter. I'm not involved emotionally as Louella Parsons is. Neither do I demand they tell me everything, or what Hopper would call the truth. I simply do not care what people do in the privacy of their lives, although no one could guess this from my column. And it's true that I sometimes mistake my typewriter for my teeth, because the more I bite the more my column will be read. And this is the sad thing about human beings. We like to read about the troubles of other people, especially if they're rich and famous. It makes us—me—you—feel, "Well, they don't have *everything* they want."

But when the heat of composition cools, usually just after the column or news story has been sent, the reaction sets in. Why did I say that? Why wasn't I kinder? And it follows as the night the day, that I feel better when I do a straightforward interview. I'm still naïve—or haven't you noticed?—and usually believe what my interviewees tell me, and for the hour allotted, fool myself that we are very close. If I am actually face to face with the stars, I find it almost impossible to write cruelly about them. It's when I don't see them, when they are vague shadows on a screen, and I hear titillating news from the army of enemies they all seem to have, that I can take potshots. I expect them to be angry, and I stay away from them until something nicer goes into the column.

And why do I take such a delight in making fun of Zsa Zsa Gabor? This girl has never really harmed me. I use her deliberately to jazz up the column, to make readers smile. I don't like her, but this should not influence me when I write about her.

Marlon Brando and I have detested each other from our first and only face-to-face meeting. It was in 1947 and he was starring on Broadway in *A Streetcar Named Desire*. I was sitting close to the stage in the third row. I reacted strongly to this raw hunk of male virility. I thought he was the best young actor I had ever seen, and the sexiest. The torn shirt and the tough accent and the shouting "Stella, Stella"; even the slobbiness. He was something original and quite wonderful. I couldn't wait to meet him.

Jessica Tandy, his co-star, was an acquaintance and I hastened backstage after the show. "You were excellent," I told her, but my mind was on Marlon. "I must meet Mr. Brando. I think he's sensational, he's marvelous. What a man!" Jessica smiled. She had obviously heard this before. "All right, just give me a minute and I'll take you to him."

We seemed to go up some stairs to his dressing room, but it might have been my spiraling emotions. The whole episode had a surrealistic quality that turned Brando's dressing room into a narrow corridor about a mile long. Far at the end stood Brando, frowning, his arms crossed. He watched us without moving. The steady stare was most discomfiting and I wondered what I would say to this rigid statue. I could have saved my wondering. When Jessica said, "Oh, Marlon, I want you to meet—" he interrupted with, "Your mother?" I fled.

When Marlon tells the story, he explains he is rather short-sighted and had not meant to be rude. Hah! Later when I told the story to Hume Cronyn, who is married to Jessica, he laughed and said, "In actual fact, Jessica might be one year older than you." He was being kind. I am older than Jessica but not old enough to be her mother, even if I had married before I was born.

Marlon is the best American film actor, and I would have liked the opportunity to talk to him about his work. But he has never given me a chance. I, with several other columnists, including what he calls "The Hat" and "The Fat One," although Louella is no longer fat, are banned from the set when he is working and he refuses to talk to us at any time. I find him a very disagreeable man. My opinion of him was confirmed by Truman Capote in his story in *The New Yorker*.

I was interested when Marlon brought a lawsuit against Bill Davidson for his sharp article in the *Saturday Evening Post*, detailing what happened during the filming of the 18-million-dollar film, *Mutiny on the Bounty*. What case does he have? He *was* difficult. His co-star, Richard Harris, spent one evening with me talking about Brando and the problems and delays he caused by his peculiar behavior and his insistence on reshooting the end of the film to give Marlon and not Harris the death scene "because *I* am the star." He was right, of course. In the code of a top actor, to give the big scene at the end to another actor is unthinkable. But he could have spared himself, Harris and other members of the cast trouble and anguish by refusing to start the picture until the script was written to his satisfaction. It is no excuse to say—as he has—"they pressured me into it." No one in a film studio today can pressure a star as important as Brando.

There have been many accounts of Marlon's treatment of the various women in his life. Some of it makes shocking reading, but most of his girls are loyal to him regardless of his behavior. I had tea one day with the French fisherman's daughter, Josanne Berenger, to whom he was still presumably engaged, although Marlon was being seen with Rita Moreno and other girls. It was at Vanessa Brown's modernistic house high up in Beverly Hills. We all sat around a table drinking tea. There had been reports that the romance was over, and during a lull in the conversation I asked Josanne, "Are you still going to marry Marlon Brando?" At that precise second, her chair collapsed noisily and she completely disappeared under the table. Obviously Marlon's spirit was in the room and this was his method of preventing an answer.

Frank Sinatra and I were good friends when he first came to Hollywood. He would flirt with me a bit and pay me compliments. He objected to what I wrote about his marriage and breakup with Ava Gardner, although I only learned of his resentment at a concert in Carnegie Hall. I stretched out my hand to shake his. He walked past me with his hands in his pockets. I grew more and more aware of his animosity, and in retaliation, did my share of barbs in the column. At one elegant party in Beverly Hills, he told the hostess that unless I left, he would. She was more afraid of me, I guess, because Frankie left.

Shelley Winters, another temperamental star, once demanded all over the Universal lot, "Where is she? I'll kill her!" She was looking for *me*. My problem is that I never remember what I have written. I'm sure she does not remember what it was all about. Neither do I. I might have written that she was overweight. This is an obsession of mine, because I gain weight so easily. With success and psychiatric treatment, Shelley has become more secure and more able to diet. After she read *Beloved Infidel*, she asked me for lunch. She was sympathetic and interested in me as a person, more than as a sharp-penned reporter. She even recommended her psychiatrist to me. We are now excellent friends.

Everyone writes about Marilyn Monroe and tries to understand her. I doubt whether any of us ever has. I was quick to criticize when she failed to report for work. And I resented the hours she wasted, especially when it was I she kept waiting.

My boss, John Wheeler, recognized that Marilyn would be a big star very early in the game. He was in Hollywood and *Look* Magazine was giving a party in the Rodeo Room at the Beverly Hills Hotel. John, who has always had a good eye for a pretty blonde, pointed to Marilyn, barely visible at the other end of the room, and asked, "Who's that?" "Oh, a starlet, Marilyn Monroe," I replied. "Do you want to meet her?" He did. He looked appreciatively into the wide-apart frank blue eyes and she looked into his not-so-innocent blue eyes with her own special intimacy. "You're very pretty," said John gruffly. "You're going to be a great star." She always remembered him and every time we met she told me to be sure to remember her to Mr. Wheeler. When she married Arthur Miller, Mr. Wheeler and his wife invited them for dinner several times. When the Millers were at Amagansett on Long Island, and the Wheelers were at Easthampton, they planned a champagne-caviar evening, but instead Marilyn was rushed to New York by ambulance and she lost the baby she was expecting. She had two miscarriages and what a pity. She might have had something to cling to in the debris of the extraordinary fame that did not make her happy.

My first meeting with Marilyn was in 1951, soon after she had signed a contract at 20th Century-Fox. She had been at Columbia Studios where she was a chorus girl in a Rita Hayworth musical. Recently, I was given a photograph from this film, showing a line of 20 girls in spangly short dresses, all with one knee up. I have asked people to pick the most interesting girl in the line and they never pick Marilyn Monroe. In those days, there was no lisp and no problems. Johnny Hyde, of the William Morris Agency, was in love with her and perhaps he advised the lisp, the wiggling and the wisecracking. She was always uncertain, although in the last years there was an outward poise hiding the inner turmoil. The ghost of her lonely, unloved past was always there. But in company, Marilyn would joke or ask about *your* problems and interests. She was extremely appealing.

In the beginning, someone, perhaps Mr. Hyde, had advised her to carry a big book on philosophy. It was unexpected—the profound book and the young girl in the beige suit with the U-neck you could really look deep down into. There was nothing extraordinary about her in private life, and I was told that without the makeup—although I never saw her without it—she was unrecognizable and not even very pretty. This was why she spent so many agonizing hours preparing for her appearances in public.

Marilyn was my guest on a taped radio show and I learned then never to underestimate her. She had not yet reached the withdrawal of the last few years, she was still attending some of the Hollywood functions. Marilyn kept us waiting only two hours—later it would be longer. I am punctual. I cannot bear to be kept waiting. I was sorry I had thought this would be a good idea. But when she appeared, breathless and apologetic and all little-girl bewilderment, who could be angry? Marilyn stumbled all over the script. We split words of two syllables into one syllable. And we redid sentences until the room at the studio looked like a tickertape office on a busy stock market day. I thought, My God, how terrible she is and how good I am. How did she ever get to be a star? The worse she became, the more brisk and competent I sounded. But when I played the tape over at the end of the long afternoon, she was so much better than I. Her hesitation was natural, her mistakes were real, you could hear her thinking. My brisk competence sounded false. She came through as a star. This was even more true of her films. She drove everyone on the set to the brink of a breakdown—when she appeared, that is. But what came through on the screen was amazingly good.

In the last year or two Marilyn used liquor and sleeping pills as the raft in her sea of uncertainty. Like many of the insecure stars, her closest friend at the end was her press agent. She did not have to put on a show for Pat Newcombe. She paid her, she was always on call. Pat gave service above and beyond the dollars and cents, she worshiped her beautiful employer and tried with all her energy to protect her from the overwhelming problems Marilyn was less and less able to cope with.

I am often asked, "Did Marilyn really mean to commit suicide?" I do not know, but she had tried it before, and if you keep on trying, there will probably be one time when help will come too late. Gruesomely, that was my prediction in London, a month before she died.

Darryl Zanuck and I have been good friends since the day of the Great Favor. Selig Adler from the New York *Mirror* called me. A well-known Hollywood star, a friend of his, had just told him that Zanuck was divorcing his wife to enable him to marry Bella Darvi. Would I check and call back? Somewhat hesitantly, I telephoned Mr. Zanuck at 20th Century-Fox. It was a delicate topic and I tried to be tactful. Darryl did not fly into a rage as I had feared. He was too anxious for me to kill the story. "I give you my word of honor it isn't true, Sheilah. They'll have to carry me out feet first before I ever divorce my wife." I relayed this to the *Mirror* and Darryl has expressed his gratitude by always replying accurately to my questions, he has always given me his news stories, and has always been helpful. You sometimes do better by *not* printing a story.

❦ CHAPTER TWENTY-TWO

THE most unusual of all the strange people I have met in Hollywood is the elusive multimillionaire, Howard Hughes. I met Howard soon after I arrived in New York from England. Jack Duff, a rich youngish bachelor who seemed to know all the beautiful models and all the rich men-about-town, gave one of his frequent cocktail parties at his apartment in the Park Lane Hotel. Mr. Hughes was an early arrival. He seemed no different from the other young, rich bachelors. Tall and thin, with no signs of future antisocial eccentricity, he circulated in Jack's living room, concentrating on the more beautiful models. He was polite when Jack introduced us. I told him I was going soon to Hollywood. "Be sure to call me," he said absently. I was obviously not his type, for as he spoke, his busy gaze drifted past me and found the face of a lovely brunette.

I telephoned him in Hollywood. My syndicate had a query about a new type of plane. Mr. Hughes was polite and businesslike. There were a few other calls for one thing or another. He was often in the news, for his film activities, aviation, and romances—at various times he was linked with Katharine Hepburn, Ava Gardner, Olivia De Havilland, Ginger Rogers, Janet Leigh, Terry Moore, Mitzi Gaynor, Yvonne de Carlo, and later Jean Peters. His big film project was the making and remaking of *The Outlaw* with Jane Russell, whose mammoth-size bust was becoming part of the English dictionary, courtesy of Howard's press agent, Russell Birdwell. He bought the RKO Studio, which he never visited. He maintained offices at the Sam Goldwyn Studio. There was the oftentold story that one day he flew over the RKO lot and gave his one cryptic order: "Paint it."

I heard a great deal about Howard from Yvonne de Carlo. "We're in love," Yvonne told me one lunchtime in 1949 at Universal. "We're going to marry." "You are?" I was skeptical. Howard's romances were so well known. "Yes," Yvonne assured me. "He wants to wait awhile. He wants us to be sure." I could see that Yvonne was sure.

It seemed unfair that because Hughes was so rich, he could lead so many girls up the garden path and I said so on my radio show and in my column, and he did not like it. Johnny Myers, whom I had known at Warners in the Publicity Department, called me. He was working for Howard, in what capacity no one was quite sure, except that he had unlimited funds and always picked up the tab. Johnny sounded friendly. "When can you have a drink with me?" "Is it about Howard?" Small pause. Then he said, "I haven't seen you since Warners." It was obviously about Howard. "Okay—tomorrow—the Polo Lounge—at five."

Johnny was a bit thinner, but more confident. Some casual pleasantries, and then it came. "You know, Howard doesn't like you linking him with all those girls. It makes him unhappy." I had to smile. Johnny kept on talking, mostly double-talk, but all very casual and pleasant. It was all so pleasant that he believed I was going to be kinder to Mr. Hughes. Driving home, I thought, What a nerve this man has. And I laid it on thicker with Mr. Hughes.

I had a call from the Hughes office. "Bill Gaye speaking. Mr. Hughes will be calling you in five minutes." I promised to wait. Then the great man was on the phone and saying in soft Texas tones, "I'd like to see you." I quaked a bit, but said, "Okay. When?" That afternoon would be fine, at his office on the Goldwyn lot. I was quite nervous. He wanted to tell me off, what else? But my curiosity was stronger than my fear. And no matter what happened, it would be another item for the column, so here we go.

Howard was courteous, offered me a drink and a cigarette, both of which I declined. (I do not smoke and have never cared for anything much in the alcohol department.) He was thinner and had grown a mustache. He was wearing his well-known not-too-clean sneakers. When I spoke, he watched my lips closely. Apparently his deafness was worse. We sat almost knee to knee and his mournful brown eyes bored penetratingly into mine. "You've come a long way since I saw you in New York," he said. "So have you," I replied, somewhat desperately. He half smiled, then—"Why don't you like me?" I almost laughed. I had expected an angry tirade. It was incredible that the great Howard Hughes cared whether I, Sheilah Graham, neé Lily Sheil, liked him. What difference could it make? Feeling more confident, I assured him, "I don't dislike you at all." "Well, then," he replied, "why are you attacking me all the time?" He seemed genuinely anxious. What should I say? That I was sorry for the starlets I thought he deceived? "I guess it really isn't my business," I said slowly. "But if you were to marry one of these girls, and they all *think* you're going to marry them, it would be a big news story." He stood up. "I'll make a deal with you. I'll be available to you twenty-four hours a day [He was almost as hard to find then as now; Robert Mitchum had been trying to reach him for weeks to discuss his RKO contract], if you'll promise to lay off the girls. It hurts me in my business. I can tip you off to some good stories. I'm in a position to know a lot of what's going on." I followed him to the door. It seemed like a good bargain. "But you must promise me one thing," I said as we walked to my car. "If you ever plan to marry, you must tell me." "I promise," he replied solemnly, adding, "And you can crucify me if I break my word."

He gave me some fine news stories, including Cary Grant's elopement with Betsy Drake. Howard was best man and telephoned me immediately after the ceremony in Arizona, giving me a beat of several hours on the wire services. But when Howard married Jean Peters, after her divorce from Stuart Cramer III (now married to Terry Moore who had expected Hughes to marry *her*), he did not give me the story. By that time, RKO Studios had been sold to Desilu, he was no longer in the business of making movies, and our last encounter had been unsatisfactory. He gave the scoop of his marriage to Louella Parsons; he could trust her to accept his condition—to use the story in her movie column instead of splashing it on the front page where it belonged.

My last contact with Howard was quite extraordinary. Bill Gaye telephoned one evening when I was ill in bed with flu. "Mr. Hughes will be calling in five minutes and please be sure no one else is in the room or able to listen on an extension." This was the usual preliminary to a call from Howard. This time Mr. Gaye repeated, "You are sure you are alone?" It must be something very important. I assured him I was alone and wearily prepared pencil and paper. Precisely five minutes later, Howard was on the phone. He could always hear on the telephone. I don't know whether he had a contraption on it, or whether his particular kind of deafness disappeared on the phone, but one could talk without having to shout.

"I've got a scoop for you, and I'd like to see you right away. I'll send a car for you." He seemed quite excited. "I have flu," I explained. "Can't you tell me on the phone? I'm feeling quite ill." He said he was sorry, but "I cannot talk about it on the phone. I must see you." In my weakest voice I said, "I'm not sure I can get up." "This is the biggest scoop of the year," he persisted. I did not want to lose the biggest scoop of the year, so, resignedly, "All right, I'll get dressed, I'll wrap up." "Do that," he said and hung up.

The car was there ten minutes later and the chauffeur took me on a most curious drive. Up the hills and down the hills and round about for some 30 minutes. Where was he taking me? I looked into the darkness and hadn't the faintest idea where we were. We stopped at what seemed to be the servants' entrance of a one-story bungalow, and looking around at the shrubs and the garbage cans and the enormous Spanish edifice outlined against the sky in front, I realized I was at the back door of a Beverly Hills Hotel bungalow, which was only three minutes from my home! Was the drive intended to confuse me? I can think of no other reason.

Howard opened the door. I settled into an armchair in the small living room, sniffling and suffering, anxious to get the story and go home. It must be something stupendous, to judge by Howard's agitated pacing up and down. He had absolute proof, he stated emphatically, that the Hollywood film official who was courting Elizabeth Taylor was a Communist. He paused for my reaction, while I waited for him to continue. But there was nothing more. I was outraged— and very disappointed. I knew of Howard's liking for Elizabeth. I also knew that she considered him an old man. She wanted his friendship, but nothing more.

"Is this the scoop? Is this what you want me to print? Of course I can't use a story like that." "But I have proof," he persisted. "But *I* have *no* proof. Besides, it isn't my job to print he's a Communist. Why don't you tell the FBI?" He ignored my suggestion. Instead, "This is a big story. If I gave it to Louella or Hedda, they'd make it a big thing." I doubted it. Even Hedda couldn't print such a story without proof, and I said, "I'm sorry, I must leave now. I'm not well."

I have not seen or talked to him since. I think he still maintains several bungalows at the Beverly Hills Hotel. He is reported to be in Las Vegas and Florida, but no one except his trusted staff really knows. Sometimes his wife,

Jean Peters, who was a gregarious young beauty-contest winner from Ohio when I first met her at 20th Century-Fox, is seen shopping in Beverly Hills. There is a rumor that they have a child, a son. When Simone Signoret was living with her husband, Yves Montand, in a bungalow at the Beverly Hills Hotel while he filmed *Let's Make Love* with Marilyn Monroe, I visited Simone and she told me that she had seen Jean Peters next door, playing on the grass with a little boy. He might have been her nephew, but it could have been her own child with Howard Hughes. I am not brave enough to try to find out.

❦ CHAPTER TWENTY-THREE

IF I am a better reporter today than when I began nearly three decades ago, if I am more careful of my sources and the checking of as many facts as time allows for the writing of a daily column, I owe this to two men, Mike Kaplan and Al Sharper, with whom I worked on *Daily Variety* in Hollywood from February 1952 to May 1953, when I learned the importance of being right as well as being read. It was a fascinating time. I was Cock o' the Walk. Louella and Hedda were eating out of my hand. I wielded the whip and I enjoyed it—mostly.

No one could understand it. Why was I taking on such a difficult job? I was an established syndicated columnist with twenty-two million readers all over the world. Except for an occasional unpleasantness with a star or a studio, there were no problems. After 16 years, the column almost ran itself. There was time for my children—Wendy was nine years old, Robert six, I was a regular attendee at the P.T.A. We had Cub Scout meetings in my house on Maple Drive. I went to most of the Hollywood parties. I played tennis. I swam. I took the children for weekend trips to Ojai, Santa Barbara and Palm Springs. Life was pleasant and easy. I am always restless when things are too easy. I always want to prove I can do something more.

A week after I started my new column in the Hollywood *Daily Variety, Time* Magazine compared my new power and prestige to "that enjoyed by a top executive producer's wife." It was much more. *Daily Variety* and the Hollywood *Re-*

porter, with a circulation of only 8000 apiece, are required reading for everyone in the motion picture industry, from the president of a studio to the merest extra. They are like babies with the bottle. They must have what they call "the trades": stars, executives, writers, directors, agents and other columnists would rather be mentioned in these two trade papers than in any 50-million-circulation syndicate or magazine in the world. And especially in the gossip column of these two trade papers.

Mike Connolly had recently left *Daily Variety* for the Hollywood *Reporter*. His successor was too innocuous to be satisfactory. The local publisher, Joe Schoenfeld, was scanning the field when he pinpointed me for the job, at the 1952 New Year's Day party in the Hollywood Hills home of Jack Hellman, *Daily Variety's* veteran byliner for radio and television.

A few years before, the very tough publisher, Arthur Unger, had asked me to write the column. Mr. Hellman had thought then, as he did now, that it was a good idea. But my children were much younger then and Unger's bite was as bad as his bark, and after playing with the idea, I told him, "The *Citizen News* won't release me." I had not asked them.

But now, as the *Time* piece stated, I would "flex my muscles." I would prove I could write the very best column on motion pictures. It would involve an enormous amount of extra work because the trade papers have to be a day ahead of the newspapers. They have to know today what will happen tomorrow, and other columnists and newspaper reporters often get their first hint of a good story in the *Reporter* or *Variety*. It meant attending every function, every banquet, every premiere, every preview, every cocktail party. It's a full-time job, and with two children and a large home, I would be a very busy woman. In fact, I already was.

In addition to my column, I still had my monthly *Photoplay* assignment, twice a month I wrote a column for *TV Guide*, I was editing fan magazine books for Dell Publications: *Sheilah Graham's Hollywood Romances, Sheilah Graham's Hollywood Yearbook, Sheilah Graham's* this and *Sheilah Graham's* that; and they were paying me $1000 each time for the use of my name and for going through and okaying the material. Later, with the success of *Confidential*, they believed they, too, had to be dirty and full of innuendo with false, misleading statements on the cover, and while correcting a *Sheilah Graham's Hollywood Yearbook* I realized that the editor had made every actor a queer and every woman a degenerate, and I threw the pencil away and wired them, TAKE MY NAME OFF. I have done nothing for them since.

When I told Sidney Skolsky—we've always been friends—that I was planning to undertake *Daily Variety*'s page two gossip column, he demanded, "What do you need it for? It'll be a hell of a lot of work." "I want something more challenging," I explained. He shook his dark head wonderingly. "Well, I suppose you know what you're doing. But be sure you get a contract for a year. You never know, if someone doesn't like you they could fire you tomorrow and you'd be left with egg on your face." How could he have foreseen my battles and problems with Joe Schoenfeld? I asked my syndicate to insist on a year's contract. They added an extra two months' cancellation clause. It meant leaving the Hollywood *Citizen News;* I could not appear in two publications in the same city. "Our readers will miss you," said Mr. Palmer. "We will always be glad to have you back." "Thank you," I said cheerfully. I doubted that I would return. *The Citizen* was small potatoes compared to the powerful trade paper.

As always with a new project, I hurled myself into a do-or-die battle. I was extremely alert, mentally and physically, taking notes and storing up nuggets of news for the day when my column would start in *Daily Variety*. Then, the week before publication, Joe Schoenfeld was rushed to the hospital with a severe heart attack. I was very upset. Not only did I like him, but Joe had promised to guide me, and without his help I was not sure I could write this new kind of column that had to be sharp with a very special trade language of its own. I consulted Sidney. "It's too late to back out now," we reluctantly agreed.

My first *Daily Variety* column was, perhaps, the best I have ever written. One item *Time* Magazine mentioned in its complimentary piece—"Errol Flynn says he doesn't worry about money—as long as he can reconcile his gross habits with his net income." This has been used many times since in other columns. I did not invent it. Errol told me himself.

My column was the talk of Hollywood in the six weeks that Joe Schoenfeld was in the hospital. I have always liked to surprise people with what I can do when I really try. I was given a free hand, but Mike Kaplan, the editor, never allowed anything to pass that he considered questionable. I would recheck, and it was amazing how right he always was. I had an item about a Howard Hughes activity from Howard himself, but Mike said, "Better recheck. It doesn't seem feasible." He was right. I had taken it down wrong. I loved working with Mike. He was an experienced newspaperman and a fantastically good editor. Al Sharper, who put the paper together, was always helpful, and it was no bother, he assured me, anytime I wanted to change an item at the very last minute. Al spent Saturday afternoons at the Santa Anita Racetrack. And I was usually there on Saturdays, searching for news from Louis B. Mayer, Betty Grable, Carl Laemmle Jr., Alfred Vanderbilt, John Huston. It was like winning the Daily Double when Al told me at the track, "This is the first time *Daily Variety* has had a good columnist. This is the first time we have given page two competition to the *Reporter.*"

Joe Schoenfeld came back and immediately started to harass me about the column. I was a seasoned newspaper-woman, but Joe treated me like an ignorant cub reporter and I resented this enormously. We had fights almost every day, usually over trivial matters. One day he called me and raged, "Mike Connolly has two hundred people at the Chaplin party; you have forty." I happened to be right, but it was hardly worth the wear and tear to prove it.

I told my problems with Joe to a British director, Terence Young, who was in Hollywood. He gave me some good advice that I did not follow. "Never charge a bull head-on." I considered Joe, who was fairly short, more like a fighting cock. He often cut my items without telling me, and I would call the printers at night after Joe had left and ask, "How short is the column?" I put in new items, which infuriated Joe the next day. But I was even more annoyed at his habit of adding stories to my column without asking me. Invariably they got me into hot water. One time Joe stated in my column that Edmund Goulding was leaving 20th Century-Fox. Fanny Holzman, his lawyer, had told me not too long before that Goulding had signed a seven-year contract with the studio. When I saw the item I called Mr. Goulding and apologized. The man who had directed *Grand Hotel* and *Dark Victory* was most forgiving. I promised a retraction for the next day, but had to fight Joe to do it.

My biggest battle with Schoenfeld concerned Lana Turner. I had been jabbing her, starting with the bit in my first column: "Lana Turner is saying that Bob Topping owes her

$82,000. Moral—never marry a trust fund." She was starring at Metro in *The Merry Widow* with Fernando Lamas. Dore Schary, then in charge of production, called me. "Sheilah, will you do me a favor?" I have always liked Dore. He is gentle and unassuming. "You know I will if I can," I replied. "Lana Turner reads your column every morning. She gets very upset and she's threatened to walk off the picture at the next crack. I'd be very grateful if you could put something nice about Lana in your column." Of course I could and would. "What can I write that will be legitimate and will also soothe her? Er—how about this—I'll say I've heard she is doing a good job in *The Merry Widow*." "That," said Dore, "will make her, and me, very happy." "It's a pleasure." I had not realized I was making Lana so unhappy.

The next morning I opened my *Daily Variety* and nearly fell out of bed. In my column, Joe had rewritten the item to read that Fernando Lamas was stealing every scene from Lana in *The Merry Widow*. I called Dore Schary at once and explained, "I did not write this." I read over what I had written, but he was naturally somewhat skeptical. Why would anyone rewrite my quite harmless piece? "I'll get Joe Schoenfeld to call you." I was almost in tears. I called Joe and demanded, "Why did you change the meaning of my item so completely? I promised Mr. Schary I'd write something nice about Lana. Now she won't come to work." As usual, he became angry. "How was I to know about your promise?" "How was I to know you would change my item?" I stormed. "Well, it's true," he replied. "Fernando Lamas *is* stealing every scene." "That's not the point and I don't believe it." Lana was not the world's greatest actress, but she was better than Fernando. He would not call Dore Schary. "And for God's sake, forget it," said Joe.

While I still enjoyed the power and the attention, I became less interested in the column. Why spend a half hour trying to word an item in a certain way when it would probably be changed or eliminated? Mostly I worked at home where I could keep an eye on what was happening with my children. Sometimes on Sunday when it was difficult to get a messenger to deliver the column, I brought Wendy and Rob to the *Variety* office and Joe would be kind to them, although they regarded him with suspicion. "It's Joe," they would say whenever they heard me shouting on the phone.

I married again for the third and last time—an American

of Polish ancestry with an unpronounceable name. I had known him for exactly five weeks when we were married secretly on Valentine's Day 1953, in Ventura County, California. We were quite different: he, gregarious and outgoing and full of fantasies; I, cautious of new friendships, reserved, and careful with my facts. No one could understand the marriage. My lawyer, Jerry Geisler, begged me to wait six months. "Ask him to change his name," he suggested when I came to his office prior to the marriage to make a will leaving everything I possessed to my children. "That will give you time to think it over." He was right, but my fiancé was most indignant. "I am proud of my name," he said. I respected him for that. Mrs. Edward G. Robinson telephoned and begged, "Promise me you will talk it over with me before doing anything." But by then, I was already married. George Lait, the publicist son of Jack Lait, on his deathbed a few years later shook his head and whispered hoarsely, "I'll never understand why you married him. You had absolutely nothing in common." The general opinion was, "It must have been sex."

I married again because I believed I was in love, and the other fifty percent was to give my children, especially my son, a father at closer range than their father in London. In fact, I had not told them of the divorce until I was able to say, "And now I can give you an American father." They were delighted and danced a little jig around my bedroom. Wendy was ten and a half. Rob was seven.

It was getting near the end of the one-year contract with *Variety*. It had been fascinating in spite of the fights with Joe. Agents, producers and stars supplied me with so much news it was a problem what to discard. I enjoyed the politeness from Louella and Hedda. They knew that as the *Daily Variety* columnist I had the last word on anything they did and I could get it in print faster, to the audience that mattered in Hollywood—the trade. I had what seemed like an interesting idea. It would be good, I thought, to write a column evaluating my year with *Variety*, the scoops, the mistakes, the enemies and the friends—a summary of the year to be used on the anniversary of the day I had started the column. But when I told Joe, he replied, "I don't believe in rehashing the past." There was a pause. "You've been with us one year, have you?" I should have had an inkling of what was in his mind, but I did not. Not until he called me the next day and said, with elaborate casualness, "I'd like to have a drink with you on Saturday—four o'clock at the Beverly Wilshire?" I knew at once I was going to be fired.

It did not take long, although he was more pleasant than I had known him since he had hired me. "I have sent a letter to NANA, giving notice of cancellation. I'm sorry." "But why?" I asked. "The column is popular. Is it that I don't work in the office? Am I too expensive?" I thought of the humiliation. I thought of the lovely power. I thought of the jubilation of my enemies. The idea of returning to being just one of the top five columnists in Hollywood instead of the Number One was hard to accept. "I'll come to the office. You can cut the salary entirely." It was $125, of which NANA gave me $75. "Please," I urged him, "please don't cancel the column." He promised to think it over. But he had already hired Army Archerd, who was Harrison Carrol's pains-taking young assistant. There would be no fights with Army. It was a great opportunity for him and he is still with *Daily Variety*. Joe has long since left to return to work as an agent, which I believe he performs with less anxiety.

Joe was kind enough to let me announce my resignation in my column and to hold off the announcement until after the big reception I had planned in my home to celebrate my marriage. My husband had invited all the big-shots. The party had been his idea. I was not sure they would come if I were no longer at the head of the class in Hollywood. I re-membered Jim Henaghan, who had written the Hollywood *Reporter* column before Mike Connolly, telling me that when he resigned to write an original movie one month before Christmas, not only were there no presents from anyone, "but not even a Christmas card." This is Hollywood, where your power is measured by the celebrities you can force to come to your parties and invite you to theirs. Looking over the 150 mostly important names who came to wish me joy, I won-dered how many would have sent regrets if I had announced the week before instead of the week after that I had been fired from *Variety*, that I was returning to my nice little column in the Hollywood *Citizen News*.

There were some lovely presents—linens, silver, glass and china, and more flowers than you see at the funeral of a Hollywood czar. Joe Schenk held court on the staircase. Mike Todd brought Evelyn Keyes—this was, of course, before Eliz-abeth Taylor. Darryl Zanuck took up a position in the crowded dining room. There wasn't a star, a producer, writer or director who was invited who did not accept. Robert Taylor came with his new wife, Ursula Theiss, Greer Garson with Buddy Fogelson, and John Wayne, Rosalind Russell, Stewart Granger ánd Jean Simmons. Marilyn Monroe arrived with Sidney Skolsky after most of the guests had gone. She spent some time with my son. I hope she gave him advice on how to handle women because Rob is now eighteen, tall, extremely handsome and is always having all sorts of complications with all sorts of young ladies.

✿ CHAPTER TWENTY-FOUR

ALMOST everything very good and very bad has happened to me around Christmastime. My son was born on Christmas Eve 1945. Scott Fitzgerald died a few days before Christmas 1940. And in mid-December 1954, the amazing offer of $5000 a week was telephoned from San Francisco by Tom McAvity, vice-president in charge of NBC television production. I had wished for this to happen, but you never quite believe it when it does.

Nothing in my previous career in television had indicated that I was worth $5000 a week. "The program," said Tom, a pleasant, efficient executive with a healthy golf handicap, "will be titled *The Sheilah Graham Show*." He was obviously crazy. "It will start January 2nd, over the entire NBC network. Can you be ready?" I am always ready. I always say Yes, and then find a way to do it. I am superstitious. If I say No I will never get another chance. So don't think of the problems, old girl. Step in where angels and wise men flee. I said, "Yes, Tom, I can do it."

I did not tell him of my first dreadful appearance on television, the TV fiasco of 1948. Someone at the Don Lee television station had had a brave idea—to have a lady commentator for Gorgeous George, the wrestler with the mop of golden curls. A feminine touch might sweeten the gore. "You will describe the match from the ringside." Later I would interview the blue-eyed gorilla in a private room off the arena. I had attended two wrestling matches in London. "They are all fixed," I was told, and I could well believe it. The phony anger, the grunting and groaning, the pounding, the torture. Then they walked away in one piece. But this might be interesting. I could semi-close my eyes and I was to receive a hundred dollars.

I knew nothing of wrestling or of television. I did not own a set, which in those days were small, expensive and unsatisfactory. As far as I could see, Gloria Swanson was the only woman brave enough for the new cruel medium. You turned the knob in a friend's house, and there she was, looking 199 years old.

"Come as you are," they told me. "Don't bother about makeup. It won't make any difference." They were so right. I arrived at the arena early, as I always do for an assignment. No one there. I went to the office. Not a soul in sight. A friend had said, "Use a darker lipstick." I went to a nearby drugstore, bought one, had a cup of tea and tried to plan what I would say. My mind was blank. But no matter. Watch the wrestling and it will come.

Back to the arena. People were filling the seats, men without coats were rushing around yelling orders, moving the great hot lights around the ring. I introduced myself to a man with a microphone. He explained the camera would not be on me at all during the bout; they would just hear me. They would not see me until the interview.

Applause, boos, jeering laughter, catcalls and hisses heralded the start of each bout and during every match—with a double portion of everything for Gorgeous George. It seemed that every man, woman and child in the audience was screaming obscenities. George stared back at them with haughty disdain.

I talked. I described Gorgeous George—his mop of golden curls, his blazing raiment, and as he stripped—"What a body!" But mostly I said, "Oh my God," as Mr. George gouged and tossed his opponent, or vice versa, and several times nearly landed in my lap. A voice hissed in my ear, "Don't keep saying 'God.' " Then it was over and I was hustled off to the anteroom. It was like a Finnish bath, with white blazing lights.

"Is this your first experience in television?" the pleasant young director asked me. I nodded and shook a pint of sweat from my face. "Don't be worried," he continued cheerfully. "It's very simple. Just follow my instructions and you can't go wrong." "Oh, I will," I promised energetically, and lost another pint of perspiration. "This is the camera," he said patiently, as though instructing a child. "And here is a mark" —pointing to an imaginary spot four inches to the left of the camera. "You will direct all your conversation to this spot. You must never look anywhere else." "Is that where Mr. George will be?" I asked. "Oh, no, he will sit on your left," he replied. It seemed odd, but I have always respected authority and this man must know. He drew up a chair next to mine for the star wrestler who had just entered. We shook hands. Mine were damp and his were hot.

It was like having my head in a vise, looking left of the camera while I asked questions of George who was on my right. When I instinctively turned to him, the director made a soft clicking noise, crawled under the camera and pointed urgently to the spot where I must look. The entire interview was a two-shot of us both, and everyone I knew who saw it thought I had lost my mind. "Did you have a stiff neck?" "Why didn't you look at him?" "Why that glazed stare?" "How can you talk to a man and look the other way?" I was furious. "No more television for me," I vowed.

I kept my word until 1951, when I was fired from my national radio show at the Mutual Broadcasting Company, when radio as well as motion pictures seemed destined for oblivion.

I had been riding for a fall. The best feature on my radio show, "What are the stars really like with their makeup off and their hair down?" had caused me every kind of trouble in Hollywood. But it was heard. Greer Garson, I was told, would stop whatever she was doing on Sunday at 6:30 P.M. and carry her portable radio with her wherever she went. Everybody in Hollywood was listening because of the sharpness of this particular feature. I tried to be fair, but when the profile was too long, the controversial lines remained while the good was oft interred in the wastepaper basket. Everyone was amused—except the person profiled. Kirk Douglas was understandably annoyed when I ended my piece on him with "Kirk Douglas is now starring in *Young Man With a Horn*. It should be a cinch. He never stops blowing it." Errol Flynn had been injured during a film scene and in my profile of him I mentioned something about the young nurse who had attended him—"Not even she is safe from his attentions." He threatened a lawsuit.

There was an unhappy experience with Lucille Ball. Scott Fitzgerald and I had watched from the balcony of his apartment on Laurel Drive while Lucille, who lived in the same building as Scott, had courted Desi Arnaz. She always seemed to be asking him not to drive away in his car, to stay. We could not understand his reluctance and sometimes made bets on the outcome. No matter which of us lost, we were both pleased when Lucille won.

One Sunday, I was short of news, and I called Lucille's press agent with the usual beginning by a columnist. "What's new?" He hesitated, then said, "Lucille and Desi are having some bad battles in New York." I mentioned this on the show. Lucille called me in a rage from New York. "I'm going to get you for this and who told you?" she demanded. "You know, Lucille, I cannot tell you," I replied. She started to cry. "You've got two children and you don't care. You say things like this about me and I will never have children." I felt dreadful and tried to tell her I was sorry, but she yelled about how she would get me if it was the last thing she ever did, and hung up. Lucille wanted children desperately. Her doctor had suggested, "Why don't you adopt a child?" But Desi did not want adopted children. I was pleased when they had children of their own.

Jennifer Jones also called me from New York and she was angrier than Lucille. She had been one of my "profiles." I had stated that David Selznick was, as usual, masterminding her picture. It was true, but she denied it and called me a liar and a few other choice despicable things. I managed to keep calm. When she paused for breath, I said, "Jennifer, you have just given your finest performance," and slammed the phone down, which was really frustrating for her because to judge by her vast intake of breath, she had a great deal more to say. We did not talk again until the night of the press preview of *Tender Is the Night*, when I congratulated her for her portrayal of Nicole. She was too old for the part then but I wanted to be nice to her.

Humphrey Bogart, furious with my profile of him, threatened to punch me in the nose the next time he saw me. I was careful to stay away from him. Not that he would have fulfilled his threat. Bogey always talked big, but face to face he was quite timid.

It was Jane Wyman who actually got me fired. Most of the information for her profile was supplied by her best friend, and her press agent, and she will learn of this now for the first time.

Jane did not hear the radio show. The offended stars never do. Nor do they see the particular column that upsets them. When Charlton Heston, for instance, was making a recent film in Rome, I wrote in my column that the script girl on his picture was flying to Hollywood for one day to complete an interrupted job for Billy Wilder. She would then fly back to Rome for one more week on the Heston picture. "How dedicated can a girl be?" I had written. Meaning, dedicated to her job. Charlton was called in Rome by his wife and his press agent, neither of whom had read the item, and informed I had stated he was having an affair with the script girl! He spent all night tracking me down, and awakened me by phone in London at five in the morning. I was exhausted, having flown in from Vienna a few hours previously. His icy "How dare you" etc., etc., sent me stumbling to a copy of the column. Then just as coldly I read him what I had written. "Nothing wrong in that," he said very sheepishly, and apologized.

But Jane Wyman had more cause to be angry. All her friends, apparently, and a few enemies had telephoned her after my broadcast. She called her lawyer, the debonair Greg Bautzer. He sent a long legal telegram to every station of the Mutual Broadcasting Network that carried my show, demanding a full retraction. Mutual's legal department ordered me to comply. The following Sunday I retracted—line for line. "I'm delighted to tell you," I told my listeners with false brightness, "that Jane Wyman is not antisocial; she *does* have some friends." And, "Jane Wyman does not break out in a rash when she's nervous. That *is not* the reason she wears a high-necked gown." I repeated everything to which she had objected, then said it was not true. The press agent who had given me the information agreed with me that the retraction was worse for Jane than the original offense. But having relieved the network of responsibility, I was tossed into the ranks of the radio unemployed.

But now, it seemed that television would wash out all other mediums of entertainment. Radio was drowning. The motion picture industry was backing away from the tidal wave, refusing to face the inevitable. Every householder's roof was sprouting an aerial and less and less people were going to the movies. Milton Berle was Mr. Television. Eddie Cantor, Jimmy Durante, Bob Hope, Jack Benny, Fred Allen, all the top stars of radio were rushing to join the "monster" that was chaining their audiences at home to the small screen, which was getting cheaper, had stopped flickering, and would soon, courtesy of the Telephone Company, be seen simultaneously east and west, north and south.

Sidney Skolsky and I took a long walk on the beach. "What's going to happen to Hollywood?" I asked him anxiously. "Will it become a ghost town?" We thought it very well might. But if you can't lick 'em, join 'em. Sidney, who is more brainy than beautiful, got himself a TV show. I used to photograph rather well. Perhaps *I* should join this new medium. I was prettier than Sidney and, as Ezra Goodman wrote in his book on Hollywood, I was young compared to my two rivals, Parsons and Hopper.

I made the rounds. No agent this time. Ken Dolan had died. Other agents had been ineffectual. No luck at CBS. It was hopeless to try the powerful NBC. The executive at ABC was on the telephone when I was ushered into his office. He was talking to John Guedel who was, and still is, in partnership with Groucho Marx. It was a long conversation. The ABC official was pleading with Guedel to let him have Groucho. He had acknowledged my entrance with a vague smile and pointed to a chair. Every so often, he would look at me or wink to make me part of the conversation, which went on and on. I thought, Oh, if only he would plead so desperately to have *me*. I gathered he was not making much headway with Mr. Guedel. Finally, he jarred the phone down, turned to me very irritably and said, "What can I do for you?" He was no longer including me in his plans, I could see that. He wanted to get rid of me fast so he could get back to the job of trying to land Groucho.

The atmosphere was not conducive for a sale, but I plunged into my talk. I was sure, I told him, that I could get the studios to give me portions of their films, or perhaps their old films. I would be hostess, interview some of the stars, and with my reputation as a Hollywood film columnist, I thought I could build up a following for motion pictures on television. His laugh was more like a sneer. He threw up his hands at my crass stupidity. "You know the studios will never give any of their stars to television. Or their films. You'll never get cooperation from the film studios."

He's right, I thought as I drove to the apartment I had rented at the beach. I was terribly depressed. No one wants me. I'm no good. I'll never make the grade in television. This is the future, Hollywood itself will go under, and this new medium of entertainment will take over and I won't be part of it. I was full of anxiety and I wept tears of self-pity.

The telephone was ringing as I entered the apartment. It was Ed Sobol, in charge of local NBC television. His words sent me rocketing to the sky. "How would the best columnist like to work for the best television station?" Just like that. I knew it wasn't a dream because Wendy and Rob had dashed in from the beach and were making such a noise I could barely hear Mr. Sobol. *"Shhh,"* I hissed at them. I thought my head would explode. I was up as high as I had been low. I must be calm, I admonished myself. "How much will you pay?" I asked in what I hoped was a fairly businesslike voice. His reply brought me down to earth. "Well," he hesitated, "you know television is not paying at all right now. We're all losing money." Oh dear, the same old story. I repeated, "How much?" He hedged. "It's a weekly show, a quarter of an hour—we can only pay fifty dollars a week. But if it goes well and we get a sponsor, we will certainly pay more." Fifty dollars! This was ridiculous. "It's too low," I said. But I was thinking as I talked. I wanted to be inside. When you are on the outside, it's almost impossible to get any kind of offer, as I had discovered. But fifty dollars! "All right," I said. "But I must have a secretary and I'll have to pay her seventy-five dollars a week. I'll do it for seventy-five." He had expected a longer argument. "Okay," he replied. "It's a deal."

When I told Helen Mack I was doing a television show for $75 a week she said, "This will hurt you. You should never work for nothing." This is the first time I have known Helen to be wrong. The chief thing is to get inside, even if you have to do it for nothing. Russell Birdwell, the public relations expert, was reassuring. "You're doing the right thing. No one has to know what you're getting."

Within five weeks I had found a national sponsor and was seen and heard in 45 major cities in America. I was on my way to the rich green verdant grazing lands.

𝔚 CHAPTER TWENTY-FIVE

THERE would be no mistakes this time. I must look pretty and I must sound intelligent. No more staring at a spot four inches to the left of the camera. With God's help, I vowed, this time I will succeed.

First things first. Bob Hope, who has always been kind and helpful in my show business career, agreed to be a surprise guest on my first show, on which I also set Don DeFore. I asked Perc Westmore of the House of Westmore Beauty Salon in Hollywood to put my makeup on personally. I looked my best, I was not too nervous, just a deep intake of breath now and then during the show. The reviewers were kind and believed I was an acquisition to television.

The next week I trotted along happily to Westmore's to be made up for the second show. Perc was ill. I was made up by one of the girls. The next day lunching at the Hollywood Brown Derby, Joe Rines, an advertising executive, told me, "Sheilah, I caught your show, and as a friend of yours"—I steeled myself for the worst—"I must tell you that you looked terrible." My smile froze. Never mind, it would be corrected. I would simply go elsewhere to be made beautiful.

Lucille Ball looked lovely on television. Harry King of Max Factor, the worldwide manufacturers of makeup, theatrical and personal, made her pretty for the *I Love Lucy* show, which had recently started and was a tremendous hit. Lucille was not too young or too beautiful in real life, and if Mr. King could do this for her, perhaps he would do the same for me. I called the Factor publicity department and told Bill Hardwicke of my problem. He was sympathetic. He would ask Harry to make me up for my show. He did a great job. I looked 1000 percent better. Harry, who could be temperamental like all great artists, was pleased that I was grateful. Yes, I could come back every week and he would be happy to apply the paint and powder.

During my third makeup session at Factor's, the idea hit me like a command from heaven: "Bill," I said to Mr. Hardwicke, "why shouldn't Max Factor sponsor me on television?" I was a Hollywood columnist, a purveyor of glamour to the public, why shouldn't they sell their fine makeup on my show? Mr. Hardwicke brought it up at their next meeting. Max Factor's agreed it was a good idea. It took a week to settle the details. My salary was to start at $400 a week. In 13 weeks it would jump to $600. And if I went the full five years, I would earn $2000 a week. From a salary of $75, in exactly five weeks.

But there is always irritation with every good job. Mine was commercials. I have never believed the jabberwocky that sponsors claim goes into their pharmaceutical products. I was having to spout absolute nonsense. I have always used

Max Factor makeup, particularly the lipsticks. But while I could memorize my entire show without difficulty, I could not learn those commercials. My brain resisted them, rejecting the mumbo jumbo. To me, a lipstick is a lipstick and my chief liking for the Factor lipstick was that it stayed on, no matter what you ate, or how nervously you bit or licked your lips or whom you kissed. It did not come off. And that was what I wanted to say. Who cared what the ingredients were? All I wanted to know, all any woman wants to know, is does it look pretty and will it stay on?

It was impressed upon me that I must never, never, on any account, forget myself and say that the lipstick contained a dye. Of course, that's the one thing I did. In one show my memory went blank. I was extemporizing wildly, and said, "This lovely, beautiful Max Factor lipstick contains a beautiful dye." Fortunately, my dreadful blunder was heard only in Los Angeles. As was the custom then for coast-to-coast shows, my program was performed live and kinescoped for the rest of the country. I redid the lipstick sales talk—in their language.

In spite of our commercial quarrels, Factor's liked my show. I had interesting news and some good stars. Danny Thomas, Ralph Edwards, Dick Powell, June Havoc, Sonja Henie, José Ferrer, and Dean Martin and Jerry Lewis. Not many women—they did not care for the crucifying kinescope.

The set was a little three-sided room furnished as my office on a corner of a large stage. Chef Milani, the locally well-known restaurateur, and his plump, comfortable wife had the fifteen minutes ahead of me. His set would be dismantled while I was doing my show. One day they dropped the gas stove. "It made a terrible noise," said Helen Mack, "but you went right on as though nothing had happened. You should have noticed it and made a joke." But the only way I could function in this terrifying medium was to blot out everything around me. I must think only of the tiny, piercing red eyes on each side of the television camera.

My contract stipulated a summer hiatus of eight weeks and I longed for it. The strain was increasing. At the end of one show, I could not remember the name of my guest for the next day. "Tomorrow my guest star will be—" then BLANK. My smile was deceptive while I prayed, "In the name of God, the NAME!" I finally said, "Tomorrow we shall have a big, big star."

I was saving money, also buying some good furniture for

the house. I could afford to furnish the dining room which for four years had functioned as an empty playroom for the children. I threw out some of the cheap junk I had bought and shopped at Sloane's for better pieces.

NBC had never particularly liked the show, and they treated my sponsors badly. Our time in the various cities was always being changed—11 changes in one week without warning. It was hard to build up a rating under these circumstances. The week before I was to return after the hiatus, with Jimmy Durante to be my guest, Max Factor peremptorily canceled the show, although I had already been informed by NBC of the renewal.

I believe I could have sued NBC, to whom I was under contract. I was not under contract to Max Factor. I had signed with NBC and they had told me to report back for the show. But who sues a giant network? And the experience had been valuable. I had established a reputation in television. The show had been popular, especially in New York, where it was seen at 11:30 on Saturday nights.

I made some well-paying guest appearances on the Jimmy Durante and Eddie Cantor shows. Art Linkletter hired me as a regular guest expert on motion pictures for his *House Party* television show. I have become more recognized because of Art's *House Party* than almost anything else I have done, including my 28 years as a daily syndicated columnist, magazine stories, radio shows, the *Beloved Infidel* book and film, and even *The Sheilah Graham Show* for NBC Television with its heavenly price tag of $5000 a week.

This money was not all mine. Five thousand dollars was the price for the package. From it, I must pay all what they call "above the line" expenses—the talent, me (I gave myself a delightful basic salary of $1,250 a week), my writers, if any, the producer (I was the producer), the director, and any filming expenses. "You will have your own company," Tom McAvity informed me. I never really knew why. But mine is not to reason why, mine is but to do or die. And I very nearly did—die, I mean.

☙ CHAPTER TWENTY-SIX

ONLY a person as optimistic as I am would have taken on *The Sheilah Graham Show*. It meant working harder than I ever had in my life. With all my other commitments, I had taken on a new 5-times-a-week radio show—*Three City Byline*. I gave the news from Hollywood, Irv Kupcinet from Chicago, Hy Gardner from New York.

But all I could think of when Tom McAvity called from San Francisco was, *How amazing . . . five thousand dollars a week*. Tom was saying, "We would like one feature of your show to be the biography of a star. We know it would be too difficult to get a top star every day. I suggest you film the biography, divide it into five parts, and show one segment a day. The rest of your show will be live." My head was spinning. I hoped I could do what the mighty NBC seemed so casually sure I could. There wasn't much time—less than three weeks to get a staff, to get ahead with some of the filmed biographies, and form a company.

My children did not have much of a Christmas in 1954. There was a tree, and colored lights around the door as usual. But except for the present-opening on Christmas morn, their mother was a glazed, dazed, preoccupied phantom. I developed a Groucho Marx crouch. There simply was not time to straighten up.

I soon learned that filming each biography would cost about $2000—a large bite in the $5000 budget. Later I used a newsreel camera and cut the cost in half. But in the early months, we filmed in a studio. The cost would have been prohibitive, but for riding "piggy-back" on the *Ozzie and Harriet Show*. When they filmed half-days, we took over their crew and equipment.

I hired Jack Mullen from the CBS publicity department to write the show with me, and a press agent, Cliff Brown, to line up some of the guests. I already had an excellent secretary, Adele Roy, who had come from New York when I started *Three-City Byline*. She was loyal and hardworking, and my children loved her.

I had my staff. I had my contract. Martin Gang, an excellent lawyer, had made sure I would be on for six months at least—most television shows had 13-week options, but the hardest part of a program like this is getting it organized, getting it rolling, and then it almost runs by itself. But at no time was it easy. We were to do the live part from NBC Hollywood at 7:45 A.M., which would mean getting up at 5 o'clock in the morning, gulping coffee from a bedside thermos flask, and leaving for the studio at 5:30. On two mornings, I saw the atom bomb redden the sky from Nevada, 400 miles away. It was an awesome sight.

Getting top names for the show was easier than anticipated. At first, I concentrated on my friends and stars who were hoping for Oscar nominations. Bing Crosby and Bill Holden were both strong possibilities for *The Country Girl*. I tried for Grace Kelly, who was actually to win the award, but she would have nothing to do with television, and in my heart I could not blame her.

The hardest man to get for a television show or for anything in Hollywood is Bing Crosby. But for an Oscar, stars who are not usually cooperative suddenly will be seen on every show, they will do every requested interview. I called Bing Crosby at his Palm Springs home and nearly dropped the phone when he replied with his usual nonchalance, "Sure, I'll be happy to do it, Sheilah." Bing would be my first biography—30 minutes of film to be seen on my show from Monday to Friday inclusive. What a coup!

There had been a trade paper story that Bing had recently signed a contract with CBS-TV, but this had not yet started and he had done practically no television at all. I was crowing like a cock at dawn, and I wanted NBC to see how clever I was and I made a dreadful mistake. I phoned Fred Wile, who was in charge of coast-to-coast programming at NBC in Hollywood. With great excitement I said, "Fred, I have landed Bing Crosby for all of the first week." Fred belonged to the Grand Order of the Pessimists. He replied, "Of course you know he signed with CBS and I am sure they will not let him appear on NBC." I cursed myself for having called him. "Look," I said, "Bing Crosby is bigger than any network. He wants to do it." I have always believed in doing things first and fighting about it afterwards.

But the world is full of people who say No. They cannot get into trouble by saying No: it's the easiest way out. I try to avoid them. Fred Wile continued, "I'll check with CBS to see what the situation is before you go to the expense of filming." I was willing to risk $2000 to have Bing Crosby on my show, but not Fred. He called CBS and they said, "Absolutely no, you cannot have Bing Crosby." They called Bing, they called his lawyers, they called everyone. And we lost him. This reinforced a very important lesson: Never tell anyone what you're going to do. Let them find out, afterwards.

But the show, as they say, must go on. What now, little girl of the big ideas? Which star is important enough to start this $5000-a-week show? I had wasted valuable time with Bing Crosby. I contacted William Holden, Bob Hope and Marjorie Main. Bob had no picture to sell, neither did Marjorie. But they were good friends and time was short. I would be able to film only three biographies before the January 2nd deadline. It was a frightening prospect.

William Perlberg, who had produced *The Country Girl*, persuaded Mr. Holden to be my first star biography. The first show I actually filmed was with Bob Hope. I knew I would not feel so nervous with him. With the excellent *Ozzie and Harriet* crew, their fine makeup man, and with Bill Mellor, who had won an Oscar, in charge of the camera, I knew that not too much could go wrong. But I was green at the job, and the 30-minute filming took six hours, which was a lot of time in the life of the always-busy Bob Hope. The cost was nearly $3000. No matter. For Bob's story, told in his wonderful comedy style, it was worth every cent. It was $500 less when I got the hang of it and filmed Bill Holden.

Later I was able to film the 5-minute segments in approximately four hours—30 minutes of film; studios sometimes took a month to film 30 minutes. The set was like a madhouse sometimes—everyone rushing around like those fast chase scenes in the silent comedies. Exhausting, but exhilarating. I have always loved a project, especially when I am the star.

NBC was pleased with the caliber of my promised star biographies and went to town on promotion. They took full-page advertisements in the trade papers about "Hollywood's Own Sheilah Graham." Somehow I found time for long photographic sessions and interviews, and the only depressing note was a blast from Terence Flaherty of the San Francisco *Chronicle* BEFORE the show began, saying I would be lousy. I *had* been terrible the previous New Year's Day on the local NBC-sponsored Tournament of Roses commentary. I am not good at commentaries—shades of Gorgeous George.

I don't know one rose or chrysanthemum from another, and it was hard to get a word in with my co-commentator, Don Wilson.

But my anguish over Flaherty's column was happiness compared to the suffering with Marjorie Main. I had really wanted a joint life story with Marjorie Main and Percy Kilbride—Ma and Pa Kettle. But he had retired. I knew that Marjorie was a health faddist. I knew that between scenes on the set she wore gloves so as not to come into contact with other people's germs. I also knew that around her house in Palm Springs she had built a high wall, as much to keep out bugs as curious tourists. But I was not prepared for what I was to endure in having Miss Main for my television guest of the week. If I had known what was coming, I would have gone down on my knees and begged her not to do it.

Margie's agent called me in the evening while I was catching up with a magazine assignment. "I am canceling Miss Main," he told me in tones of outrage. "She has never done television and we could get $50,000 for her first show." She was doing mine for nothing. "But everything is planned for the morning," I spluttered. "I have the crew all set. It's costing me $2000 and I can't cancel at this late hour. "She is not an ad-libber," he continued coldly, "we must not jeopardize her future in television." "But she has promised—" "I'm sorry," he said in un-sorry tones, and hung up.

I called Margie. She, too, was sorry, but had to admit, she said, that her agent was right. "But you promised." I was near tears. "My dear, I know, but I am not good at ad-libbing and my agents won't let me." In a choking voice I said, "Margie, you're bigger than your agents. They will do just what you tell them to, and you just cannot let me down, Margie, you cannot." There was a pause. She didn't want to do it, and I knew it was Margie who had begged her agents, "Get me out of this." But she's a goodhearted woman, and my grief was genuine. Finally, reluctantly, "All right, I'll do it." "Thank you." I put the phone down and felt suddenly faint.

But there was no time to collapse. On with the show, let work be unconfined. I worked far into the night, finishing the magazine story and planning the television biography of Marjorie Main. I read everything I had written about her and worded my questions to make the answering of them as simple as possible. I tried to sleep. But in my dreams, she wore enormous gloves and I was asking her questions and she would not reply.

We were to film at four in the afternoon. Margie had a whole day in which to change her mind and I was worried. I called her at eleven in the morning and suggested it might be a good idea if I came over after lunch to rehearse the show, "So you will know what I am going to ask you." She was still dubious. "I shouldn't do this," she repeated several times. "You'll be great," I assured her. She didn't think so. "I'll be over soon," I said hastily.

Marjorie had a one-story very small house in West Los Angeles. I have never seen so many things crammed into so small a space. There were paperbacks, scrapbooks, scripts, magazines, bric-a-brac, clothes all over the bedroom, dining room, living room and kitchen. The *pièce de résistance* was a large massage table in the center of the living room. "Wait a minute," said Margie. "I must relax." She draped herself face down on the table and hung limply like a sack with her head loose over the top. She breathed deeply, with eyes closed, for five minutes. Then she got down and told me in that postnasal drip voice, "Wa-ell, I've been thinking about the show and I have a good idea. My neighbor's little girl will come on at the beginning." My eyebrows rose. "You don't have a thing to worry about. We've already re-hearsed it. After we talk awhile, she'll hop on one foot and say, 'Auntie Margie, I have to go—you know.'" My anguished "But—" was cut short by the arrival of the child. "This is the nice lady I told you about—Sheilah Graham," said Miss Main, trying unsuccessfully to take the little girl's hand and steer her toward me. The child glared at me and wouldn't budge. "All right," said Margie lightly. "Let's re-hearse what we did this morning." The girl, who must have been about four years old, whined, "I don' wanna." "Come along," said Margie semi-severely. "You know what we have to do." "I don' wanna," repeated the moppet. I glanced at my director, who had come with me, and I thought, Heaven is taking care of this in its own way. Margie, now very exasperated, screeched, "Come to Auntie Margie!" The child burst into loud weeping, shouted "I want my mama," rushed out and did not return.

But that was only the beginning. With every question, Margie first groaned, "I am not an ad-libber," then went off on a wild torrent of unconnected sentences and we simply were not getting anywhere. She and her agent were right. Marjorie was not an ad-libber. I stifled a groan. "Now, come on, Sheilah," said Miss Main severely. "You've got to relax." And she put *me* on the massage table and made me hang with my head down and go all limp and close my eyes for five minutes. I was much too nervous to derive any benefit from it, especially as she continued saying, "I'm not an ad-libber, I shouldn't be doing this." With my head over the table, I tried to reassure her. "You're marvelous, Margie. You're going to be a tremendous sensation." "You think so?" —skeptically. "I know so, Margie"—wearily. I was beginning to wish that she had never been born and I had never met her.

It was worse at the studio. I was afraid to let her out of sight and we drove there together. Waiting on the set were the usual complement of crew, cameramen and makeup people. Seeing them, Margie stated, "I won't do the show unless everyone leaves." "They can't leave. They are the crew," I explained through clenched teeth. And suddenly it was enough. She could go to hell or Timbuctu. I shouted, "If you don't want to do it, you can leave right now." It was suddenly quiet. Margie took a long look at me, at the silent people on the set, and in a gay, surprised voice said, "For gosh sakes, where's the makeup man?" It was one of the best biographies we did. Never be fooled by a pro. When they are on, they perform.

🕊 CHAPTER TWENTY-SEVEN

THE Arlene Frances *Home Show* was ahead of ours. A soap opera followed us. Our rating was often higher than either of them. But we never landed a sponsor. I had every top star in Hollywood on the show, stars who, in the nighttime, had enormous ratings—Red Skelton, Jack Benny, and Dean Martin and Jerry Lewis. The five segments with Dean and Jerry were hilarious. But on that week, we actually lost a point. There had been rumors that the famed partnership was dissolving. "We will never break up," said Jerry during the only serious second on the show. "We couldn't break up," said Dean, swinging an imaginary golf club on Jerry's head. When I turned back to Jerry, his face was right next to mine, and I almost hit him on the nose. When I was talking to Dean, Jerry, in a loud aside to the back of my head, said, "You need a shave." It was very difficult to do this show because most of the time I was dissolved in helpless laughter. No one at NBC could understand the lost rating point. Maybe so much laughter was a little hard to take at 10:45 in the morning.

The John Wayne life story was filmed in San Francisco where he was making *Blood Alley* with Lauren Bacall on a tanker, which was supposed to be a war vessel off China. Wayne had a very helpful press agent, Bev Barnett. Bev is dead now. He died at about forty of a heart attack. (So many people in the motion picture industry, with its tensions and pressures, seem to die young, of heart attacks.) The boat was rocky, and Bev supplied me with seasick pills as the smelly deck heaved up and down while I shouted my questions above the wind and the noisy sea gulls. We used John's crew and equipment and this saved us money.

But we had already cut our biography costs by going outside the studio to the homes of the stars, using the mobile newsreel camera. It was much more interesting, for example, to film "The Liberace Story"—he was then at the full flower of his glory—at his home in the Valley, by the side of his piano-shaped pool, with candelabra inside and out. We filmed his completely mirrored bathroom, where everything was in the shape of a piano, even the toilet, I believe. I guess it was a case of hitting the right key.

We newsreeled Edward G. Robinson at home with his marvelous art collection, which had not yet been divided by divorce, and Eddie explained the fine points of his beloved Cézannes and Degas. We went inside and outside of My Little Margie's—Gale Storm's—fabulous new quarter-of-a-million-dollar home in the Valley and included her husband and children. Also, the Gordon MacRae home with their children. When we covered Lou Costello's home for the biography with his partner Bud Abbott, I put my own children in the pool for some everlasting background shots. By this time, Martin and Lewis had broken up as a team, and I asked Bud and Lou, "Will you ever break up *your* partnership?" "Never," said Bud positively. "Sheilah," said Lou, "when we get mad at each other, we put on the tape recorder. And if you ever *listen* to yourself having a fight, it sounds so silly, you just have to laugh. Oh no, we will never break up." As you know, they did.

The schedule was hectic. After the morning show, we had a meeting to discuss the next. Then I wrote my column. The afternoons were for filming. At 5:30 the radio show. After dinner with Wendy and Rob, I helped Rob with his homework, discussed the day's adventures and problems with my daughter, memorized the television show, and tried to be asleep by 10:30.

It was fortunate that I had such a big house. I gave over the breakfast room to Jack and Cliff, my secretary had the den. I worked in my bedroom upstairs—a big, light room. With Wendy doing homework in her room, Rob in his, and my new housekeeper, Anna, in the kitchen, the whole house vibrated with concentrated toil.

A big feature of *The Sheilah Graham Show* was the live guests—stars like Dick Powell and Kirk Douglas. I had written some nicer things about Kirk since the *Young Man With a Horn* crack on radio. Red Skelton's contract with CBS prohibited filming a show and he willingly appeared for us at the unearthly hour of 7:45 A.M., having spent most of the night drawing comedy sketches of his new home, which he exhibited and explained. In one sketch, the new freeway ran slap through the middle of the house. Sweet Red. I saw him in Zurich, when he was touring the world with his wife and daughter and his son who was dying of leukemia. Red the clown, Red the child, Red the gentleman.

Studios were loosening up as I had hoped they would. I was able to get scenes and trailers from current films and scenes from old films. I fell in love with Laurence Olivier's Heathcliff all over again when we showed a scene from *Wuthering Heights*. Mine was the first television show to feature Greta Garbo—a five-minute scene from her memorable *Camille*. We would find reasons for using film scenes from past movies, such as "The Ten Best Pictures of the 30's." Cecil B. DeMille had a 50th anniversary. I presented him with a plaque as the Greatest Film Producer of Our Time, while our newsreel camera turned at the DeMille Gate at Paramount. I found that if you gave an award, you could get almost anyone.

We had some contests. Rosalind Russell's comedy about Las Vegas, *Girl Rush*, was about to be released. Paramount's promotion department offered, on my show, a free trip to the studio and a dinner date with Liberace for the girl with legs as beautiful as Miss Russell's, displayed generously in her film. Someone entered the legs of a horse. We gave the photo-

graph to Roz's husband, Freddie Brisson; he showed it to his
wife and they both had a good laugh.

I was getting very tired. I was still memorizing the show;
I was still afraid to take a chance. But it was getting harder
to learn the lines. A TelePrompTer was suggested, but I have
never been able to use this blessing for busy TV commentators. I can see to read without glasses, but 18 inches away,
the world without my glasses—contact lenses irritate my eyes
—is a furry blur. So every night, for two hours, I beat *The
Sheilah Graham Show* into the Sheilah Graham head. It
seems ridiculous to me now. What did it matter if I made
some mistakes? It would possibly have made the show more
relaxed. But in all my life, only one person has said, "Sheilo,
don't be afraid, slow down. I will help you," and he was not
around in 1955.

There had to be a blow-up and it came when Sheree North
was late for the 7:45 A.M. performance. Sheree was then an
important star at 20th Century-Fox. She was the blonde between the Betty Grable and Marilyn Monroe eras. In her
about-to-be-released picture, she was playing a beatnik role.
I thought it would be amusing for us both to talk the lingo
from the film and she had promised to come in early to
rehearse this with me. She did not arrive until halfway
through the show. During the film break I explained what I
had in mind. Sheree looked at me blankly. She was not quite
awake and suddenly I could not stand the tension, the pressure, and I shouted, "Get her out of here. Get her out." There
was a great hush of alarm, but they took her out. I would
have to fill five minutes. I was in tears, as I always am when
I am temperamental, and the makeup was running a bit.
What now, little girl? You got yourself into a fine fix this
time. You have nothing memorized. Five minutes to fill, and
you know how long that can be. Forever.

"Are you all right, Sheilah?" The director's voice was anxious. "Ten seconds," said another voice. I had wondered
what I would do in the event the "live" guest did not turn
up. With the back of my hand, I wiped away the twin rivers
of mascara trickling down my cheeks. "Stand by." The two
little red lights went on. I smiled into the camera—I too am a
pro and when I'm on, I'm on. I glanced down at the Hollywood *Reporter* and *Daily Variety* that were always on the
desk, and in a calm voice said, "These are Hollywood trade
papers." I discussed news items and the tidbits in the gossip

columns of Army Archerd and Mike Connolly. It was one of my best shows.

But it had to end. It is always a surprise to me to discover I am not superhuman, that I cannot twirl the world by the tail as I advised the shy Tony Perkins to do when he first came to Hollywood—not indefinitely, that is. I have to put it down sometimes and step aside.

After eight and a half months, I informed John Nelson, in charge of NBC daytime shows from Hollywood, "I must give up the show." He gave a barbecue party in my honor and asked me to stay until they found a replacement, which they did after another five weeks. And oh, the blessed mornings when I could see the children before they went to school, and the evenings when I did not have to memorize film facts and figures. I missed the heavenly money, but I had a jewel of a house on the wide sandy beach at Trancas —10 miles north of Malibu—to show for the months and months of unbearably hard work. The house was built to my specifications. It was a dream come true with its wide sundeck, large sliding glass windows, large fireplace, three bedrooms, two baths, a gleaming built-in kitchen. And with a deep turquoise blue rug in the living room from Sloane's.

In a state of collapse, the star of *The Sheilah Graham Show* disappeared from the network, into the Scripps' Clinic at La Jolla (near San Diego), for a two week check-up—my two-week annual vacation from the column. I told everyone at NBC, my family and those who worked for me, "I don't ever want to hear the word 'work.' I'm so tired I may never work again." I installed Wendy, Rob and the good Anna Bayer, the housekeeper who had come to us from Zurich, into a beach cottage nearby.

As I entered the door of the clinic, there was a call for me from NBC in New York. They were preparing *The Perry Como Show*. "We want you to interview a star every week." Wearily, from the habit of years, I said, "What will you pay me?" For a ten-minute interview, they would pay me $2000 a week. I could not have done it then if it had been $20,000 a week. "Later perhaps." They agreed to wait for me until I was ready. The Como show was an instant success. NBC decided it would be foolish to tamper with the format. They would not need me with my star interviews. But at the time, I could not have cared less. Besides, there was something else to worry about—my divorce.

At the start of the TV show on January 2, 1955, the marriage had been somewhat shaky. The strain of the impossibly difficult, well-paying burden was to finish it.

It was a grueling battle. I made six agonizing appearances in court until George Delacorte finally got us together and settled the matter. If only lawyers would allow the two most concerned to discuss the situation as human beings who had once loved each other, people would be saved an enormous amount of grief and money. In the divorce settlement, I surrendered my jewel of a beach house. As George said, it was a case of giving him the house, or giving up my sanity. I don't have a beach house today, but I believe I am still sane. I don't believe I will ever marry again. I agreed with my daughter when she said recently, "Let's face it, Mother. You are not good at being married."

After the divorce I got fat deliberately. I did not want to be attractive to men. And this distressed Cary Grant. He decided to help me. Cary is not only enormously attractive, but more than any star I know, he goes far out of his way to help people in distress. A middle-aged woman press agent in Hollywood has many problems. Cary calls on her frequently to discuss them. Ingrid Bergman can never forget his outspoken support and cheerfulness when the rest of the world, columnists included, were throwing stones.

I was with Cary in his dressing room at Metro one afternoon soon after my divorce and I prayed I would not burst into tears as I had the day before when I was interviewing Marlene Dietrich at her home. "You are very tired," Marlene had said in her low voice. "Go on, cry." She had held me against her like a mother with a child. I must not bawl in front of Cary. "What is your next film?" I sobbed. How dreadful. Stop it. You're a tough reporter. Control yourself.

I'd like to be able to say that Cary took me in his arms. He did not. He talked unconcernedly of a number of things and in a few seconds I was able to damn the flood and apologize. He was called for a scene. "Please don't go. We must talk," he said casually. I was in his dressing room most of the afternoon. We talked about my children, my broken marriage. He told me of the discipline and will power that are necessary to accept the good and bad things in life; the satisfaction of work well done. He had not liked everything I had written about him—he had called me one day in a fierce rage and threatened legal action unless I immediately retracted what I had written. I did—his anger had scared me into a blue funk.

"I'm going to send you some books that I think will help you," he promised. They were delivered to my home a few hours later. The main idea in the books was do not dwell on past mistakes. Look to the future. You can get what you want out of life by going after it. I have always believed this, but I had been so full of energy-draining self-pity I had forgotten the credo by which I live.

When I read that Cary and his wife, Betsy, were hypnotizing each other for various reasons—to stop smoking, to sleep—I, half in jest, half serious, asked him to hypnotize me into not eating so much. He looked into my eyes and I looked into his and he said quietly, "Think of yourself as thin. You are thin." I said, "Yes, Cary, I am thin. I am thin." When I arrived home, I rushed to my dressing room mirror—alas, I was still fat.

I doubt whether anyone could really hypnotize me. Especially on the subject of food. My unconscious had told me it is better for me to eat when I am exhausted or unhappy. When I am rested and calm, I can diet. And when I tell Cary that I have lost weight and feel well, he says, with friendly satisfaction, "Ah, you like yourself now."

III

☙ CHAPTER TWENTY-EIGHT

How could I, with a passion for anonymity in my private life, have written the story of my time with Scott Fitzgerald and the childhood I had discussed in America only with Scott? *Beloved Infidel* would not have been written but for two other books—Budd Schulberg's best seller *The Disenchanted*, published October 1950, and Arthur Mizener's biography of Scott Fitzgerald, *The Far Side of Paradise*, which came out a few months later.

I met Budd early in 1939 during the preparation for Walter Wanger's film, *Winter Carnival*. The producer was dissatisfied with Schulberg's script and for the sum of $1,500 a week he had hired Scott to work with Budd and give some gloss to the production, part of which would be filmed at Wanger's alma mater, Dartmouth College in New Hampshire. Budd, recently graduated from Dartmouth, tall, gangling, seemingly shy, stuttered rather painfully. He was always knocking things over and apologizing in a mumble of words. His father, B. P. Schulberg, had previously been head of Paramount Studio Production. Budd had been raised in splendor and opulence in Beverly Hills.

This fact was of great interest to Scott, who was to transpose some of Budd's youthful acceptance of Hollywood as the normal way of life into producer Brady's daughter Cecilia in *The Last Tycoon*, who "accepted Hollywood with the resignation of a ghost assigned to a haunted house."

Soon after Scott's death, Budd visited me in Hollywood. He knew how unhappy I must be, he said. He had already been quite busy recounting in print his experiences with Scott at Dartmouth and in Hollywood. He seemed to have recovered from his shyness, but there was no question about his love for Scott. It was more than love, it was reverence. And later I was quite interested when I learned that Budd was writing a novel about his brief time with the author who

139

had been resurrected as the darling boy of American literature.

When *The Disenchanted* was published, Budd sent me
an advance copy with an affectionate greeting—"To Sheilah,
who will understand what I have tried to say." I did not
understand, and I do not have the book with its affectionate
greeting. I threw it away after reading half and scanning the
rest with increasing anger against Budd that he could be so
cruel to a man who had only been kind to him. It was such a
one-dimensional portrait of Scott. It showed him at his very
worst, whining, antagonistic, boastful, exhausted. It simply
was not true. When he was drunk, perhaps, but Budd had
also seen Scott sober. Budd's hero-villain Manley Halliday
drank himself into the grave. But as Budd knew, in that last
year, Scott had stopped drinking completely. Scott had been
hard at work on *The Last Tycoon* and was optimistic about
its success. He was not the miserable man in Schulberg's book.
How could Budd, who professed to love Scott, who seemed to
regard himself as his heir, present such a dreadful image of
him to the world? And it would be believed, because Budd had
appointed himself the Fitzgerald spokesman. There was not
a radio or television show or anthology about Scott that did
not include Budd's opinion about the late fascinating Fitzgerald. I resented *The Disenchanted* as did many of Scott's
friends, the people who had known and loved him. It was
outrageous, the minor writer criticizing the genius.

I received a call from Scottie requesting my help. "Will
you tell them in the studios that we will sue if anyone at-
tempts to film Schulberg's book?" she asked. I knew one
producer who was interested in the book and I passed on
Scottie's message that there would be a lawsuit. It has not
yet been filmed, although I doubt if Scottie would mind it
so much today. It was only moderately successful as a play,
and Scottie, who disliked the book as much as I did, thought
the play less objectionable. In fact she enjoyed Jason Robards
Jr.'s performance very much. I did not see the play. On this
particular subject I am less open-minded.

My first knowledge of *The Far Side of Paradise* was the
letter I received in January 1948 from Arthur Mizener, telling
me that for the past four years he had been at work on a
book about Scott and that he would never have undertaken
the biography without first consulting Edmund Wilson, who
had advised him to talk to me. He had also talked to Budd
Schulberg, he wrote, who had told him at length how much

Scott had depended on me. He was returning to Princeton on a fellowship and he wondered if I could visit him there.

In his next letter, Mr. Mizener apologized for continuing to intrude on my privacy, but he had heard that when Scott had died in my home, his secretary and I carried him back to his own apartment—so there should be no scandal, I presume —and then telephoned for the doctor. How absurd, I wrote back. My only concern had been to get him a doctor, the fire department with oxygen, anyone who could revive Scott as fast as possible. As for the invitation to see Mizener in Princeton, I explained that my children were small, I rarely left them, and I had no plans to come east. But I would help him all I could if he would write me his questions. For a start I sent him the true account of Scott's death. For many weeks afterwards I answered his numerous queries by mail.

When *The Far Side of Paradise* was published I was sure that all the biographical facts were correct, but I was surprised at the author's lack of real understanding of Scott. I had heard, of course, about the pranks and drinking of the twenties and thirties. I had lived through some wild times myself with Scott and I had often wondered about the man Scott had been before we met. At one time he was a whole man, good, bad, kind, cruel. But in my time with him, the good and the bad had separated somewhat. He was all good when he was sober; the Manley Halliday of *The Disenchanted* when he was drunk. But a biographer has to present both sides, and it seemed to me that both books had failed to give the full view of Fitzgerald. In spite of the publication of *The Last Tycoon*, which proved that Scott had been working industriously when he died, they both gave a distorted impression of the man he had been at the end. Both failed to acknowledge his attempted comeback—a failure, I suppose, because he died before completing his book. But there was a greatness about the failure nonetheless and cause for rejoicing. He had not ended with a whimper. Edmund Wilson had thought the unfinished book might have been the best that Fitzgerald would have written. Many other critics and reviewers were of the same opinion.

Would no one ever write the truth about those last years? Of Scott's belief that he would regain his position as an important observer of the contemporary scene, that he still had something to say, and that he could say it in better prose than any of his contemporaries? It seemed they all admired his work, but the man was regarded as an immature idiot to the

THE REST OF THE STORY

moment of his death. Fascinating at times, oh yes, they gave him that, but what a pity he had careened drunkenly to his grave—Dorothy Parker's "poor son of a bitch." Of course he had been unhappy over his literary obscurity and bad health. But he was distracted from it like a child who has lost a parent and receives a toy. Scott's toy was his continuing enthusiasm and interest in people and events.

It was important to put the record straight. If I died, no one would know of Scott's comparative tranquillity, his maturity at the end of his life, his calm pleasure in his book, his confidence that he was doing good work. And above all, perhaps because I hated his drinking so much, that he had been sober for so long. But could I write a book about my time with Scott Fitzgerald? I was busy 24 hours a day it seemed. And how much could I tell? I had to consider the effect on my children. What was good taste, what was bad? Perhaps this was a story that could never be told.

And then, as always, the thought, the idea, became a fact. In the autumn of 1955, Woodrow Wirsig, editor of *Woman's Home Companion*, called on me. He wanted my autobiography. "You have a story worth telling," he informed me. I thought, He must have heard about Scott Fitzgerald. Very few people knew of my association with Scott. I only discussed him when I was asked direct questions. Charles Jackson, author of the alcoholic story *The Lost Weekend*, worshiped Scott and came to see me when he was in Hollywood for the filming of his book. We talked of Scott, but it was a strain for us both.

I had discussed Scott with Kenneth Tynan, the London critic. He had come to Hollywood for *Punch* Magazine, and one of his assignments was to interview a Hollywood columnist. On the advice of Mrs. James Mason, who had said, "Oh, don't interview Hedda Hopper or Louella Parsons, they've been done to death, why don't you talk to Sheilah Graham, who has a fresher viewpoint," Mr. Tynan interviewed me in my house on North Maple Drive.

Soon he was talking sympathetically about Scott Fitzgerald, and the pity of his early death, and asking all sorts of questions. I was startled, but he was gentle and quiet and I said, "I will tell you but you must not use any of this in your story, because I have never talked of Scott for publication." I should have known that a good journalist, whether it be for *Punch* or for a Hollywood gossip column, finds it hard to resist a good story and a sharp ending. I told him, "He died at three o'clock on a Saturday afternoon." And rather flippantly, to cover the emotion—"He was a gentleman." He used this as the last line of his interview, as in my early insecure days as a journalist I might have done.

I had thought I would be silent about the years with Scott. I had my children, Scott was in heaven and all was well with the world, and I did not want to bring up agonizing memories and suffer all over again. But it was inevitable that I would write about Scott.

Soon after Mr. Wirsig's visit, Jerry Wald, the producer at 20th Century-Fox, was lunching with John O'Hara and told him, "I'm planning a film biography of Scott Fitzgerald. You were a good friend of his—would you like to write it?" (When I had gone on my lecture tour in 1939, Scott had wanted a kitten for company. He interviewed several cats, but told me later he had settled for several lunches with O'Hara.) Jerry practically fell off his chair, he told me, when O'Hara said, "If you really want to know about Fitzgerald, the best person to talk to is Sheilah Graham." "What has Sheilah to do with it?" he asked, surprised. "They were in love," O'Hara told him. Jerry's round jaw dropped. He thought he knew everything about everybody in Hollywood, but this was something he had never heard of. What an amazing thing, Sheilah Graham, Hollywood columnist, and Scott Fitzgerald, the darling of the twenties, the legend of the fifties.

Jerry, one of my best contacts for news in the studios, called me in great excitement and discussed his conversation with O'Hara. "You must write a book," he begged. "As a matter of fact," I replied, "I have started something. Woody Wirsig, of *Woman's Home Companion*, wants my story for his magazine—not only about Fitzgerald, but about why I came to America, why does a young Englishwoman come here? What does she expect to find? Did she find it?" Jerry was polite, but barely listening. He was interested only in Fitzgerald. He was on a literary bender—James Joyce, Hemingway, Wolfe, Fitzgerald. He hoped to be the first to siphon Scott to the masses.

"Jack Goodman of Simon and Schuster is in town," he told me with growing enthusiasm. He had not been quite sure whether O'Hara had been pulling his leg. Graham and Fitzgerald—it was farfetched, but apparently true. "He agrees with me, your story would make a fascinating book—and movie."

"I have already written thirty typewritten pages for

Woman's Home Companion," I told Jerry. He called Jack
Goodman with this good news. Jack read the thirty pages,
and on this basis was anxious to give me a contract for a book.
"How about *Beloved Infidel* for a title," I asked him, "after
the poem Scott wrote for me?" I recited it from memory. I
had another suggestion. When Scott died, and I was full of
poetry I had enjoyed and memorized for him, there was something about the War of the Roses I had learned at my orphanage that returned to my mind. I only remembered the
first lines:

> He is dead, the beautiful youth—
> The heart of honor, the soul of truth.
> He, the life and light of us all,
> Whose voice was blithe as a bugle call.

This was Scott, I told Mr. Goodman, as later I told
Andrew Turnbull when he was planning his Scott Fitzgerald
biography. Mr. Goodman was much taken by the lines. "*The
Beautiful Youth,*" he mused. "That's a good title." But we
finally were sure, as was Jerry Wald, that the book should be
called *Beloved Infidel*. It had been Scott's own title for a
5000-word short story I had written about him which I had
called "Fled Is the Music." Scott had blue-penciled the title
and written "Beloved Infidel" in its place, and with several
brilliant strokes of his gifted pencil, had enhanced the story.
In the first "Beloved Infidel" Scott had died. He was a
painter. He told me that someone else had written a story
about him, that he had died and he had also been a painter.

I was at the beach again, in an apartment—adequate, but
not as beautiful as the beach house I had lost in the divorce.
I wrote fast and furiously, bearing hard on my pencil—I think
faster when I write in longhand—propped on the pillows on
the divan facing the sea. I decided to write my story as a
book first, and Wirsig could take what he wanted for his
magazine. Within a month I had written a hundred pages.
Not in continuity. Big chunks of Scott at the beginning, then
to the orphanage, Scottie, my acting and journalistic careers.
I wanted to give Mr. Goodman a sample of all the important
facets of my life. I had much to tell, it poured out of me, a
nonstop rushing of words. I sent a copy to Mr. Wirsig and to
Mr. Goodman, and awaited their verdicts.

Wirsig had been disturbed to learn I was now writing pri-
marily for a book. Dammit, it had been his idea. He did not
like my 100 pages, he told me with a certain pleasure. I

hoped for a better reaction from Jack Goodman. One of the readers at Simon and Schuster predicted a smash best seller. Another described it as "a bedroom confidential." Mr. Goodman said I had been too hard on myself. I usually am. I have what I hope is an exaggerated view of my shortcomings and motives. "Perhaps you should undergo psychoanalysis," suggested Mr. Goodman, who, I was told, had extensive sessions himself. "You believe you are unlovable. A collaborator perhaps would give you a better perspective." I was deflated and depressed. I had written with all my energy and all my heart and it was wrong. A bedroom confidential. That was the last thing I wanted.

Jack Goodman continued: "I think Gerold Frank would be helpful for your book." I had read *I'll Cry Tomorrow* on which Frank had collaborated with Mike Connolly and Lillian Roth and while the behavior of the heroine had amazed me, I had not been able to put the book down until I finished it at 3 in the morning. "But my story isn't like that. I have never been drunk," I replied somewhat dubiously. But it *had* been the number one best seller. (I wonder at what moment the money becomes interesting and you want to make a profit on what began as a noble idea?) I knew that Mr. Frank had recently completed the Diana Barrymore book, that Warners had already bought the movie rights, and that he was in Hollywood to work on the film script. "He'd be excellent—if you can get him," said Jack. I would try.

Mr. Frank was cool when I explained why I had called him, but he came to my house, listened, and was careful not to commit himself. He was not sure if he wanted to "do" another woman. He was not sure if he wanted to collaborate with anyone again. And lest I should think that collaborating was all he had ever done, he assured me he had written for *The New Yorker*. The solemn, bald, middle-aged, somewhat impatient man had the two *New Yorker* pieces with him, and I was not sure who was trying to convince whom. But his Lillian Roth book had held me. Jack Goodman, of the excellent publishing house of Simon and Schuster, had recommended him, and I was keen to get him. The best he would promise me was "I will think about it." He gave me all his reasons for not wanting to do my book, among them, "I'm not sure the reading public would be interested in the life of a Hollywood gossip columnist." That really shook me because I wondered myself. "But I *know* my story about Fitzgerald will be very interesting," I persisted, as though I were trying to sell a cherished painting by an obscure artist. "I'll have to think about it," he concluded with a sort of querulous antagonism.

Woody Wirsig wrote me that the best way to do my story for him would be to get it all down on a tape recorder. And while Mr. Frank was making up his mind, I decided to try once more without him. In seven days I poured at least a hundred thousand words onto a dozen reels of tape. It was like confessing to a psychoanalyst. At times it was a painful experience. When I talked of my hair being clipped in the orphanage, I burst into tears. I was surprised that I wept more while telling the tape recorder of my childhood than I had while actually living it. It was exhausting to delve back into the past, it was living everything over again, the feeling of abandonment at the orphanage, the lack of warmth and love there, the lies I told later to cover my tracks trying to escape all the dreariness. I said to Woody, "I seem to have done so many devious things in my life." He soothed me with, "You were simply trying to survive."

I was glad it was different for my children, that I could work at home, that I was there when they left for school in the morning and when they returned. It was not often that I went to a party or a film preview before they went to bed. I was glad I could be available to them at all times, that they could interrupt me no matter what I was doing, even if it was just to say "Hi." I loved to hear Wendy eagerly running up the stairs to my bedroom where I worked when she returned from school, and to know that Rob was rushing out to play with Jerry Showalter, his best friend, who lived on the corner at 601 North Maple Drive.

"You have done well," Woody assured me. "I'll have it typed while you're in Europe." I was going there as usual in the summer to write about the numerous films in production. "It's very good and will require very little editing. When you come back we will have the contract ready for you to sign." I would be paid $30,000. What fun. And all done in a week.

And while I was in Europe, Woody Wirsig lost his job and soon afterwards *Woman's Home Companion* folded. What was I to do with more than 100,000 words on 600 sheets of white paper, covering most of what I had done or thought— a life story that was not publishable in its present form? In spite of Wirsig's optimism I knew I had produced a rambling, verbose manuscript and I anticipated Jack Goodman's comment: "It will take a great deal of work to make it a book." My confidence as an author was nil. I was depressed and disillusioned. The dream was gone. Also $30,000. Perhaps this was a story that indeed should not be told.

"You're wrong," said Jack Goodman. He personally would talk to Gerold Frank. I remained in the East and Gerold again came to see me. He still was not sure, but he listened and, without much enthusiasm, asked questions and thought that perhaps he would do the book. Jack was pleased. He prepared the contract. Before we could sign, Jack Goodman died. We had an interview with a pessimistic woman editor at Simon and Schuster, and Gerold Frank stopped wavering. He withdrew from the project. He was kind but firm. "My agent, and my friends, have advised me against it," he told me.

Extremely depressed, I returned to Hollywood. What had made me believe I had something interesting to say? It was apparent that I was not going to write *Beloved Infidel*. But I was reckoning without my inability to give up—and Jerry Wald.

❦ CHAPTER TWENTY-NINE

I HAD been home a week when I telephoned Mr. Wald, of the slightly crumpled cherub's face, at 20th Century-Fox. I *did* have a worthwhile project, and somehow it must be done. I said, "Jerry, you've always believed in this book. I can't seem to get it off the ground. Would you be interested in it as an original story for a movie?" "Come right over," said the blessedly enthusiastic Mr. Wald. When I arrived at his office, Harriet and Irving Ravetch, a top writing couple, were there. Jerry was already telling them the story. He prodded me into repeating some of the incidents I had previously told him. He liked especially the story in which Scott and I, dressed in evening clothes, had rented a car, with chauffeur, to discover that "The Diamond as Big as the Ritz," based on Scott's short story, was not premiering at the Pasadena Playhouse Theatre but was being presented in a studio upstairs to a handful of students. Tears glistened in Jerry's emotional eyes while I spoke. He laughed continuously over Scott's poem for me, "France, by Big Shots," written to make me remember important events in French history. He repeated "The Huguenots, two lousy snots"—he could not continue for laughing.

It was settled, or seemed to be. The three of us would write an original screen story of the life of F. Scott Fitzgerald. When Mr. and Mrs. Ravetch left, Jerry fixed his immediately less emotional eyes on me and said briskly, "Now we must get down to business. We will draw up a contract." He called David Brown, head of the story department, and told him to expect me right away.

After a few pleasantries, the usual time-wasting preliminary to every business deal, Mr. Brown shifted in his seat and asked me, "How much do you want?" I was prepared. On the way over, I had decided what my price would be. "I want a cottage in Connecticut," I told Mr. Brown firmly. As Frances and Albert Hackett said later, Scott would be delighted to know he was getting me out of Hollywood. Besides, I had promised Wendy, at Rosemary Hall in Greenwich, that I would find a way of living part of the time in the East.

It was a most unexpected situation. No one had ever wanted to barter a life story—or any story—for a cottage in Connecticut. Head man Buddy Adler was in New York and after several urgent calls to Mr. Wald, Mr. Brown said to me, "It's unusual, but Mr. Adler will be back on Thursday. We will discuss this with him. Er—how much do you think a cottage in Connecticut will cost?" I had thought of that too. "Fifty thousand dollars," I replied.

Jerry Wald could never wait for anything, especially for a contract to be signed. He loved to see his name and his multitudinous projects in print. Even when he was in the hospital and until the very last illness, he was always calling reporters and columnists with tidbits of news. I had barely left his office when he telephoned Tom Pryor, then Hollywood correspondent for *The New York Times*, and informed him, "I have bought an original story, *Beloved Infidel*, from Sheilah Graham about the last years of Scott Fitzgerald." Jerry's enthusiasm was contagious and Tom teletyped the news to New York.

In New York that Friday night in November 1957, Gerold Frank had gone to the theatre. On the way home he bought the *Times*, and at the very top of the dispatch from Hollywood he read that Sheilah Graham's *Beloved Infidel*, the story of Scott Fitzgerald, had been bought by Jerry Wald. He telephoned me as soon as he reached his apartment. "I have reconsidered," he said. "I want to do your story." "You are too late," I replied. This time *I* was kind, but firm, because unexpectedly it was also going to be a book.

That same Friday, in the afternoon, Wald had contacted Donald Friede, of World Publishing, and suggested that he might want to publish *Beloved Infidel* on the understanding that Jerry had the film rights. Friede was most enthusiastic. He telephoned me immediately and said, "I want your book, and what do you want as an advance?" Originally Jack Goodman was to have given $2,500, but whenever I have the advantage I take a chance and double the price, and I said, "Five thousand dollars." How the situation had changed! It had all happened so suddenly and swiftly, the result of my desperate call to Jerry Wald but a few hours previously. Verily it hath been said, "God helps those who help themselves." But this was fast, even for God.

Mr. Friede assured me I would have my $5000 advance. "But I will have to verify it with Mr. Zevin [the president of World Publishing]." He would call me about 1 o'clock on Saturday.

Then the usual reaction. Could I write a book? I had expressed some doubt to Mr. Friede, and he had promised to come to Hollywood within a week and get me started, but even with his help, would I have the time and competence to write a book about Scott? And how much should I tell about myself? What would Edmund Wilson think? Or Scott's daughter, or his agent Harold Ober? Or Scott himself? I was full of doubts, and somewhat pleased to hear Gerold Frank begging for the job of collaborator. But I repeated, "It might be too late." I explained about Mr. Friede and World Publishing. "You must let *me* do it," Gerold insisted. All his indecision had vanished. I listened with interest as he outlined how the book should be done. It sounded good. I wondered, *is* it too late? Apart from whether I could do the book, *when* would I do it? Wendy was flying in from school for Thanksgiving, and Christmas was coming—and I was still very tired from the daily television show for NBC and the harrowing divorce which followed. The elastic in my brain had been overstretched. "You always snap back," Eddie Mayer had once said admiringly, but now I felt more like a tired girdle. The thought of the vast amount of extra work involved in writing a book overwhelmed me. Gerold persisted,

"This is *my* project. I understand it." He did, but I reminded him, "You turned it down." "I know," and his voice was angry. "My agent persuaded me. This is the last time I will listen to my agent."

Of course *The Times* story of the sale to 20th Century-Fox had something to do with Gerold's change of mind. It had made it seem a worthwhile project. He needed this assurance. Gerold Frank was never quite sure he was doing the right thing until contracts had been signed. Then it was the only thing in his life. "I'll let you know tomorrow morning," I told him. "I'll have to talk to Mr. Friede."

It was a fascinating morning. Gerold called me with a complete and excellent outline for the book. Friede, who was angry with the emergence of Gerold, assured me, "You can have the five-thousand-dollar advance right away." Jerry Wald called and was impishly delighted with the stir he had created. "I make things happen," he crowed. "Gerold understands the story," I told him. "He would use my early life as well. He believes it will give depth to the Fitzgerald part." "That's all right for the book," said Jerry somewhat dubiously, "but I am only interested in you and Fitzgerald."

I was taking telephone calls from New York all that Saturday morning. Rob wandered in and out of my room asking, "Who is it now?" First Gerold, then Donald—Gerold pleading, Donald pleading and angry by turns. He even called Gerold and told him, "Stop bothering her, you're making her ill." The deal was finally clinched by supersalesman Bill Buckley, then a vice-president of Holt & Company, to whom Gerold was committed for his next book. Gerold would collaborate with me, and Holt would give us an advance of $11,000—$5000 to Gerold and $6000 to me. I had promised to pay $1000 to Mr. Wirsig for his earlier assistance. I agreed to give Gerold 50 percent of all income from the book and film, although the movie rights were bought but for the signing. I like money and I could have had it all, but it has never been really important to me except to spend freely, perhaps because I have usually been paid well for my work.

So bring out ye jolly old tape recorder again and in almost the same words that had gone into the Woody Wirsig version, I t.   y story to the wart on Mr. Frank's nose, while the tape at 607 North Maple Drive rolled on and on.

Bill Buckley flew to Hollywood to clinch the film deal with Jerry Wald. Bill, soft-spoken, pleasant, and a sharp trader. Luckily the contract with the studio had not been signed because of the complication of the cottage in Connecticut. We ran into an unexpected game of cat-and-mouse. Every time Buckley brought up the subject of the contract, Jerry Wald would nod and beg earnestly, "Tell me what you want. Name the price." "How much will he pay?" Bill asked me. I did not know. It was not a question now of a cottage in Connecticut. We knew we could get $50,000. The titillating imponderable was, could we get $500,000?

Jerry was demanding that we name the price. Bill was trying to find out what he would pay. Meanwhile, word seeped through to Metro and Warners that, in spite of the stories in *The New York Times* and elsewhere, no deal had been signed with Wald. Mysteriously, they all knew I had been willing to settle for a cottage costing $50,000. Warners offered $60,000. Metro offered $70,000. And just as mysteriously, Jerry Wald knew all this—he must have had a spy in every office. He offered $75,000.

Mr. Buckley, Gerold and I had a conference. "Jerry *has* to buy it," I insisted. "He's committed. We need not accept a cent less than $150,000." It was tremendously exciting. A real fortune was hovering. The publisher decided to start at $300,000. "He'll never pay it," I told him. "We can always come down," he soothed. At the next session with Jerry, Bill dropped his bomb. "The price for the book is $300,000." All of a sudden Jerry Wald was as vague as a cloud. He just wasn't there. He was floating in his own protected paradise. But I knew we had him, although Gerold had not yet put one of my tape-recorded words on paper. It was a delicious game of high financial poker. I am always calm and clear when I have the advantage. I wish I could be as calm and clear when I do not. Then I would be a real poker player.

Jerry called me, and pleaded in anguished tones: "Sheilah, what are you trying to do to me? Look, I'll give you five per cent of the profits on top of the $75,000." It was an interesting thought, but profits are often mythical in Hollywood because of the huge overhead charged to the picture. I had been in Hollywood long enough to understand the word "gross." I thought fast. "Instead of five percent of the profits, Jerry, how about one percent of the gross? That would really mean something." He almost wept. "I can't, I'm getting top stars and they will want a percentage, and this five percent is from my share." He went into facts and figures, none of which I believed, but I was grateful to him and I wanted Jerry to have the movie. He continued, "Look, I'm trying to give you an annuity for your children. Don't you want your children to have an annuity?" "I do," I assured him—what a lovely idea! "I'll call you back." I consulted with Bill and Gerold. We agreed on $100,000 and 5 percent of the profits. And because he had publicized the project so much before the deal was signed, Jerry Wald agreed to pay $100,000, with an immediate down payment of $7,500 for the option, which Buckley insisted must be exercised within 30 days after receipt of the manuscript. And now, on with the book. Forget the money. We must have a good book. It was the third week of November 1957. We must be finished by August 1958 for a November 24, 1958 publication date.

❦ CHAPTER THIRTY

GEROLD Frank could pass for a successful banker. He is of good height, well built, and his baldness somehow gives him an air of stern solidity. He has little personality of his own. Perhaps this is why he is so good at losing himself in other people's lives. He can be pompous, but his small, slightly upslanted brown eyes reveal a shy, sensitive, kind man. No matter what dreadful deeds have been committed by "his ladies," he manages to translate them into terms of noble necessity. The wart on his nose hypnotized me. Perhaps that is why it was there. Soon after commencing his later, unsuccessful book with Zsa Zsa Gabor, he had the wart removed, and I rather resented that.

Gerold's own life has always, I am sure, been highly respectable. I believe he would have liked to be more unconventional and with some encouragement I think he might have been, but he married his Lillian quite early, he is devoted to her and they have two grown-up children. His desire to be dashing and a bit wicked has perforce been satisfied vicariously in the lives of the people for whom he has served as a catalyst in print. He is in love with his prose, and during our several heated arguments at the end when I wanted to cut some of the sentimentality, it was like telling Shakespeare to eliminate all of the sonnets and all of the plays. Gerold has a hushed-cathedral attitude toward his writing. He cannot bear criticism—how many of us can?—and he was desperately unhappy when *Time* Magazine referred to him

as a "non-book writer." I sometimes think he wrote *The
Deed*, about the assassination of British High Commissioner
Lord Moyne, in revenge for what the London reviewers did,
unfairly I thought, to his contribution to *Beloved Infidel*.

Gerold is the noisiest ghost ever to glorify a troubled
conscience. He is forever giving out interviews about this
and that personality with whom he has worked, and while
most of it is complimentary, most of it is nonsense. But he
is a good technician. He *can* put a book together. He *can*
write well. If he wants to write a good book on his own,
I believe it would help him to have some psychoanalysis to
help him lose his fear of God knows what, to see beneath
the image he creates of himself and of other people's lives.
I am glad I am doing this book myself. But I'll be lucky if
it does as well as *Beloved Infidel*.

It was a twilight experience "combing my memory," as
Gerold put it, and retracing the places and people of my
three and a half years with Scott. It had all been so long
ago—eighteen years. Old incidents bloomed again. Old pain
and pleasure made me smile and sigh. I gave Gerald a list of
people Scott and I had known together. He had already interviewed Arnold Gingrich of *Esquire*, with whom I had not
been in contact since December 24, 1940, three days after
Scott's death, when I had written to him about four unpub-
lished Pat Hobby stories.

> I think you have four Pat Hobbys left. Against two of
> them, "Two Old Timers" and "Mightier Than The Sword"
> —on his copies, Scott had written *Poor*. As for "College
> Days," this was written during a drinking binge and he
> did not read it to me, so I don't know whether it was as
> good as the best Pat Hobby or as bad as the worst. Would
> it be asking too much of you to refrain from publishing
> the two Pat Hobbys he had marked *Poor*? It breaks my
> heart to have young people, who didn't know how good a
> writer Scott could be, read those bad ones and say,
> "Oh, so he wrote that sort of thing? I wonder why they
> made all that fuss about him?"

Arnold replied that everything Scott had written should
be read. Recently a book of "Pat Hobby" stories was published. Some were very good, some very bad. I know they
were all interesting to admirers of Fitzgerald. But I personally do not believe that every word written by Scott

Fitzgerald should be published. Perhaps I am wrong, but some of the Pat Hobby stories make me wince, as they did Scott.

I told Gerold of the doctor who had attended Scott during the first two years in Hollywood. He could give him an enormous amount of information. The doctor refused to be interviewed. And with good reason. I had once written to him: "The only way to save Scott is to get him to a hospital where he cannot get liquor. Everything else is utterly futile and you know it. . . . If you can do nothing to save him, in the name of God find someone who can."

Dr. Clarence Nelson, of Scott's last year and a half in Hollywood, was glad to see Gerold, and told him of the time Scott had awakened after a feverish night; his arms entangled in his pajamas, he had imagined in his half-asleep state that he was paralyzed. "The result of your drinking," the doctor had said to him. "The good Lord tapped you on the shoulder."

Gerold called on Walter Wanger, but Walter did not remember anything, he insisted, of the dreadful experience of *Winter Carnival* with Scott. "Everything was beautiful, nothing went wrong." He could not even remember Scott's being drunk, which, of course, was absurd.

Dr. Richard Hoffman, the psychiatrist I had called to see Scott in New York after Dartmouth and *Winter Carnival*, told Gerold something I had not known: that Scott craved liquor because there was a deficiency of sugar in his blood. Isn't all drinking and compulsive eating a desire for comfort and fast energy, which is contained in sugar and starch? But it made me wonder whether a doctor could have cured Scott of his drinking. I doubted it: not unless he could also cure him of the weariness and the anxiety. Dr. Hoffman praised me very highly to Gerold and this surprised me. He had been so interested in Scott as a man and patient that I thought he had been unaware of me, hovering anxiously in the background. But in a note from Gerold dated November 30, 1957, he repeated Dr. Hoffman's tribute:

Never in my experience as a doctor have I met a more devoted, dedicated person than the young lady was. She completely negated herself to help this man, with whom she had obviously fallen deeply in love. She took care of him with utter dedication. . . . Nothing meant anything to her but Scott's survival. She was perfect in the way she cared for him.

I did not realize I had been so devoted. I remembered more my unhappiness and anger when he drank. And his sweetness to me when he was sober.

Nunnally Johnson, the writer and director, remembered vividly the party at Malibu where Scott had locked him into a room and finally letting him go, had said, "You'll never return." "Why not?" Nunnally had asked. "Because I am living with my paramour!" Scott had shouted at him. This was the first I knew of this, and when Gerold told me, I was angry with Scott and would not understand the frustration that had caused the outburst. How dare he call me his paramour? Even if he were drunk and being dramatic, he had no right to say this. When I told Edmund Wilson not long ago how upset I had been, and also of my distress at being referred to in some of the reviews as "Scott Fitzgerald's mistress," he said quietly, "You were not his mistress. You were his second wife." Had I loved Scott less, I could have pressured him into getting a divorce from his poor demented Zelda. He needed me, and he wanted to marry me. "Zelda and I should never have married," Scott had told me. "We were wrong for each other. She would have been happier married to almost anyone else. She was beautiful and talented. It was her tragedy that she could not bear to be overshadowed by the attention I received from my early books. For instance, she hated it when Gertrude Stein talked only to me, while her companion Alice B. Toklas talked to her. She had a compulsion to compete with me. She could not as a writer, so she decided to be a famous ballerina and studied with the Russian ballet in Paris. But it was too late for her. And when she realized this, instead of accepting the fact and bending with it, she broke."

How could I, who loved Scott, give him the added burden of abandoning Zelda? In my less attractive moments, I sometimes wish I had. As his widow, I would have served as his shrine. Scott, when he started to write *The Last Tycoon*, had wanted to add a codicil to his will, leaving me whatever money might come from the book. "I want you to have the first chapter and the plan, it might be worth something." I had answered, "Scottie and Zelda might need it—I can take care of myself." Zelda died before the Fitzgerald re-

surgence enriched his estate to the tune of $50,000 a year
during the past ten years. I mention this now so you will
know I was never a mistress. I was a woman who loved
Scott Fitzgerald for better or worse until he died.

I took Gerold to the places where Scott had lived. At the
house of the big binge at Malibu, the owners allowed us to
wander at will. A new patio had been added, but the little
captain's walk on top of the house was still there, with the
carved-out crescents in the wooden shutters. I could almost
breathe the heavy scent of the flowers with which I had
filled the sitting room and the good smell of the cookies
Scott's housekeeper Flora had baked continuously at my request. I walked along the beach with Gerold, took off my
shoes and kicked at the water as I had in the days with
Scott.

Gerold and I visited my apartment in Hollywood where
Scott had died. "I lived here once," I told the woman who
opened the door. She recognized me as the columnist and
was quite interested. I was surprised at the smallness of
the apartment. I had thought of it with its two spacious
bedrooms as quite large. Here was the room where he died.
Had he ever really lived?

I took Gerold to the Edward Everett Horton estate in Encino—Belly Acres. The fastidious Scott had hated that name,
and I was under strict orders to keep it secret. Scott's house
no longer existed. The new freeway had swallowed it. The
Horton house was still there, very run down. And where
were the pomegranate hedges and the two magnolia trees
named Herbert and Gloria, planted for the early romance of
Herbert Marshall and Gloria Swanson? The small roses no
longer bloomed riotously everywhere as in Scott's day.

I was happy with my *Beloved Infidel* project. It was absorbing to retrace the years and look back at the uncertain,
vulnerable girl who had been so much in love with Scott
Fitzgerald. Finally, with a snip here and a tuck there, the
book was finished, and Gerold came to California with the
manuscript. I read it through most of one night. I did not
like the writing in the first section. It was oversentimental-
ized. I could almost hear the violins. It read like a fan
magazine. "We have to rewrite some of it," I told Gerold
in the morning.

With our August deadline coming, Bob Lescher, senior
editor at Holt, came to town and with Gerold fighting for
his prose all the way, we managed to cut and change a great

deal of the first part of the book. The second half, the part concerning Scott, was almost exactly as I had dictated it into the tape recorder from the notes I had written about Scott immediately after his death—not for the purpose of writing a book but to remember him, to remember our conversations, our time together. After Bob left, the indignant Gerold put some of his sentiment back, but not all.

As Woodrow Wirsig had been, Gerold was fascinated with my early life. I was not sure it belonged in the book about Scott Fitzgerald, but Gerold had convinced me it would make my time with Scott, my need for him, more understandable. I eliminated some of the people in my early life to save hurting them—this was not the most conventional story—and we used some fictitious names for the same reason, and changed some locales.

I was pleased when my children were undismayed that I had not been the rich society debutante they had thought I was. I had never quite told them this, but they had assumed I had been cherished and well educated and that I had never been poor, because they were never poor. I was anxious telling them, "We had no money when I was a little girl and I was raised in an orphanage." "But Mother," said Wendy, "this is the great American story—you start poor and then you get rich and famous. There's nothing wrong with that." I told them my real name, and Wendy replied. "I like it. When I have a daughter I will call her Lily." But the project itself bored her, and I cannot blame her.

The name of Scott Fitzgerald was heard constantly in our house at this time. Rob quite enjoyed Gerold Frank's comings and goings and during a lull in writing, Gerold, a former Ohio State chess champion, taught Rob some moves he used to good advantage against Wendy, which added further fuel to her dislike of the whole thing. I am still not sure whether Wendy has read *Beloved Infidel* all the way through, although recently she read *The Last Tycoon* and, like Zelda Fitzgerald, did not care for the heroine too much. Rob read the book, and saw the film as soon as possible at an early-morning showing in New York—practically the only person in the theatre—and assured me he had enjoyed the film as well as the book. Wendy came around to Fitzgerald in college, and appreciates him now perhaps more than Rob. Her complete capitulation came last summer: "I'm thinking of Scott Fitzgerald for my honor papers at Bryn Mawr. He's the best of the American writers." I was very pleased.

In August, the publishers sent the finished script to Jerry Wald. The project had been emotionally dehydrating, and I was tired. I took Wendy and Rob to Sun Valley. We all needed a breather. We skated and swam and rode horses, but I was nervous and restless, and ate enormously and continuously. Fortune and freedom were hanging on Jerry's decision and I was glad when we returned home. It seemed incredible that I could make this huge amount of money and I waited for Jerry Wald to tell me whether he would follow through on his option and have 20th Century-Fox pay the other $92,000 for the book. The days passed and no call from Jerry, who usually telephoned as predictably as he used to breathe. Alas, he no longer does. He died two years ago.

I discovered by a chance conversation with Rachel Brand at Martindale's bookshop in Beverly Hills that Jerry had mimeographed a dozen copies of the manuscript and it was making the rounds: Rachel had one, also the book editor of the Los Angeles *Times*, an agent, Jerry's secretary, his press agent, and the Lord knew who else. Like other Hollywood producers, Mr. Wald needed reassurance.

I did what I swore to myself I would not do—I called him and said, "I can't stand the suspense, Jerry, have you made up your mind yet?" Jerry lied in most honest tones, "Gee, Sheilah, I haven't finished reading it." He had been forced to pay $100,000 and we would wait for it. The day before the option expired, with Gerold in New York and me in Hollywood calling each other twice a day to ask "Have you heard anything?" Jerry Wald made up his mind. "We are picking up the option," he told me. "Congratulations." *Phew!* I felt lightheaded and rich. Now that the suspense was over, it seemed inevitable and quite delicious.

Holt was so sure of a best seller, the first edition was 20,000 copies. It was sold out before publication and another 20,000 copies were rushed into print. Usually a book takes six months from the time the manuscript is completed to publication date. Ours was pushed through in three months.

The first review was glorious, from Robert Kirsch of the Los Angeles *Times*. I loved his line, "The same enchanting quality which all great novels possess." Rachel Brand called me: "Get *Time* and *Newsweek*," she crowed. "Great." This was surprising because *Time* had already slapped the project several times. They had referred to me as a "tattler-prattler," they had jeered and sneered, and as I don't enjoy this I had decided I would not read the *Time* Magazine review. I was sure it would be bad. But now I dashed to Gunther's Drug Store in Beverly Hills, excitedly took the magazine from the rack and tore it open in the shop. Ah, the lead book review. I was transfixed, humiliated, ashamed. They called the book cheap, they called me vulgar; it was like someone hitting me hard on the back of my neck. Lord, what have I done to Scott Fitzgerald? I wanted to show what a fine, mature person he was during the years I had known him, and now I had dug a pit and buried him in it. I had damaged irrevocably the man I loved so completely, and I prayed "Dear God, don't let the other reviews be like this." If they were, I would hide for the rest of my life. But I could not run away. I would have to face people. You cannot run away when you have two dependent children. This is *Time* Magazine. The bad review was a foregone conclusion. *I'll send a telegram for publication.* Some lines from a Shakespeare sonnet flashed into my mind. "Love's not Time's fool though rosy lips and cheeks within his bending sickle's compass come."

"Ach, don't bother," Jerry Wald advised, but I felt raw and depressed. I remembered the woman editor at Simon and Schuster who had thought the book would be in bad taste. I remembered everyone who had said, "Don't do the project."

Newsweek was better than *Time.* But because their man in Hollywood had seen some of my Scott Fitzgerald material—Jerry Wald had made photostats of everything I had from Scott—he chided me for not using it all.

Jerry had given out stories about a hidden cache of a hundred letters Scott had written me. I had exactly four letters. Scott and I had been together most of the time, and when we were apart he sent me funny notes or telegrams. "Never mind," said Jerry when I called him on this, "I'll write ninety-six letters and who'll know the difference?" I had to laugh, it was so preposterous.

There was a letter Scott had written that I wanted to include in the book. Gerold had thought it would slow up the story, but I am the boss now and I will show you the letter. An Englishman had been pestering me for dates and when I would not see him, he wrote me a rude letter with his various past projects printed across the top on the sides of the page. He addressed it to:

Miss Mussolini Graham
1530 North Kings Road
Hollywood

Dear Miss Sheilah Graham:

It would appear to me you are lacking both in sportsmanship and also good manners, in other words you are getting exactly like all the other British who reside here. When I last saw you at ——'s house, it was left you were to have dinner with me on the Friday evening. I waited specially for you, but you neither communicated with me or left any message, but went off to Chicago.

I have 'phoned you many many times since, and to say the least you must have had some of my messages.

It is a matter of complete indifference whether I meet you or not, but at any rate you might have had the courtesy to have communicated with me.

> With kind regards:
> Yours sincerely,

Scott was amused when I showed it to him. "Do you mind if I answer it?" he asked me. This letter is dated October 6, 1937:

3d Football Team St. Paul Academy 1910	Ex-1st Lt. Infantry Headquarters Co. 1917	Ex-employee Baron & Collier Carcards, 1920

Worked Unsuccessfully
       on

Redheaded Woman   Dear Mr.
with Jean Harlow   Unable to match the apt phraseology in
     1932   your letter to Miss Graham of recent date,
               I can only repeat it: "You show both poor
Won FIELDMEET   sportsmanship and bad manners"—the
   (Junior)   former because when a girl neglects two
NEWMAN School   dozen phone calls it is fair to suppose you
     1912   didn't make an impression—the latter
               because you wrote such a letter at all.
AFFAIR   It is nice to know that it is all "a matter
(unconsummated) of complete indifference" to you, so there
   with   will be no hard feelings. But you worry
ACTRESS (1927) us about the state of the English colony

WROTE
22
Unsuccessful
stories 1920
offered to
*Saturday
Evening
Post*

in Hollywood. Can it be that there are
other telephones that—but no—and any-
how you can always take refuge behind
that splendid, that truly magnificent indifference.

Very truly yours,

(signed)   F. SCOTT FITZGERALD

Play *Vegetable*
Ran 2 weeks
ATLANTIC CITY
(with Ernest Truex)
        1923

I flew to New york a few days before the publication
date. It was enjoyable, walking on Fifth Avenue, to see
Beloved Infidel in the windows of Scribner's—Scott's publishers—and Doubleday and Brentano's, and wondering with some
apprehension, what will the *Times* and *Tribune* say?

The New York Times gave the book an excellent review.
"I hope it sells a million copies," said reviewer Charles
Poore. John Hutchens in the *Tribune* was almost as enthusiastic, and his last line pleased me enormously: "We
now must write another ending to the story of Scott Fitzgerald, and for Sheilah Graham this should be triumph
enough." This was why I had written the book. So they
would know that Scott was not a defeated man at the end.
Don Mankiewicz, brother of Scott's *Three Comrades* producer Joe Mankiewicz, headlined his review in *The New
York Times* Sunday Book Section, KATHLEEN REMEMBERS.
He praised the book and he praised me as a fine export
from Britain. I recited Christina Rossetti's lovely poem,
"When I am dead, my dearest," lingering on the last, "And
if thou wilt remember, and if thou wilt forget." I was glad
I had decided to remember.

It certainly seemed that we would have a great success.
The book was reviewed at great length and depth all over
the country and in Canada. Eighty percent were in the
rave class, ten medium, and ten very bad.

With some trepidation, I had sent an advance copy of
Beloved Infidel to Scottie Lanahan and to Edmund Wilson.
It was a Sunday, and I had been at the beach. On my re-

turn, my answering service informed me of Scottie's call, with an operator's number in Washington, D.C. I was worried. Was she pleased, was she angry? I discussed it at length with my secretary, Adele Roy. "Why don't you call her and find out?" Adele suggested. Scottie's first words were like a hymn at heaven's gate—"I love the book, Sheilah, and Daddy would have loved it. It's a marvelous story and you have written it with great taste." She had wept twice, she told me—when the society woman at St. Moritz had said, "You're an adventuress, aren't you?" and I had replied after an anxious pause, "Yes, I am." And in the last chapter, when her father was dead, and I had driven to the party at Dorothy Parker's and the car would not go forward, only backwards. I was tremendously relieved that Scottie liked the book. I had wanted to please her, as Scott had wanted to please her when he wrote *The Last Tycoon*.

I received a letter from Edmund Wilson. "I think your portrait of Scott is the best that has yet been published. . . . And the part about your own life is fascinating. I shan't go on at length, because I have done a review for *The New Yorker*, which ought to be out soon. I am enclosing a list of errors which you should have corrected in a new edition. Sincerely, Edmund Wilson." Perfectionist Wilson's list of my errors included:

P. 27—4th paragraph, 3rd line: Insert *a* after *to*.
P. 153—8th line: No hyphen after No; hyphen after Que.
P. 219—3rd paragraph, 6th line: Night should be nights.
P. 307—2nd line: Insert *a* after *at*.

I rejoiced and was enormously proud when a few weeks later I read the eleven beautiful columns in *The New Yorker* in which Mr. Wilson made me feel that I was an admirable person, as Scott had made me feel I was valuable. I had needed this reassurance.

Later when the book was published in England, J. B. Priestly referred to me as a modern Becky Sharp. He hoped I would one day write my story alone. The *Daily Telegraph* referred to me as a "female Gatsby." The cheaper press decided to be shocked. They called me ruthless, greedy, sleek as a fat cat. They were convinced I had clawed my way to the top. I had always believed I had climbed on my smile. The dignified newspapers—the *Times, Observer* and *Telegraph,* and the evening papers—praised the book very

highly, although, except for the *Times*, they united in de-
ploring the style of Gerold Frank. With the cheaper press
horrified—a typical comment: "We cannot understand why a
wealthy Englishwoman would write such a book, and why a
reputable British publisher would print it"—and the better
papers recommending the book, *Beloved Infidel* was the number one best seller in England, and I was Topic A for
two weeks.

I received thousands of letters in America and from England. I heard from Buff Cobb Rogers, who was in a New
York hospital dying of cancer. It was Buff who had taken
me to her home in Santa Monica after Scott died, who gave
me her bed, who enveloped me with the warmth of her
kind heart. She wrote:

> I cannot disappear without telling you what a very ex-
> traordinary person I have always found you. When I first
> met you, I thought you were a girl, golden and gracious,
> but that never if I lived to be a thousand would I ever be
> able to reach under the façade and find a friend, or
> even someone whom I might conceivably understand.
> . . . What I am trying to say, clumsily, is that men
> who know something about people, and did not grade
> them either by Chase Manhattan Bank or girls' finish-
> ing school standards, would have been fascinated by Lily
> Shiels—men like my own father, men like Nunnally, Eddie
> Mayer, Ogden Nash; women like me, like Dorothy Parker,
> like Clare Boothe—we would have known that it was not
> only wonderful that you appeared to us, lovely, gracious
> and well mannered as you are, but that the road by
> which you reached us, the things you learned as you fairly
> fled down that road, made you one of the most romantic
> and interesting women of your time. What a shame, what
> a waste, my dear, that we summed you up merely as a
> pretty girl with a gift for industry and a disagreeable
> ability to say a cutting thing. . . . It took Scott the genius
> to make her known to herself and us.

There was more and it was signed, "With respect, your
always affectionate, Buff Cobb Rogers." Very soon after, before she went into the coma that preceded her death, Buff
whispered to her husband, "When it is over, there are two
people I want you to call in California—Nunnally Johnson
and Sheilah Graham." Rest my dear, kind, generous Buff.

There was a letter from a Mrs. John P. Hawkins from Oklahoma. She had been Scott's nurse during his last bad drinking bout in 1939. "The picture of you and Scott in Mexico, you say it was the only one ever made of you together. I have a much better one of you than you have in the book. He is not wearing a hat and it is very clear of both of you." Did I want it? I wrote her by the next mail. The photograph was the last ever taken of Scott, in the garden at Encino, against the white picket fence "looking like little gravestones in a confederate graveyard," as Buff had described it on her first visit to Encino. He was to die a year later and death was on his face behind the sad worn smile, the perpetual pencil behind his ear, the check sports coat. And I holding his arm and smiling gaily into the camera, and not knowing.

A Mrs. Ruth Ann Armstrong wrote that her husband had known Mr. Fitzgerald at Princeton and had made her read everything of Scott's before he would marry her. She suggested I could do a great many people a tremendous favor if I would write down his reading program for me, my education which had been so painstakingly prepared by Scott on a dozen or so foolscap size sheets of paper—the history, literature, poetry, art and music courses in The F. Scott Fitzgerald College of One. I still have the books, although I thought the plans and the order for reading, with all the detailed instructions, had been lost. I was delighted to find them again among some other things he had written for me in the F. Scott Fitzgerald papers at Princeton.

There was a letter from Mrs. Margaret Turnbull in whose home at La Paix, near Baltimore, Scott had lived from the spring of 1932 until the fall of 1933. She was so pleased to learn from *Beloved Infidel* that Scott had not been lonely or bitter at the end of his life, that we had fulfilled each other's lives in a complete and beautiful way, that he had a comforting hand to hold at the last.

I heard from Judith Hurt Armitage in Ireland—pretty, blond, blue-eyed Judith, who had introduced me to the Eton-Oxford young set and opened the door to my "society" period in England. She was angry with me. "You don't say whom you married, or how old your children are."

Captain the Honorable Jack Mitford—before his death early in 1964 he had succeeded to the title and was Lord Redesdale—was most intrigued. "I hear you have written *two* books. Please send me a copy of each. Love, Jack."

The Marquess of Donegall, the Earl of Belfast, Viscount Chichester, Baron Fisherwick of Fisherwick, Hereditary Lord High Admiral of Lock Neagh, had only one complaint— "The best photograph I ever took (in the sun of St. Moritz) you credited to Jack Mitford!"

"Would you have liked me as much if you had known of my real background?" I asked Jack when I was in England for the publication of the book. Jack, white-haired and incapacitated from a serious accident in his car, replied, "Of course," and called me affectionately a "clever puss."

I put the same question to Donegall and received the same reply. He had imagined, he told me, that I was the daughter of a country doctor. I had not had a cockney accent, he assured me. Furthermore, he was still fond of me in spite of the *Beloved Infidel* revelations and gave a cocktail party in my honor, something he had not done in the old days. I met and liked Maureen McKenzie, the attractive blond woman he wants to marry.

A traveling salesman fell in love with the girl I was in the book and made it his number one sales project to track me down. Not only me, but everyone who had ever known me, from Scottie to John Wheeler to Jonah Ruddy and every blessed one of my three husbands. The pen salesman finally caught up with me at the Warwick Hotel in New York. He had telephoned from Kansas City, stated he was "Bob Scott," that he was the book reviewer for the Kansas City *Star*. He interviewed me on the phone and I replied to everything he asked about me and my children. Two days later, he was in the lobby of the Warwick, and could he come up? As soon as I opened the door and saw the heavy porcine face, I thought, Is he really a book reviewer? "Have you done the interview yet?" I said, after asking him to sit down. "I have a confession to make," he said. "You are not a book reviewer?" I replied, measuring the distance to the door. "No." "Then what are you?" "A pen salesman, but I had to meet you. I have read *Beloved Infidel* and I have fallen in love with you."

"But that was twenty years ago!" I reminded him. "How old are you?" I asked. "Thirty-one." I must widen the gap. "I'm old enough to be your mother," I said severely. "You're as beautiful as you were in the book," he insisted.

I stood up. "I have an appointment." "Please, when can I see you?" "I'll call you," I said and almost pushed him through the door.

But while the book and the aftermath had been on the whole deeply satisfying, the film was to be a complete disaster.

❦   CHAPTER THIRTY-ONE

I HAD but one life to give to my producer, and Jerry Wald ruined it. Not intentionally, I am sure, but through the usual Hollywood crime—starting without proper preparation. Deborah Kerr had received the book in Switzerland from Buddy Adler, head of production at 20th Century-Fox. "I read it in one sitting," she told me later. "I wired Buddy at once. 'Why didn't you sent it to me sooner? Of course I'll do it.'" She was curious to know, "Did you ever graduate from the Scott Fitzgerald College of One?" No, I told her. Graduation had been planned for June 1941. Scott had died six months before. She cabled her agent Joe Schoenfeld, my old nemesis on *Daily Variety* and now with the William Morris Agency: DON'T DELAY. GET ME THE PART OF SHEILAH GRAHAM IN BELOVED INFIDEL. Joe was amused, remembering our battles. I was flattered, although I thought Deborah was too controlled, too thin and too ladylike. "Jean Simmons would be better," I told Jerry Wald. Or Marilyn Monroe—a sudden inspiration while I lingered in my bath that night. Our lives had been similar in some respects.

Everyone was asking me who I thought should play Scott Fitzgerald. "Richard Basehart," I replied without hesitation, and those who had seen him as the tender, sensitive, doomed fool in *La Strada* knew what I meant. But Jerry Wald smiled indulgently and said, "Oh no, we'll have someone much more important than Richard Basehart—how would you like Gregory Peck?" Greg was a big star and I have always found him very attractive, but he was absolutely wrong for the part. He is tall and not too flexible. Scott was rather short, enthusiastic and always open to new ideas. Even Bing Crosby would have been better. I have always found sensitivity in Bing's face. But 20th Century-Fox had a picture commitment with Mr. Peck and he agreed, reluctantly, to play the part. Eddie Albert was signed to be Robert Benchley, Philip Ober for John Wheeler, and John Sutton for the part of the Marquess of Donegall. Except for Ober, it was the miscasting

mistake of the decade. And the script by Alfred Hayes was
no better.

When you have sold your story to a motion picture company, you have sold your soul to the devil. They can change
your name, the title, the story, they can make you fictitious,
they can make you real, they can cut anything they like, add
anything they like, they can sell you to television, they can
sell you down the river. All they cannot do, according to the
contract, is hold you up to public ridicule and scorn. And 20th
Century-Fox managed this too. Even important authors like
Hemingway and Faulkner had no rights about how a film was
to be made, or who should star in it, once the story was sold.

But Jerry Wald wanted my approval, perhaps because I
was a columnist, or he might have been unsure, or maybe he
genuinely wanted me to be happy. He sent me the script and
called me the next day at 7:30 A.M., impatient for my reaction. "Well?" he started. "Thank you for sending me the
script . . ." I hedged. "Yes, yes," said Jerry impatiently. "You
didn't have to," I continued. "What did you think of it?" He
was bursting to know. "I think it's dreadful, since you ask my
opinion." I was angry and upset. "Which part of it?" "Every
part." "Tell me now, don't wait until the preview, when it
will be too late." I drew a long breath and plunged—"Alfred
Hayes is a cynical writer. [He had made his reputation with
Girl on the Via Flaminnia, and was rated an authority on
love.] He doesn't believe that love can be simple. He
doesn't like the two leading characters, and if you don't care
about the hero or heroine, you don't have a picture. He has
taken the warmth and depth out of the characters. *She's* a
nagging shrew and *he's* the whining failure of *The Disenchanted*. Hayes has no understanding of Fitzgerald. He's
made Donegall a conventional silly-ass Englishman. He's not.
He would never wear a monocle. Eddie Mayer was a highly
cultured man. Hayes has made it seem that he would talk
out of the side of his mouth. He has completely missed the
whole idea. Only people who have read the book will have
even the faintest idea of what it is all about." I could hear
Jerry's pen scratching away as I talked. "Is that all?" he asked
pleasantly when I stopped. "No. It would take a week to tell
you all that is wrong." "Then you must work on it for a
week," said Jerry happily. It was impossible to dent this man.

I was put on the 20th Century-Fox payroll for seven days
as a script writer with a salary of $300 a day. I was given a
two-room office in the writers' annex, with a new typewriter,

lots of typewriting paper, carbons and pencils, and some leftovers from Luther Davis, the last occupant. I was given a secretary. I worked hard. Twice in that seven days my secretary dissolved in tears and complained that I was overworking her. But this was my life and Scott's, and I had to do my best to save us. They must understand about Scott, the painstaking education he had tried to give me—there must be more than just a supercilious scene where Scott chides Sheilah for reading the last page first. And most of the happy incidents in the book had been left out.

There were some good scenes and these I did not tamper with. One I liked very much—the fifteen-year-old Lily, fresh from the orphanage, her nose pressed against the window of a jeweler's shop in Bond Street. And during her daydreaming, two men in top hat, white tie and tails materialized in the windowpane. "My dear, I would like you to have this diamond necklace," said one. Lily's eyes widened with pleasure, " 'Ow nice"—and then, recollecting her prim purity, "I'm not that kind of a girl, I'd 'ave you know." "And how about this diamond ring?" said the other toff. "It's loverly," the girl sighed and turned around to smile at the men, but they had vanished. The scene had also vanished when I saw the finished film.

At the end of the week, I turned in a hundred and fifty closely typed pages. I put back mostly what had been in the book—my earnest reading of my lecture to Scott and his staff at Encino in the doorless rooms that fitted into each other like a child's box of squares, each one getting smaller; the fiasco of Scott's visit to Chicago to help me with my radio sponsor, ending violently with Scott knocking the sponsor down. It was all there in the book for which they had paid $100,000.

Jerry Wald told me that Buddy Adler thought my scenes were excellent and would improve the film very much. They gave them to Mr. Hayes, who must have tossed the hundred and fifty pages into the wastepaper basket—none of it was used. I can almost hear him saying, "These amateurs!"

A few weeks later, Jerry sent me the second draft. I called him in tears. "May we have a meeting in your office with Mr. Hayes?" "Of course," Jerry replied, pleasant as always. And with the script writer there, I said to Jerry, "Mr. Hayes does not like Scott Fitzgerald or Sheilah Graham, do you, Mr. Hayes?" Mr. Hayes was honest. "No, I don't," he replied. "I think, Jerry, you should get another writer," I said. That was fine with Mr. Hayes, but he remained another two months on the script.

A few weeks before production, when Gregory Peck refused to make the picture without drastic changes in the script, Jerry hired Robert Alan Arthur and then Sy Bartlett for fast rewrites.

"Postpone the picture," Gregory begged Wald. "I will be available when you want to do it, but we must have a better script." "We can't," said Jerry. "We'll lose Deborah Kerr if we don't start now." And this, my friends, is how pictures in Hollywood are sometimes made.

It was better under the circumstances, I thought, to have nothing to do with the film. I decided it was a good time to take off for Europe to cover the motion pictures abroad. I stayed in Europe that summer with my children for eleven weeks, writing my column as I went.

Cassell's, the British publishers of *Beloved Infidel*, held a press reception for me at the Savoy Hotel July 23, 1959. Some executives of 20th Century-Fox attended. "When will the film version be made?" a reporter asked. A 20th Century-Fox official told him, "It has been postponed to November." This was typical of the ineptitude and confusion at the studio. That very morning, I had received a cable from Jerry Wald: SCOTT FITZGERALD MEETING SHEILAH TODAY. TOO BAD YOU'RE NOT HERE. The film had started before I had left Hollywood. It was in the last week of production when I returned.

There was good news from Jerry. "Deborah Kerr is great. She gives an Academy Award performance." Several others said the same thing. I was delighted to be proved wrong. The comments about Mr. Peck were not so favorable. He had been striking out like a wounded animal, battling with Wald and the director, but not with Deborah. It is impossible to fight with this charming lady, which was another reason why she was wrong for the part. Poor Gregory, he was regarded as a Grade-A stinker. He had merely been fighting for his life as an actor. Several bad roles and even Gregory Peck could be through.

It is a custom in Hollywood, when there is some doubt about the excellence of a film, to put together 20 minutes of the most dramatic scenes to show to selected columnists and top reporters before the actual press reviews. These scenes can give an erroneous impression of the complete picture. In the 20 minutes from *Beloved Infidel*, the hand-picked press saw the scene in which Scott tries to kill his Sheilo with the gun actually being fired, which was not true. And the scene on the beach where she confesses her fake background. Of course this meant putting Deborah into a swim suit. She had worn a swim suit with Burt Lancaster in the Oscar-winning film *From Here to Eternity*. The film had given her a new sexy image. It had succeeded once, they hoped it might succeed again.

The Chicago episode had been emasculated with Deborah pleading, "Oh, Scott, oh Scott," and Gregory, under the impression that he was drunk, smiling a strained constipated smile, instead of the real-life stronger effect of Scott swinging at the sponsor.

But everyone said it was great and everyone said that Deborah Kerr would win the Oscar—even Joe Hyams of the New York *Herald Tribune*, who usually has better judgment. The sea scenes at Malibu were superb and it was possible to fool these molders of opinion from the 20 minutes shown. But not Tim Horan, promotion director of Bantam Books. He knew that Deborah would not win the Oscar. "It's the worst picture she has made in a long time and she looks bad as well," he told me. Mr. Horan was justifiably concerned, because his office had paid an advance of $25,000 for the paperback rights. And a first printing of 500,000 was in the works.

20th Century-Fox followed the same procedure with *Tender Is the Night*, showing favored reporters 20 minutes from the film. Bantam was so sure the complete film from the Fitzgerald novel would be a success, they paid Scribner's $50,000 for the right to print one million copies in paperback, for one year only.

The film history of *Tender Is the Night* is typical of what can happen financially. Judge Biggs, executor of Scott's estate, had written me on July 5, 1946 that he had just disposed of the "talkie" rights of *Tender Is the Night* to David Selznick for $17,500. He had accepted the low offer because Zelda had become ill again and it was necessary to institutionalize her again, perhaps briefly, perhaps for a long time. Of course, $17,500 was too little, but they needed the money. Selznick had bought the book for his wife, Jennifer Jones. He would make it at M.G.M. Years elapsed, Metro now owned the property. They also owed money to Mr. Selznick. In lieu of cash he accepted back his screen rights to *Tender Is the Night*. In 1956 he sold the property to 20th Century-Fox for $300,000. How Scott could have used all that lovely money.

The picture, made in 1961 and released in 1962, with the now middle-aged Miss Jones as Nicole, was a failure in spite of the 20 minutes of exciting excerpts.

I was not invited to the previews of *Beloved Infidel* and I did not want to go. Jerry Wald called faithfully with reports—all good. Perhaps it was true. I telephoned Gerold Frank, who would share in the 5 percent profit, and repeated Mr. Wald's cheering words. I took to pad and pencil. If the picture made 1 million dollars, our share above the $100,000 would be $20,000. And for 2 million, $40,000. Before I put the pad down, I had retired and was living like a millionaire on my coupons, stocks and shares. It was almost exhausting to be so rich. But was it as good as Jerry Wald claimed? Was there anything in the film that would embarrass me? Suddenly, urgently, I had to see it. Jerry promised I would attend the next preview. It came and went and he did not call me. There must be something I would not like. I insisted on seeing it at once.

For no reason whatever, Jerry slipped the unscored *Beloved Infidel*, in a bad color print, into the San Francisco Film Festival. The critics did not like it. Ah, there *was* something the matter. This was why Jerry Wald did not want me to see it.

There was to be one more preview in Long Beach, which is halfway between Los Angeles and San Diego. I insisted on attending. I wanted to see the film alone. I wanted to lose myself in the story and get the full emotional impact. But there were two carloads of people going to the Long Beach preview—Jerry Wald, his wife, his secretary, her husband, the director Henry King and his wife, the cameraman Leon Shamroy, the film cutter and Lord knows who else. We stopped on the way down and had a noisy dinner with everyone making jokes. I was nervous and apprehensive, but tried to join in the inconsequential chatter.

When we arrived at the theatre, I said firmly, "I will sit away from you all." Sure, they clucked sympathetically. I took a seat near the back and as the lights dimmed, my heart was beating very fast. It had practically stopped by the time the picture ended. I had been completely uninvolved. A bit of a gulp when Scott died, but that was all. This was my life —actual names, actual events—and I felt absolutely nothing. Was it because I was too close to it? Why didn't I feel something? "Did you like it?" I asked the woman sitting next to me. "Oh, yes," she replied enthusiastically. I thought, I must be wrong. It's because it's my story, that's why I feel numb.

The lights went up. Jerry Wald, Henry King and the others gathered around me, watching my face intently. "Well, how did you like it?" Jerry demanded. I felt sorry for them, they were all so eager for me to like it. "I didn't feel anything," I confessed. "Perhaps it is because I'm too close to the story." They were disappointed, but chorused, "Yes, yes, you're too close." Then I was angry. It was a bad picture, and that was why I had felt nothing.

"I do think, Henry," I said to the complacent director, "that it drags. You should cut at least thirty minutes." He smiled a contented experienced smile and replied, "I love every foot of the film." I thought, Christ, these Hollywood directors—they love every lousy foot. Eddie Mayer had once said to me, "A good writer must murder his darlings"—the phrases he falls in love with that are unnecessary to the story. The prevailing disease of directors, especially in Hollywood, is they will not cut an inch of film—not until the critics have complained. *Lawrence of Arabia* would have been a great film if it had been 30 minutes shorter. Twenty-two minutes were cut from the 4 hours 5 minutes of dreariness known as *Cleopatra*—after its critical pannings and fewer praisings.

So Henry loved every foot of *Beloved Infidel.* I hoped I was wrong. But I was right and when I attended the big charity premiere in New York and the theatre was packed with people in evening clothes and I was photographed with this celebrity and that celebrity—and I was *the* celebrity, I was the star, and no one knew where Deborah Kerr left off and Sheilah Graham began—I knew I was right. It was a dreadful film and most of the critics murdered it. Our dear friends at *Time* Magazine had another field day and this time I agreed with them.

But if the picture was bad, the advertising campaign was shocking.

I was staying with the Franklin Laceys—he co-authored the book of *The Music Man* with Meredith Willson—in their rambling pretty house overlooking the Ojai Valley, about 80 miles from Los Angeles. Before I went to sleep I was leafing through the new *Life* Magazine and jerked up when I saw the ghastly advertisement. Gregory Peck and Deborah Kerr kneeling on the sands and in big letters above, THE UNSWEETENED SINS OF SCOTT FITZGERALD AND SHEILAH GRAHAM. My heart was leaden. I thought, It's bad enough to say these

startling shocking things about people who are dead, but I'm
alive and this isn't true and it wasn't like this at all.

Franklin and Gladys were anxious the next morning when
they saw how distraught I was. We sat on the sun-drenched
stone steps and the leaves stirred softly as the breeze changed
their patterns. The world looked lovely and I was miserable.
Usually the sun or the sea can cure me of depression. But
this was a dark heavy shadow. The Laceys agreed with me
when I said, "I must do something, I must stop it." It was
Sunday. I telephoned Spyros Skouras in New York but could
not reach him. Nor Charlie Einfield, who was head of publicity. I sent telegrams to both, stating that under the terms
of the contract I would sue. It stated specifically that I could
not be held up to public ridicule or scorn.

Charlie Einfield wired promptly: DEAR SHEILAH, PLEASE AD-
VISE HOW IN VIOLATION (STOP) WILL CORRECT IMMEDIATELY.
Then another telegram: DEAR SHEILAH, YOU KNOW I WOULDN'T
DO ANYTHING IN THE WORLD TO HURT OR OFFEND YOU (STOP)
SO PLEASE TELL ME WHAT YOU WOULD LIKE ME TO CORRECT
AND I WILL IMMEDIATELY DO SO. WARMEST. CHARLES EINFIELD

The next day I called Harry Brand at 20th Century-Fox.
I am always losing contracts and I could not find my contract
for the film. I asked Harry to send me a copy and told him
why. "I will not," he replied. (He was a rich man and could
afford to snub powerful columnists.) "Why should I send
you a copy of the contract when you're planning to use it to
sue us?"

They knew they had a turkey in the oven, and had gone all
out to make the advertising as sensational as possible. LET
EVERY LOVER BE THE LAST. . . . S. stared at me from every
newspaper and magazine—always with me (Deborah) in a
tight swim suit crying in Scott's arms, on the beach at Malibu.
From Sheilah's agonized expression and Scott's concern, you
could only deduce that he had raped her and she was full
of pain and he was full of remorse. "Let every Lover be the
Last" had been a line in Scott's poem, "Beloved Infidel," but
taken out of context it had a different meaning. I worried
about the effect on my children, especially Wendy in her
good boarding school in Greenwich. The advertisements
gave the wrong impression of the picture—and me. Because
of the fuss I made, the cheap, misleading words *did* stop.

There were no profits. Later, I received a cost sheet from
20th Century-Fox. It should have gone, I suppose, to Holt,
who were handling all the finances. I read it with great

interest and saw that the picture had earned $3,000,000. Good, I thought, there'll be something more for us after all. I read on—charged against the picture was $5,000,000. Of course they jazz up the cost—advertising, distributing and heaven knows what. According to their books, the picture had lost $2,000,000, but it was my well-educated guess that *Beloved Infidel* with the prints, advertising, exhibitors' fees, etc., had cost $3,000,000 and they broke even. I was glad I had not been cajoled by Jerry Wald into accepting $75,000 and his "annuity for your children." The only person who will give an annuity to my children is me, and it won't be much, because I believe in living well, and I believe that after educating my children to the very best of their ability and mine, my financial obligation to them is over. I have told them this and they understand it.

The *Beloved Infidel* project was a healthy one, although it did not earn half the money Jerry Wald proclaimed it would. Jerry gave interviews stating I would make half a million dollars, much more than Scott in his lifetime had earned from the total sales of *all* his books. Even the very accurate *Fortune* Magazine, in a story about best-selling authors, put our profits at $250,000. Actually the total has been about $150,000, which is good. But after the 10 percent to Holt, acting as agents, and the 50 percent to Gerold Frank, I was left with about $70,000. The book continues to sell, especially in the soft cover, of which there were several editions—about 800,000 copies to date. Only recently when I attended the premiere of *Tom Jones*, the star, Albert Finney, whispered into my neck, "I'm reading your book—I love it."

So much had happened to me in Hollywood. It was time for a change. Rob, nearly fourteen, was enrolled for the fall at the Putney School in Vermont. I had promised Wendy, when I sent her to boarding school in Connecticut, that I would try to have another home for us in the East as soon as I could. The state of the film industry now made this almost essential. It was no longer centered in Hollywood. There was more production in London, Rome, Paris, Athens and Madrid, with a sprinkling in New York and the Far East. Stars of the caliber of William Holden, Deborah Kerr, David Niven, Richard Burton, Yul Brynner, and Jack Palance had taken up residence in Switzerland. You saw more stars on the Via Veneto in Rome than on Hollywood Boulevard. The sound stages in London were so full of American productions that the British producers were forced to the South of France and Yugoslavia to make their films. Hollywood was no longer the movie capital of the world. With a hundred series grinding out in every studio and at NBC, CBS and ABC, it was now the television center of the world. And with the jet age in full blast, I could fly to wherever films were made. I did not have to live all the time in Hollywood.

IV

I LOVED my home at 607 North Maple Drive, Beverly Hills, California, where I had lived with my children since the winter of 1947. It was part of me. A friend. I was safe. The walls were our devoted guardians. Late in 1957, I had spent $15,000 on alterations—putting in a new ceiling to hide the heavy Spanish beams in the two-story-high living room, squaring the round Spanish archways, installing new, beautifully gleaming aluminum screens on all the dozens of windows, and building a new beige-gray brick fireplace with a dark slate hearth in place of the ugly stucco protuberance. All the rooms were repainted in fresh, pale colors. In Wendy's bedroom, pretty flowered pale pink wallpaper, dainty curtains. All new furniture, a tufted turquoise blue headboard to go the length of the twin beds. Rob's room, painted yellow, thick cocoa brown drapes and bedcover, an armchair, new lamps, a set of four framed seascapes, and a big new desk with a map of the world over it. I don't believe I consulted either of them too much. This was *my* idea of comfort for a boy and beauty for a girl, and they humored me. Wendy was pleased with the new colors and furniture. Rob rarely discusses this sort of thing, but he seemed to like his new room.

When all the mess of plaster and painting was done with and all the new furniture installed, I had an unexpected relapse. I felt guilty. It was too beautiful for me. Could I afford to live in such splendor? With Wendy at school in the East and Rob leaving in the fall, what would I want with such a big house that now represented a large investment. With most of my money tied up in the house, what if anything happened to me? I decided to put it on the market.

Mrs. Jolson of the Lawrence Block real estate office in Beverly Hills brought over the sales contract. But I found it impossible to sign the document. It was like writing a death warrant for a beloved friend. Mrs. Jolson had experienced

176

this sort of squeamishness before. "Seller's nerves," she called it. She left the papers. I was to call her when I was ready to sell. As soon as she left, I tore up the contract and sighed with satisfaction, looking at my lovely walls and new drapes and furniture. Of course I could afford it; what made me feel I could not?

But once you have made the first stab at the body, it begins to die. The walls are a little less friendly, they get thinner, the love and warmth disappear. Neither of you cares so terribly about the parting. In three months, I called Mrs. Jolson back, and with *Beloved Infidel* a winner, and certain I would live part of the time in the East, I signed the papers, and was impatient with her for not finding a buyer right away. Two weeks before her 90-day option expired, Warren Cowan of the public relations firm of Rogers & Cowan paid $65,000 cash for the house as a present for his bride-to-be, Barbara Rush. I had some bad moments when they stomped all over the house. "We'll knock out this wall." . . . "Put a bar here." . . . "Enlarge the dining room." How dare they cut up my lovely house? And my staircase. It was Barbara Rush who would walk down the stairs as a bride, not my daughter Wendy.

I was to vacate Maple Drive on the 21st of June. Warren and Barbara would be married on the 22nd and hold their reception in the house, which would be empty except for the carpets and drapes and the few pieces of furniture they had bought from me—the black ebony grand piano, everything in the maid's room, and my comfortable, almost new, king-size bed—for $1000 the lot.

In May, I flew east to visit Wendy, and together we looked at some New York apartments. They were either too small for us, or the large ones were impossibly expensive. That night in our bedroom at the Warwick Hotel, Wendy burst into tears and said, "I don't want to live in a hole in the wall." Without hesitation I replied, "Of course you don't. I'll buy a house in the country." The cottage in Connecticut. Westport would be the best place. It had two summer theatres and several stage and film personalities lived there—the David Waynes, the Arthur Kennedys and let us not omit Countess Jolie Gabor. And there was the Long Island Sound for swimming. Scott and Zelda had lived there almost 40 years previously, although I was unaware of this.

I had already corresponded with Bill Chamberlin of Amy Finneran's real estate office in Westport at the time of my early plan to sell *Beloved Infidel* for a cottage in Connecticut (I have never allowed the grass to grow under my feet). Before returning to Hollywood I visited Westport, looked at houses with Mr. Chamberlin, a helpful, spare, graying, crew-cut New Englander in his mid-forties. Actually he came from Pennsylvania. I liked him immediately. In fact, I tentatively marked him in my mind as a prospective escort and, who knew?—a possible husband. He was to marry that summer. I liked Mrs. Chamberlin immediately, as I had liked Bill.

One house was possible, although it would take a lot of painting and doing over. But it was solidly built, set in the center of two acres of grassy land with big trees and stone fences marking the boundaries from the other expensive homes in the area. The "cottage" was large, four bedrooms, three bathrooms, a dining room, a good fireplace in the living room, a paneled study, an 18′ x 18′ screened porch, a huge kitchen and three-car garage. The price—$45,000.

On the theory that people always ask more than they will take, I told Bill, "At $40,000 I would be interested," and flew back to Hollywood. Four long-distance calls from Bill, each time coming down a bit. I stood firm. Then—"Sold, for $40,000." I had not really been sure, but now I was delighted, and immediately sent a deposit of $4000. I would bring the rest, a check for $36,000, on my way to Europe. I had only seen the house once, but I have never, it seems, had time to take time. I must always decide right away, not always successfully.

And now the packing began in depth. Josephine and I discarded, rescued, then threw away again—magazines, books sent by hopeful authors through the years, paperbacks, old clothes, old papers, a mountain of odds and ends that had accumulated during our 11 years in the big house, which now died rapidly, without a fight.

In the midst of the chaos, Wendy decided she wanted a last look at the old homestead, a last sleep in her bedroom. "I must pack my books and clothes myself," she insisted. Wendy, who had wanted me to live in the East, was now rather sad about leaving the house in Beverly Hills. She came home for the final two weeks on Maple Drive.

We would spend the final summer in Europe where I could do a more interesting column than in Hollywood. On our return to America we would take up residence in Westport, Connecticut. Josephine would precede us there by a few days to greet the furniture vans, unpack everything and look after us for the month before Wendy returned to Rosemary Hall in Greenwich, and Rob started at the Putney School in Vermont. The house would be painted white inside and outside while we were away.

I put my Chrysler station wagon in storage and sent our Dalmatian, Tony, to some friends near Ojai. And we left Hollywood and again I wondered, would I ever come back? I did, many times. I even bought another house, with an Olympic-size swimming pool, which I again sold for $65,000.

Twenty-three years had elapsed since I flew into Los Angeles on the hot Christmas Day of 1935. Soon after, there had been Scott. I had married twice since his death. It had been deeply satisfying living with my two children in the sun. My career had bloomed. I had made some eternal friends—Alan and Helen Hooker of Ojai; Franklin and Gladys Lacey; Helen Ainsworth, so fat and so kind; Michael O'Brien, who wanted desperately to have an acting career, but did not; Ted Berkman, Phi Beta Kappa, whom I had first met at the New York *Mirror* in 1933 and who did my spelling for me; a few press agents, especially Johnny Campbell; my first secretary, Pat Duff, and my last, Adele Roy; Maureen O'Hara, the strong-faced beautiful Irish girl. She never missed my annual Christmas party, which had started originally for Rob's birthday, December 24th.

How many of the friends I had made among the movie stars would stick? I felt that no matter what the future held, whether I had a column or not, Bob Hope would be glad to see me, Jerry Lewis would always have an open door, Oscar Levant would still offer me his tranquilizer pills as he had at the preview of *Tender Is the Night*, Jack Benny would appear for me if I had another television show—we had featured his biography on the occasion of his usual thirty-ninth birthday—and Rosalind Russell would always be ready to take up our marathon conversations. Roz had danced the Cha-Cha-Cha with my son at a supper dance at the Beverly Hills Hotel. "You remind me of Lance" (her own son), she told him when she came over to be introduced. "Come on, let's dance." They had really moved, as Rob would say, and the other dancers had stopped to watch and applaud. On the same night, Lawrence Weingarten, an important producer at Metro, asked me in a fairly loud whisper, "Would it be possible to test your son for *Jamie McPheeters*?" I was perturbed when Rob slowly turned his head to give the producer his handsome profile. He was too good-looking and Hollywood was too soft. The snows of Vermont would be good for him.

I was glad that Lana Turner and I were friends again. We had met at a party in the house of Esther Williams. Sitting next to each other we had started to talk. I felt shocked when she told me that her daughter Cheryl had asked her, "Why doesn't Sheilah Graham like you, Mama?" "How dreadfull I'm sorry." I meant it. Pecking out items on my typewriter, I had not thought of the effect on the children of these people.

I thought of Judy Garland. I had known her since she was fourteen, when she used long words she did not understand and was writing poems to Oscar Levant. I remembered when her husband, Sid Luft, had threatened to punch me in the nose for something I had written about him. I automatically disliked the men who took over the careers of their talented wives. Now Judy was not in films, and she was in and out of her marriage with Luft. Early fame had not brought her satisfaction or happiness.

Stars had come and gone and some had died. Norma Shearer, a top star when I had arrived in Hollywood, had long since given up her career. She had been Queen of the Metro lot in 1936, when her husband, Irving Thalberg, was King. I had discussed *The Last Tycoon* with her. "Of course, you know that Monroe Stahr was based on Irving," I said. "Yes," she replied. "I was quite angry about it. My husband was not like that at all." Monroe Stahr was Scott's idealized version of Thalberg. Perhaps Stahr was more Fitzgerald than Thalberg.

Claudette Colbert had eloped a few days after I had flown into Hollywood. It had been a front-page story. Now she was no longer a film star. Neither were Irene Dunne, Nelson Eddy, Jeannette MacDonald or Loretta Young. Carole Lombard had crashed to her death in 1941 when I was in New York, pregnant with Wendy. John Garfield was dead. He had come to Hollywood in 1937. I had liked him very much. He was so hopeful and naïve, and making political speeches all the time. I had interviewed William Powell on his forty-seventh birthday in 1936. We had dined at his house and afterwards he read me a 40-page poem. He was now almost seventy and living in retirement in Palm Springs with his "Mousie." Jean Harlow, whom he had loved, had died during my first Hollywood summer.

In the beginning I had envied the stars and resented them because they seemed to have so much with so little effort, and I have always had to work hard for what I have mined from the hard rock of my experiences. Only now am I beginning to realize that what I disliked in them is what I dislike in myself—conceit and temperament, brashness and insecurity. And let anyone get fat, you read of it in the Graham column. All except Ann Sothern. Her fat is the aftermath of the two years' hepatitis that almost buried her. I have never been cruel about illness. But if Elizabeth Taylor gets fat, or Judy Garland, or Anita Ekberg, the old scalpel comes out and I cut them up in the column. It is because I despise my own lack of will power on the question of calories. I, like these others, am a compulsive eater—when I am nervous, angry, or depressed. And I have come to realize that all of them, the Elizabeth Taylors, the John Waynes, the Frank Sinatras, the Ava Gardners and Robert Mitchums —even the Marlon Brandos—are not vague shadows on a screen; they are real people and they have the problems of real people, and some are worse than mine and they need help as I need help—and what this recent understanding will do to my column, I shudder to think.

✌ CHAPTER THIRTY-THREE

THE summer in Europe was over, and the Chamberlins were at the airport to meet us and to take us, with our 13 pieces of hand luggage, to our new home and our new life in Westport, Connecticut, where the ever-dependable Josephine awaited us. Everything was still in packing cases, because the furniture had been late in arriving. We were tired, irritable and discouraged. Bill called a young handyman he knew, although it was nearly midnight, and all through the night we unpacked, put beds together, and became angry about chipped, scratched and broken furniture. Our new life had started on the wrong foot and it more or less stayed that way.

Benjamin Franklin stated, "Two moves are as good as a fire." Every move, certainly from coast to coast, is costly, apart from damage to furniture, which is insured but never quite the same after the repair job. There is always so much to be done in the move to another house. Some things don't fit and there are always unexpected hidden expenses.

The house, of gray stone and white clapboard, had a basement, also a large attic with a huge electric fan that could turn Rob's room into a refrigerator when his door leading into it was open. The attic itself was stiflingly hot in the summer, icy cold in the winter. The basement, where I soon installed two new exquisite machines for washing and drying, was always cold. Our water came from the well in the basement and it was cool in the taps.

There was a huge furnace in the basement, fed with the most expensive oil—my winter bills were enormous. In that first winter, the hole that had obviously already existed in the furnace grew bigger. The heating gadget broke, and if Bill Chamberlin had not passed by while I was in Hollywood and seen the back door wide open—we were also robbed— the entire house would have been more damaged than it was. There was water, water, everywhere, because the pipes had all burst their dear little selves.

Then, of course, the cesspool went wrong on a Sunday. No one seemed to know where it was—the former owners were playing golf and could not be reached; and try to get a plumber in Westport on a Sunday. They would not do it for a native and certainly not for a stranger who was automatically regarded with suspicion by those damn Yankees. I had to install a costly new cesspool.

Josephine returned to her family and home in California, and I tackled the impossible task of getting a housekeeper. There was nothing to be had locally—for a brief few weeks I suffered with a maid from Stamford, and her husband must have loved breast of chicken, because our chickens never had them. They went home with her in the car with her husband, and he was so big and strong-looking I was afraid to draw the little matter to her attention. I was glad when she told me she was leaving for some reason or other —probably for bigger breasts of chicken with another family.

I remembered my good luck with Anna Bayer, whom I had discovered in Switzerland. On my next trip to Europe, I contacted the friend who had found Anna for me. Yes, she knew of another wonderful girl—Jeanne Boray. "Perhaps she could cook a meal for me in Geneva," I suggested when I called Marie from London. On the basis of the meal, I would decide about bringing her to America. I was going to Israel to cover Otto Preminger's picture in Haifa, *Exodus*. I could stop off on the way for my dinner.

I had prepared the menu in advance—Wiener schnitzel

with string beans and the crisp fried potatoes that Anna used to make, and Anna's heavenly open apple tart with a cream base for dessert. "Jeanne is very nervous," said Marie hesitantly at the Geneva airport. "Do you mind if you only have the dessert—the apple tart—with her?" I was disappointed, but the main thing was to know if she was a good cook and this I could learn from the tart.

Jeanne and her parents and younger brother watched me while I ate a generous portion. "It's delicious," I told them appreciatively. "The best I ever tasted." They exhaled a collective sigh. Jeanne was not on the quota, but I could bring her to America, pay her fare and she could live with me as a guest and help me with the housework and do the cooking. I would supply her with pocket money and teach her English. She spoke French and we could communicate in that language.

Jeanne arrived on a Friday. "No work for you until dinner tomorrow," I told her, literally licking my lips. With the prospect of delicious meals, I could afford to wait. I wanted Jeanne rested for my small dinner party with the Chamberlins and another couple. Jeanne and I went shopping in Westport. I bought a pot roast and red cabbage. Anna's pot roast and red cabbage were sheer bliss. "What do you require for the apple tart?" I asked. "We must buy a pie crust," Jeanne replied firmly. She was searching wildly for the pie crust department. I hurried after her. "What do you mean, *buy* a pie crust?" I demanded. "A good cook in America," I told her severely, "always makes her own pastry." "I have never made a pie crust," she answered. "But that lovely apple tart in Geneva," I spluttered. "I bought it," she confessed. I won't go into the pot roast and red cabbage fiasco, except to say they were both fried in fat with onions. I was sick all night. She stayed a week and my French improved, but everything else deteriorated.

When the children were home—I could not afford to bring Josephine east all the time—I did the cooking and cleaning with some slight help from Wendy. She dislikes household chores for the same reason that I do—it's never finished. You cook, clean and then have to do it all over again. I am a fairly good cleaner because of my early training as a maid in England, but I will never like doing it.

If I had the time to experiment, I might be a good cook because I enjoy eating. But I have never had much time.

My fiascos in the Westport kitchen were a joke with my friends. At Christmas, I cooked a turkey, not knowing that the liver and guts were in a bag hidden deep inside the rib-cage of the bird; while scooping out the prepared Pepperidge stuffing at the table, I startled my guests and myself by unexpectedly dishing out the grimy paper bag.

I set fire to the kitchen. Wendy and Rob were home and I was cooking lamb chops in a frying pan. The blaze suddenly leaped to the ceiling. The fat had caught fire. Rob rushed to pour water over the flames, which made it worse. In the excitement I dashed upstairs to call the fire department, Wendy tried to call from downstairs, and we managed to put the phone out of order. I sent Wendy on her bicycle to one neighbor, and Rob to another. When they pedaled back, I yelled frantically, "Don't go near the house, the kitchen might explode." The entire Westport fire department of three trucks arrived to find the fat in the kitchen had burned out. There was no fire, just blackened walls and ceiling. I still insist I kept my British calm, although Wendy and Rob insist I panicked.

I loved the idea of my two ancestral acres in Westport, until I tried to find a gardener. There was simply no one to be had. I spent days visiting nurseries and begging for a man to mow the vast expanse of grass. They were all too busy. When Wendy and Rob were home, I paid them to mow, but they were not home often. The machine was heavy and hard to manipulate, in spite of the power. One good thing, it *did* keep my weight down. The sweat poured off me. To the Chamberlins again for rescue.

"I know someone," said Mary helpfully. "But I must warn you, Franz is a strange character. He's an Austrian and well educated. But he looks at you strangely sometimes. I'm not sure, but I think he drinks." With two acres of grass looking more and more like a field of shaggy Shetland ponies, I begged Mary, "Get me Franz—at any price."

He was dark-skinned with piercing, bulging, watering, red-veined brown eyes and untidy black hair. He looked like a wild brunette Santa Claus. And he was just as friendly. He had obviously seen better days. When Jeanne was with me, he spoke to her in perfect French, and his German, she told me, was *hoch Deutsch*—the educated class. He was a good gardener, when he came. But he only came when he needed money. He would work an hour or so, sometimes three hours, then he always had a pressing appointment somewhere and

I would not see him again until the next day, when we
would go through the same routine. I had expected to be
somewhat afraid of Franz. I was not. I liked him. I even
tried to reform him. These were the only times he did not
like me. I can still see the glare in the red-brown eyes when
I said, "Franz, you are too intelligent to drink so much."

In the two springs of my time in Westport, a caterpillar
blight was on the land and ruined many of the trees. They
formed in gray, opaque, dirty sacs in the forks of the
branches and as they came to life you could see them swarming inside the sacs, then bursting forth to devour the tree.
There were millions of them. The trick was to burn them
while they were still in the sacs. I have a horror of little and
big things that creep and crawl, but with Rob I would attempt the hopeless task of burning out the intruders, thrust-
ing long flaming matches into the center of the sac. Sometimes the caterpillars were already alive and it was horrible
watching them drop to the ground and crawl away, mostly to
my 18' x 18' screened porch, where the slate floor would be
covered with them.

The summer brought a different unpleasantness—the mos-
quitoes. It was warm in the house after the broil of the day,
but we could not go for walks in the cool evenings or sit
outside, or play croquet or Ping-Pong by the light of the
lamps I had installed, because we would be bitten all over
the exposed skin, and some that was not, by the voracious
monsters. Wendy especially. There is some hidden ingredient
in her skin that challenges a mosquito. He must get at it
or his evening is a failure. They even penetrated the walls
of her bedroom and she would never know on going to sleep
how many red welts she would wake up with, on her nose,
her eyelids, her head, her hands, legs, neck and arms. I
drenched her every night with every known powerfully
smelling anti-mosquito stuff, but it didn't make much difference. Rob was immune. The buzzing beasts never bothered him.

The final straw—you take it and you take it and then you
moan, "Get me out"—occurred on Christmas Eve, 1960. The
Chamberlins, with the members of their family, open their
presents on Christmas Eve. They asked us to share in the
fun and have some grog. It had been snowing very heavily
and the back roads were like iced glass with the snow piled
in small mountains on each side. I was bringing Bill and
Mary my Christmas present—a four-quart bottle of Scotch.

I was careful to park the Chrysler station wagon (which had been driven to Westport for me by a friend) partly on the snow bank in front of their Cape Cod house, out of the way of skidding cars. With Rob holding the big bottle firmly with both hands, we were walking carefully up the small slippery path when we heard a loud crash, very close. The bottle was my first thought. No, Rob was still hugging it. I looked back and incredibly our station wagon was an upside down V, with another car deep into the entrails in the back. In mighty outrage I skeetered down the path. Standing uncertainly in my furry snowboots I yelled, "What the bloody hell is going on?" to the man who was emerging unscathed from the wreck of his car. Everyone in the house rushed out—they had heard the crash and my howl of pain. "Look what this damn fool has done." I turned to them for sympathy. "Hi, Jack," said Bill. It was a neighbor. "I dropped some cigarette ash on my knee and looked down for a second," Jack explained sheepishly. Bill brought us into the house. I telephoned an obliging Italian who owned a nearby garage. It was Christmas Eve, but he came to inspect the Chrysler. "It's broken in half," he diagnosed. "I believe it's finished." He towed it away the next day.

The insurance companies, mine and Jack's, declared the car a total disaster. They would pay me $700, the dealers' price for a 1955 Chrysler de Luxe New Yorker station wagon that had retailed at $5,200 and had marked up only 45,000 miles. "No," I told them. "I love the car, you must save it." The engine was undamaged; it had fortunately been buried deep in the snow bank. But the roof and most of the inside were broken. "I want my car back—you can repair it," I insisted. A Chrysler garage in New York did such a good job that the car, given up for lost, made the journey back to Beverly Hills without any trouble whatsoever.

I could not take any more. I had had enough of New England and Westport. I could not bear another traffic jam—at 8:30 A.M. when the Westport businessmen commuted to New York, and at 6:30 P.M. when they all came home. The quiet of the five weekdays and the noise of the weekends. I flew to Hollywood and left the house for Bill Chamberlin to sell.

I was lucky again. A woman saw the house on Thursday, brought her husband on Saturday, I flew back to sign the papers on Tuesday, and on Thursday I had a check for $45,000 in my happy hand. I had fulfilled my dream of a cottage in Connecticut. Quite obviously, I was not the cottage-in-Connecticut type. I'm a town girl. But if I had not gone to Westport and tried it, I might have felt robbed of a delightful experience. Some people long for a farm and chickens; I longed for a cottage in Connecticut. I am glad I tried it and I am glad I will never do it again.

There had been one gratifying personal incident during the hell of Westport. On Saturday, November 14, 1959, I drove from Westport to Princeton University where I left all my mementoes of Scott, including his recording of "Ode to a Nightingale," on which he had written, *A bigger and better Barrymore*. My children came with me for the little ceremony in the Princeton Library. President Goheen made a speech of thanks, told some anecdotes about Scott, and after lunch at Scott's old club, Cottage, we had the best seats in the stadium at the annual Princeton-Yale game. Remembering Scott's love for Princeton and football, I felt I had made a good bargain—all my visible memories of Scott for four tickets on the 50-yard line.

Wendy was sorry to leave Westport. She hates change. She gets attached to her furniture and the way things are arranged, and she makes no secret of her feelings. It has always been harder to know about Rob. Only rarely does he reveal what he is thinking. It takes a great deal to make him explode. He will stand up for his rights when he believes that Wendy or I, or both of us, are taking advantage of his easygoing nature. But he will go along with most projects, if not with most ideas. I was pleased, albeit a little apprehensive, when he took on a middle-aged bigot four years ago at the home of a friend near Westport. She was cursing Negroes and particularly hated what she called "their yellow eyeballs." She was saying, "Negroes should never be integrated. They are good only to be servants, nothing else." Rob was fourteen at this time. "You are wrong to talk that way," he said in the sudden hush. "What do you know about Negroes?" she snarled somewhat tipsily. "I know there are good Negroes and bad, just as there are good and bad white people," said Rob, looking straight into her quite angry eyeballs. Wendy added her quota of disapproval. The woman turned on her with "you silly little . . ." Then *I* sailed into the fray. "She's drunk," I interrupted loudly. "Take no notice of what she says." Our host took her protestingly away, while her husband implored, "Be quiet."

I had discovered almost at once that it was impossible to write my column in Westport, which I only used for weekends after renting a small apartment at 30 East 62nd Street in New York. Film stars were always coming to the city, the head offices of most of the film companies were in New York, I was in a continual stream of news, and it was just a few hours to Hollywood or Europe. I was getting better news items and I was happy when Charles McCabe, publisher of the *Mirror*, told me, "Your column is getting better all the time."

I gave my usual Christmas party in the New York apartment. As a film columnist, I felt I should have a sprinkling of stars, glamorous raisins in the plain pound cake. A party without stars is a better party. Everyone is equal. No one has to be catered to. But I wanted my friends, from Westport especially, to be impressed, to be able to say at their dinner parties, "Joan Crawford was telling me last week . . ." "Tony Perkins isn't a bit like you'd think he'd be from seeing his movies . . ." Or, "Joan Fontaine is more beautiful in real life than on the screen."

I had never asked Joan Crawford to my Christmas parties in Hollywood, where I had a larger selection from which to choose at that time of the year. While Joan called me "dearest" and "darling" in her notes to me, I had never believed that she liked me. I telephoned her and after the merest pause, she said, "Yes, I'd be delighted to come." On the day of the party, December 22, 1959, Joan called in the morning. Aha, she's canceling. "May I bring the twins?" she asked fervently. "How old are they?" I replied. "Thirteen." It was a bit young for Rob, who liked older girls, although he was celebrating his fifteenth birthday. I had already invited Joan Fontaine and her teen-age daughter, Debbie. But I did not want to lose Miss Crawford, who continued, "You see, I don't like to be away from them at Christmas."

"Love to have them," I said heartily.

An hour before the party, Miss Crawford called. What now? "Do we have to dress?" she asked. *Phew.* "No," I said with forced brightness, keeping an eye on the party preparations. (A friend had loaned me her man servant to tend the bar. He had already tended his own bar needs and was quite drunk.) Well, we were sure of at least one movie star.

At the height of the party, at that pleasant stage when

everyone has arrived and no one has left, Joan was at the door with the twins, she in mink, they in huge furry coats. I offered to help them remove their combined fur. "No," said Joan. "We only stopped by to say we can't come. We have to go to a dinner party." *Oh no you don't,* I said silently. Taking a firm grip on her wrist, I led her, with the tall twins following in her backwash, to every guest in my crowded living room. The tour took almost twenty minutes. Then I let her go.

Joan Fontaine's blond, blue-eyed Debbie had been sitting sulkily by her mother—of course Rob had taken no notice of her. Debbie suddenly lit up like a Christmas tree when Tony Perkins appeared. She floated happily toward him and Joan took my hands warmly and said, "You don't know what you've done for me, Sheilah." With moist eyes, she explained that Debbie had not wanted to come to New York for Christmas with her mother. She had wanted to remain with her friends in California, where she lived with her father, television executive William Dozier. "She has been very difficult and dreadfully unhappy. Tony is her idol. She's mad about him. You've *made* her vacation. Thank you. Thank you."

John Wheeler usually says No first, and later, sometimes, Yes. He said No when I first told him I would be in London in the spring of 1961, around the time of the wedding of Princess Margaret Rose to Anthony Armstrong-Jones and should I cover it for NANA? Just before I left for Europe, John said casually, "If you're going to be in London, do you still want to cover the wedding?"

Dorothy Kilgallen would be reporting the wedding for the New York *Journal American* and she was bringing over a whole trousseau of beautiful dresses. I have always had a healthy respect for Miss Kilgallen's ability as a reporter, ever since we worked together on the *Journal* thirty years ago—Dorothy writing the news, I in charge of the feature angles of the story. Dorothy was only seventeen years old then, but already gave evidence of becoming the top crime reporter in America. I watched her dash in and out of court during the Hauptmann trial for the kidnapping and murder of the Lindbergh baby—as I watched her speeding in and out of the Old Bailey while we were both covering the Dr. Ward trial. We paired for many murder cases in the early days. One time in Dedham, Massachusetts, when three M.I.T.

students and a pretty minister's daughter were involved in a murder, there was no room for me at the few hotels and Dorothy invited me to share her double bed. I could not sleep and spent most of the uncomfortable night sitting up looking at her sleeping eyelashes, wondering how she got them so long and upward-curling.

With Dorothy in London for the wedding, would I hold my own? She is always so confident before the story. I am not, until I have it. With no offense to Miss Kilgallen—she will always be a better crime reporter than I am—I am better at getting interviews with the people in the case. Whom could I interview? Princess Margaret? I remembered enough of being a Britisher to know it was impossible. Royalty does not give interviews. Armstrong-Jones? I made inquiries among his friends. They all liked him but because of his leap into the royal ranks, he too had become inaccessible. Where was the soft underbelly of the situation—as Winston Churchill used to say in the war. "Jackie" Chan? She had been Tony's favorite girl until shortly before the announcement of his engagement to Margaret.

Jackie had been appearing on the West End stage in *The World of Suzie Wong*. She had taken a long leave of absence to avoid the press, which then camped on the doorstep of her Chelsea apartment. Her number was in the telephone book and I called and called. Each time a Chinese lady's voice said, "Miss Chan is not here." But I never stopped calling, always saying, "This is Sheilah Graham of Hollywood." Two days before the wedding, the Chinese voice said, "This is Miss Chan." "Please, I'd like to have lunch with you to discuss your career," I said. If I had said "to discuss Tony," she would not have agreed, as she did, to have lunch with me. We *did* discuss her career, and I later interested Ross Hunter in offering her a role in *The Flower Drum Song*. During our lunch, oh so carefully, I brought up the name of Mr. Armstrong-Jones. To my surprise she discussed him very frankly. And I had another scoop.

When I returned to New York I heard that Dorothy had also been after Jackie. I had perhaps an unfair advantage because of my Hollywood label.

From New York, it was easy to fly to Rome where Elizabeth Taylor and Richard Burton were starring in a forty-million-dollar production titled *Cleopatra*. The producer, Walter Wanger, and I have never liked each other. I have found him deceptively polite and fiercely antagonistic behind my back. My dislike of Wanger began when Scott and Budd Schulberg were writing *Winter Carnival* for him. Scott was ill and I flew with Schulberg and him to New York, where they would have a story conference with Wanger. We had told Budd to be sure *not* to mention that I was along, but unthinkingly when Wanger asked who was on the plane he replied, "Sheilah Graham." "She's a bitch," Wanger snorted. Scott, who had been drinking champagne all the night before on the plane and gin all that day, loped up to Wanger, put his face close to his and said in a monotone, "I wouldn't say that if I were you." "Sheilah Graham is a bitch," Wanger repeated. Scott's beautiful nose was now one-eighth of an inch from Wanger's. He repeated, quietly, "I wouldn't say that if I were you." Wanger realized the situation and at once backed down. "I was joking," he said, and later suggested I should be the technical adviser for a picture he was planning on Elizabeth Arden. He did not make the picture, and of course, I was never his technical adviser.

Elizabeth Taylor and I were definitely not on speaking terms on the three occasions I was in Rome while she was making *Cleopatra*. I went through the motions of trying to get an interview with her. You never know and you have to try. She would not see me. She would not see any member of the press and she used a choice four-letter verb in telling the press what it could do to itself.

I have known Elizabeth for a long time. I was there when she was born as an actress in Hollywood. The gentle, sensitive twelve-year-old girl of *National Velvet*. Who could guess what her future would be? She was really too beautiful for her own good. When she was fourteen or fifteen, I was in the commissary at Metro when she burst in wearing a tight sweater over a perky little skirt. Every man in the place, including Orson Welles, stopped eating to stare. She was lovely, soft, with great promise in her body.

We had our first, rather one-sided battle after one of my radio broadcasts. I had stated that Howard Hughes was flying Elizabeth and her mother from Las Vegas to Los Angeles. Neither of the Taylors heard the Sunday night show, and the busy troublemakers had told Mrs. Taylor that I had implied something more.

Elizabeth was giving a party that Sunday at the Mocambo for the young singer Vic Damone, on whom she had a violent crush. Vic told me recently they were planning to marry but he was called into the Army, "And she met Nicky Hilton."

"Phone call, Miss Taylor." I watched the beautiful girl walk to the telephone booth and smiled at her as she passed. She returned with her violet eyes blazing, stopped at my table and demanded, "How dare you say those things about me on your show?" I was very much taken aback and said, "Obviously, you did not hear it," and continued talking nonchalantly to my companion. I have never fought with children.

We became friends again. In Hollywood, you are friendly with the stars according to what you write about them. If it's complimentary, they like you. If it's not, they detest you, and I must have written some nice things about her, because when she married Nicky Hilton, not only were she and I on good terms, but her mother and I were bosom friends, Hollywood style. We talked every day on the telephone, and I visited her frequently. During and after her honeymoon with Nicky Hilton I received a blow-by-blow account from her mother.

I had taken my daughter Wendy to the wedding at the Church of the Good Shepherd. I thought it would be interesting for her to see a Class-A star wedding. The church was smothered with white flowers of all expensive kinds—the Crown Princess of Hollywood was marrying the Crown Prince of the Hilton Hotel Empire. I thought, He's a Catholic, she is not. For his sake, I hope the marriage lasts. Among her bridesmaids was Debbie Reynolds—from whom the bride would one day filch Eddie Fisher.

Later, there was her mad pursuit of Michael Wilding. He did not want to marry a woman as young as Elizabeth, but she was determined. Her I-get-what-I-want pattern was emerging. The day after her divorce from Hilton, she flew to Wilding in Paris. There was an item in my column that Elizabeth was paying for the honeymoon. Michael, as usual, had no money. He had not wanted to marry. But who could resist this beautiful girl?

Wilding gave her some culture and two children. Then she was bored—ready for the dynamic Mike Todd. The explosion occurred somewhere in Virginia, while she was starring in *Raintree County*. Flamboyant, free-spending Mike. He put his plane at her disposal and bought her expensive presents. She was impressed. He was as wide open as Mike Wilding was closed in. It was Mike Todd who taught her she could get anything she wanted. But he forgot to tell her to be careful of what she took.

Elizabeth has always given her heart, and soul, with her body, to the man she loves. When she was Mrs. Wilding she wanted to stop making films and concentrate on his career, which had taken something of a dip. She would open a hat shop in London, she told him, to keep her busy while being the little housewife for Mr. Wilding. He wouldn't hear of such a sacrifice.

For Mr. Todd she almost gave her life, helping him publicize *Around the World in 80 Days*. She was very pregnant when I saw her at the London charity premiere. Everyone, all the dukes and duchesses and belted earls, had been invited. The British loved Mike Todd. For them, he was the typical, successful, noisy, big-spending, boasting, amusing American. After the show, there was a party in the Todd tradition at the Battersea Pleasure Gardens. He was sending the British aristocracy across the Thames on barges, each barge equipped with an orchestra and bar. On the day of the premiere, the rain came down as I have never seen rain, not even in California. Todd could have sent his distinguished guests to Battersea on the less picturesque buses over the bridge, covered and warm. Instead, he bought up every available raincoat in London. While I waited for the barge with my escort, Elizabeth and her party disembarked from a Rolls Royce—Elizabeth in a beautiful white dress with her ermine jacket trailing in the mud and the flooded road. The rain poured down on her uncovered head and her pregnant body. It is my opinion that her exposure to the storm this night was responsible for the difficult birth of her daughter, Lisa Todd, and for her nearly fatal illness two years ago. Elizabeth is a brave woman. When she flew to Mexico to marry Todd, her back was in a brace and she almost fainted during the ceremony when she attempted to stand up from her wheelchair. It took courage to marry Eddie Fisher in the teeth of millions of supporters for Debbie Reynolds. But even before she threw him out, she had become completely indifferent to public opinion.

I had interviewed Richard Burton in New York, and it had been pleasant. Elizabeth would not see me, perhaps he would. Napoleon asked of one of his generals, "Is he lucky?" I am lucky. I am also alert and ready to grasp the opportunity when it comes. I first tried calling Burton at his home. His male secretary barred the way. Should I go to the villa on Antica Way? If I were at the door, he would see me. But I am not Hedda Hopper and that would be the last resort.

THE REST OF THE STORY

I had a call from an Italian friend, Alfredo Quoma. "I was at the airport and bumped into Burton. He was seeing his wife, Sybil, and their two daughters off to London." Alfredo had never met the actor before, but he introduced himself and told him, "A friend of mine, Sheilah Graham, is very anxious to talk to you." Richard replied, "I know, but I have been warned by Mr. Wanger and our publicity man Guilio Ascarelli not to see her." I was angry, but now I knew who the villains were—Wanger and Ascarelli. Gathering up my most righteous anger, I telephoned Ascarelli from my room at the Grand Hotel. "Richard Burton says he wants to see me but you won't let him. Is this true?" Ascarelli spluttered and fumbled at the other end of the line. "It is Burton who doesn't want to see you." "It is you and Wanger," I insisted. And then came the chance remark that resulted in the interview. I had heard dozens of stories about the senseless extravagance in the picture. I had heard about the eighty-one standby cars, the luxuries running into hundreds of thousands of dollars, the wasted millions of dollars. "I think," I said, "the shareholders will be very interested in my story of how their money is being spent. Good-*bye*." And hung up. What I did not know was that the stockholders were having the annual meeting the following week. And number one on the agenda was the extraordinary number of dollars poured into *Cleopatra*.

Ascarelli called me back. I would barely let him speak. "I've waited for you long enough, and now I'm going out for lunch." "At least," he begged, "tell me where you're having lunch." "I'm not a bit interested." But I was. "It makes no difference," I said, "but I'm having lunch at Capriccio's. Good-bye."

When I arrived at Capriccio's there was a message to call Ascarelli and I knew I had won. At six o'clock that evening, in a private room on the ground floor of the Grand Hotel, I had an exclusive interview with Richard Burton on the subject of Elizabeth Taylor for the North American Newspaper Alliance syndicate and for the New York *Mirror*, which headlined in thick black type on the front page: WED LIZ? NO. IT'S ALL IN FUN—BURTON. At that time he believed it.

In Rome, the only topic of conversation was The Romance. Everyone had a story. I was visited by the head of the *paparazzi* (the literal translation is pesky fly), the word coined in *La Dolce Vita* to describe the brazen photographers. Short, squat, wearing his well-known black leather jacket, he told me in fairly good English that he was paid high prices for his information and photographs. He intimidated me. He looked like the Mafia. I told him, "I do not pay for information, but my syndicate might, if it were interesting enough." Then he told me an amazing story which I did not believe, and that he had a photograph of Elizabeth and Burton to prove it. Even if it were true, it was not a story I would use.

After the *Mirror* exclusive, Walter Wanger acceded to my request for an interview with him. He took me to dinner at the exclusive Taverna Flavia with its small tables on the narrow sidewalk. Mimo, the young owner, was very attentive and later sent me an enormous basket of flowers with an invitation to come to his restaurant for lunch on Sunday. Mimo gave me a feast—big green ripe figs and pink fresh prosciutto, a thick vegetable soup, roast chicken—a specialty of the Taverna—a fantastic salad, cheese. I was just about to plunge into the strawberries and cream when I keeled over in a faint. That morning I had taken one of those little peach-colored pills to lose water and weight. I am allergic to them. The same thing had happened to me one Sunday night at Luchow's Restaurant in New York.

During the lunch, the hovering Mimo had told me that the young waiter who brought the food as I sat in the white sunshine was a favorite with Elizabeth and Mr. Burton, that he went often to their home as a friend and to serve at their parties. When I was able to leave, the waiter preferred by the lovers, and who spoke English well, was delegated to take me home. I lay back in the car with my eyes closed, inhaling deeply. But the opportunity was too good to pass. I was alone with a man who had seen Liz and Dick in the raw, so to speak. As the car turned in at the Excelsior Hotel driveway, I opened my eyes and asked him weakly, "Do you think Elizabeth Taylor and Richard Burton will marry?" He was profoundly shocked. He had thought I was on my deathbed, and for a dying woman to ask such a question! He regarded me sternly, and, alas, silently.

❦ CHAPTER THIRTY-FOUR

"YOUR children are the best thing you have ever done," Mrs. Charles McCabe told me a few years ago, after we dined with them in their attractive house in Greenwich, Connecticut. Nothing cottagy about this place and they always seem to have good servants, so that eating there is a pleasure. I often think of her words: *the best thing you have ever done.* How much have I done? How much do any parents do? Obviously a great deal—for better or worse. The young are at the mercy of their parents, of the kind of people they have become from the circumstances of their own childhood. But as the children get older and learn that the parent is not omnipotent, that mistakes are made and continue to be made, then comes the re-evaluation. From worshiping the parent, children sometimes go too far in the other direction. There is often real hate and contempt. A friend of Wendy's at Rosemary Hall regularly stuck pins into a photograph of her mother. This sort of thing usually straightens out and there is a pleasant intermediary relationship in time, if we are lucky. It depends a great deal on how the silver cord is cut.

I have only realized lately that I was wrong in believing it did not matter very much for Wendy and Rob to be deprived of the presence of a father while they were growing up. I thought a father was not very necessary after nature had used him in her scheme to continue the race. I thought, I have great energy, I can do it all. I can be father as well as mother. My son especially has suffered from this error. A boy needs a father or he will either rely too much on his mother, or not "mind" a mother as much as he would a father, who represents authority. In the manner of many mothers I have been over-strict, and then sometimes for a period become over-soft. A father is necessary as a balance between these extremes.

With my own father's death when I was a baby, I have, in effect—because my children do not often see their father, who lives in London—caused the same situation for them, although the consequences have not been the same. Usually a girl who has been robbed of her father's presence seeks him in marriage with an older man. I did. Johnny, my first husband, was more than twice my age, and I still love him as I would a father. "He's your slave," Wendy once said. Perhaps he is—he is my European representative and I pay him a monthly salary. But what is more important than money, he knows there is someone in this world who loves him and cares what happens to him. I am also *his* slave. I need his unjudging love, his anger against those who are unkind to me, his pleasure in my triumphs. He is the first person I look for when my plane lands in London. And I was sick with worry on one occasion when his kind familiar face was not peering through the customs exit after my flight to London from Madrid. I was sure he was ill and I spent hours searching for him and was lightheaded with relief when I found him at his sister's home in the country. He had not received my cable from Spain.

But despite the absence of a father, my daughter Wendy will have none of a May-December match. When a thirty-four-year-old writer wanted to marry her, she gave me her reasons why she would not accept him. "In the first place I'm not in love with him, and secondly, I don't *have* to marry an older man." Wendy is now twenty-one and any male over thirty is an older man.

We have been very close, my daughter and I—perhaps too close. Parents cannot be friends on the same level with their children. Children think differently, they like different things, their wants are different. I fell into the trap of thinking I could be a friend on the same level with Wendy. There must be some distance, so that when disagreements arise you can use your maturity and experience to give the best help and advice to your child.

In California, I had never allowed Wendy to make mistakes, as we discovered when she had an essay to write at the Bel Air Town and Country School, titled "My Greatest Mistake." We racked our brains all evening to find a mistake she had made, let alone a great one. I had robbed her of the experience of suffering. We ultimately invented a mistake. But the only way to grow is to make mistakes and to profit from them. You can tell your children about your own errors until they are bored, but they will not profit from them. They refuse to benefit from your experiences. Apparently everyone has to learn from their own. This was one reason why I had sent Wendy east to school in Connecticut.

Wendy telephoned me from Rosemary Hall in Greenwich the first Saturday after I had returned to California. It was six her time, nine mine. She had a problem, "Do I have time to wash my hair before dinner?" she asked me in troubled tones. "When is dinner?" I replied. "At six-thirty." "You must decide this yourself," I told her quietly. "What do you think?" She thought not. She still calls me sometimes when she has a problem—always collect, and it does not matter if I am in London or California. I always accept the calls because I know she is still not entirely free of me. A relationship as close as ours is hard to weaken, although we have fought with violent anger that leaves us both shaking. Hardly at all now. The time of the big struggle lasted about three years. It was over before she was twenty.

A worthwhile son tries to destroy his father, Scott Fitzgerald told me once. When my extremely worthwhile daughter Wendy went through this phase, I clung to Keats for rescue. "No hungry generation shall tread me down."

"I don't like to go with you to your friends," Wendy would say. "You are always the center of attention, you talk so much, and they talk to you, not to me." Of course I should have let her stay home, as she preferred to do. But I took her with me. My not too unconscious thought, "She's so attractive I like people to know she's my daughter." I don't do this anymore—partly because I have grown in understanding, chiefly as the result of our epic fight when Wendy metaphorically put her knapsack on her shoulder and said, "I'm leaving home."

It was soon after I had sold the Westport house and we were all in New York crowded into my new one-room apartment at 20 East 68th Street. Rob was sleeping at the nearby Westbury Hotel, Wendy at the Barbizon Hotel for women on Lexington Avenue at 63rd Street. But the daily proximity in the apartment had frayed our nerves. I, doggedly doing my column in one part of the room, while they entertained their friends and twanged endlessly on their guitars, or had the record player going full blast.

The cause of the quarrel was silly. I accused Wendy of conspiring with Robert to stay out late when he should have gone back to the Westbury. After some shouting on both sides, Wendy said, "I'm leaving home." "If she goes, I'm going," said Rob. They both left. At midnight I telephoned the Barbizon. There was no answer from her room. She was probably with Rob. An hour later I called the Westbury. No answer. At two, I called both hotels again. Ha, they were trying to frighten me. But I *was* frightened. For the first time in their lives I did not know where my children were. Now hold on, steady, in any case Wendy is probably with Rob. She is a decent, sensible girl, she will not do anything stupid. You can trust her. You *must* trust her. I paced up and down the apartment. Don't start calling around. You don't want people to know you have behaved badly. She has put up with a lot from you. But they didn't have to vanish. They are both good children and what have I done? I feel like a murderess. Don't be absurd. You know she is all right. Rob will take care of her. She's such a little girl. They might be walking the streets. The gangs. Stop it. Go to bed. Stop worrying about them. Take a sleeping pill.

I was dozing off at about 3:30 A.M. The loud ring of the telephone. Wendy's best friend. "I know you'll want to know that Wendy and Rob are here with me." Great relief. "Do you want to talk to them?" Outrage. "No, I'll talk to them in the morning." I was drowsy from the sleeping pill. The telephone again. "Mom." Wendy at her softest and most contrite. "I'm sorry." "*I'm* sorry." "I'll come home in the morning." We laughed. But in spite of the pill, I was awake most of what was left of the night. Wendy had cut the cord and when I had decided to go to sleep, so had I. We would never be quite so dependent on each other again. She would never need my approval quite so much. Of course it is still not quite severed. I look forward to the time when we will both be free, while still loving and respecting each other. This will happen, I am sure, when she falls in love and gets married. One marriage only, I hope, in spite of my Hollywoodian slip a few years ago, when I said to her fervently, "Oh Wendy, I do hope you will be happy in your marriages."

Sometimes to comfort people who have not had children, I say, "You're lucky, children are a problem from the time they are born until the time they kick you in the teeth and go on their merry way." They usually reply, "Yes, children are ungrateful, they take everything and give nothing." It is true, they are ungrateful, as we were, but they *do* give something back. It varies, depending on how lucky you are— in my case, a reason for working, a reason for living, a light showing the way to the future—if the atom bomb does not destroy our traces. And a limitless satisfaction.

Rob does not confide in me very much, although we all have times of airing our grievances. Sometimes late in the evening and with no one else there, he will open up and tell me about the books he enjoys (Sartre, Fitzgerald, Dylan Thomas) and music (Bach, Kurt Weill), his conversations

with his close friends, Bill and Eric, and a bit about some of
the girls who always seem to be falling in love with him, and
vice versa. How sure he was that he was in love forever two
summers ago in Venice. He sixteen, she just turned seventeen,
the granddaughter of the ex-wife of a famous film star. When
Rob left to join Wendy in Spain, the girl came with us to the
bus that would take him to the plane. He waved to her until he was out of sight. She and I were standing a few inches
apart on the sidewalk, but he waved only to the girl. I felt
depressed. He had known her exactly 3 weeks, he had known
me all his life. I had cherished and loved him and his last
wave before flying off was to the girl.

"You're jealous" Rob accused me, when I brought this up
in London later. He added with a grin, "You're so jealous, you
can hardly see straight." I *was* jealous, although it took my
first visit to a psychiatrist in London for me to believe it.
"Natural reaction," he assured me, and explained the function
of a mother, to do everything for her son—for another woman's
benefit. "And be glad he falls in love. It's a compliment to
you. It means he likes women." I clung to his words for comfort. But there was no doubt about it, I *was* jealous. I had
always thought I would be an ideal, understanding mother-
in-law. After Venice I was not at all sure.

Rob has since been even more in love with another girl. A
soft pretty fifteen-year-old blonde with a high rosy color,
whom he described to me as "a Botticelli." It must have been
the psychiatrist, because I accepted her much more calmly.
And now there is another girl. And there will always be a
girl. Thank goodness. Rob has the irresistible combination of
tremendous good looks, sensitivity, and the gentleness that
big men sometimes have.

Last spring, Putnam published Robert's book *Journey Behind the Iron Curtain*. He had spent 8 weeks with a school
group in the Soviet Union. On his return home, John Wheeler
had him write five articles on his experiences for NANA. Of
course, I helped him. Several newspapers used the articles
on the front page. The same week that the Boston *Globe* was
featuring my son's articles on page one, they dropped my
movie column. They were more interested in Russia than in
Hollywood. The editor of the *Globe* called Rob at the Putney
School and gave him a standing invitation to write for the
paper "on any subject you choose." He was very elated when
he told me this during the Thanksgiving vacation, but I had

something more exciting to tell him. "Putnam wants you to expand your articles into a book." He jumped to his feet. "Gee, that's great." "Calm down," I said. "I don't want you to start unless you believe you can finish it. This book must be *your* book. I will guide you and edit when you have finished but that's all."

After several discouraging starts, the first chapter was finished. There were twelve short chapters completed when he returned to school after the month-long Christmas vacation. The book was finished the following June. *The New York Times* rated it above John Gunther's two books for teen-agers culled from his *Inside Russia* best seller. Of the five books for teen-agers, four written by adults, the review by Harry Schwartz, the *Times* expert on Russia, stated: "By far the best introduction to Communism is teen-ager Robert Westbrook's *Journey Behind the Iron Curtain*. The point that comes through in young Mr. Westbrook's tale, and which escapes other more learned literature in the field, is that Communists are people too, good people and bad people, pleasant people and boors." I sent a copy of the book to President Kennedy and received a thank-you note with a handwritten postscript: *I shall read it with interest as I did your own*, signed J.K.

Bob entered Columbia last fall, but in spite of his book, he is not sure he wants to be a writer. I personally think he would make a good psychiatrist. He certainly understands *me*. I rarely receive letters from him although when he is in love, the girl might get a letter a day. But he wrote me a long letter from the Putney School when he was sixteen. I had been complaining rather monotonously of feeling tired. "I've been doing quite a bit of reading in psychology," he wrote, "and I find it a great help in solving some of my problems. Let me talk about a little of what I've learned, for I think it could help you. For instance, did you know that the most basic sign of emotional disturbance is constant tiredness? A person can sleep and rest, but he will never lose his fatigue. This is because a neurosis takes up so much physical and mental energy, whether you're aware of it or not. It will leave you with constant fatigue unless you can solve your problems. . . . I hope if you have time you will read a book, *Our Inner Conflicts*, by Karen Horney. It contains a lot of helpful material. . . . Love, Rob."

I loved his concern for me. I *have* been quite stormy in the past ten years and significantly, when Rob, some seven years ago, soon after my divorce, was asked to draw his impression of me, he drew an earthquake.

My children and I have always been frank about sex. One of the advantages of having had my kind of life is that there is no falseness on this subject, or undue interest in it. When Wendy was about ten, she asked me to tell her about what we call The Facts of Life. I tried not to be clinical but to stress the beauty of love and creation, and also give the facts. When Rob was about the same age, he came home from school one day and said, "Mom, you said that when I have a question about sex I can ask you." "Of course," I replied, wondering what was coming. "Two boys at school said that you can't have a baby without . . . [He paused, never having used the strong Anglo-Saxon word before.] Is that true?" I swallowed. "In a way, yes, but that's an ugly word for something very beautiful, something as beautiful and strong as life itself. In fact, it *is* life." He looked at me rather slyly and said, "You have two children. Does that mean you did it twice?" I nodded. He regarded me with great interest for a few days, then it all went into his general knowledge of the subject. Perhaps a father could have done better. But I think I was adequate on the subject of sex.

It was always hard for Wendy, as a child, to leave home, but Rob has always wanted to. When he was six, I sent him to summer camp in the mountains near Flagstaff, Arizona, for ten weeks. If I had not gone to fetch him, he would probably still be there. One of his great friends from the age of five was Timmy Getty, the same age, and the son of Paul Getty, reputedly the richest man in the world. They learned to swim together in his mother's pool at their luxurious home on the beach at Santa Monica. One Sunday, Mrs. Getty said, "Robbie, any time you want to spend the night with us, we'll be delighted to have you." Rob looked around the luxurious room, with the butler bringing cookies and Cokes, and replied, "Thank you, and if you want me to stay until I'm grown up, I will." He was quite ready to abandon me for the life of the millionaires.

Soon after Timmy's ninth birthday, the red-haired, freckled, engaging boy developed a tumor on the optic nerve. It was dreadful to see him stumbling at our Christmas party, trying to shake hands inches away from the hand. And singing Christmas carols in his gruff voice, while Wendy and Bob took turns at the piano. When Timmy's condition became worse, his mother took him to New York where for two years he underwent a series of operations that left him totally blind. On Timmy's twelfth birthday his father, who had a fear of illness and of traveling, called him in the New York Hospital from Paris and told him he had given him a fine present, a trust fund of one million dollars. "Shucks," said Timmy when the conversation was over, "I'd rather have a hamburger with onions." When Timmy and his mother were to return to their home in California, the doctor suggested plastic surgery "to tidy up the scars." Timmy died during this minor operation. His heart simply could not take another operation. I was glad when Mrs. Getty, after her divorce, married again, and had a daughter to comfort her.

✝ CHAPTER THIRTY-FIVE

WENDY and Rob will soon be on the road of their own choosing. My job with them is almost done. As long as I live, I am available for consultation or advice. Or perhaps I will be going to them for advice. I hope I have some good years left. I still have great energy and many plans. I am thinking of buying another beach house in California. I have rented a large apartment in the East Sixties with a view of all Manhattan. I have finally succeeded in liking New York City, with its ever-soaring explosions of steel and glass. It is perhaps the last home I will provide for my children.

The time has come to think of my future. What do I really want to do?

I hope I will continue as a columnist, which takes me the length and breadth of the United States, and all over Europe. I enjoy returning to London at least twice a year, although I have now given up revisiting the places of my childhood. In fact, they no longer exist. The orphanage has been pulled down and the children are boarded with real families. Gone forever are the barracklike cold dormitories. No more cropped heads for the girls. And the East End has been cleaned up to the point where I cannot recognize the old neighborhood. In fact, when I took my children on a journey to Stepney and showed them where I had lived, they were rather disappointed. I had painted a Dickensian street. "This isn't so dreadful," said Wendy. "Where are the reeling drunkards?" asked Rob. I pointed to the big brewery at the top of the street, with the huge clock. "Well, that's still there," I said defiantly. I will never go back. I no longer have to reassure myself that I can leave if I want to. I have left.

I had thought that if I were rich enough to stop having to earn my living, I would go to college or take courses with a tutor. I would open the door wider, deeper, into history, art, literature, music and poetry, to which Scott Fitzgerald gave me the key. If I had more time I would study the origins of words, of languages, or races, for these have always fascinated me. But I am aware that I must have the discipline and the turmoil of my job. I have worked too long with a deadline to be able to be too loose and free. I'm like a convict who has been so long in jail; I wouldn't know what to do on the "outside." I like projects. I have been happy with this project. It has been absorbing and satisfying writing my book by myself, snatching hours from my work. I know that with more courage, I could have found the time to write *Beloved Infidel* without a collaborator. It might not have been as good, but I wish I had tried.

Arthur Mizener in his London review of *Beloved Infidel* for *The New Statesman* expressed the hope that one day I would write my own version of *Beloved Infidel*. It is an intriguing idea. *The Letters of F. Scott Fitzgerald*, edited by Andrew Turnbull, have recreated many incidents, from the time I met Scott in Robert Benchley's sitting room at the Garden of Allah on Bastille Day 1937, to the day he died in my Hollywood home on December 21, 1940. Especially the letters to Scottie. At the end of the long letter of July 7, 1938, Scott's P.P.S. asks his daughter to read the letter a second time because he had written it twice. All of Scott's letters were meant to be read twice, at least. They were written for posterity, and how well he succeeded. This particular letter was written twice because the first version would have made Scottie hate her father for all time. It was violently abusive. "The chief thing is to get her in Vassar, not to get your feelings on paper," I remonstrated when Scott finished reading the letter to me. "You don't want to antagonize her, you want to help her." He had been furious with her latest escapade. With another Ethel Walker School student she had thumbed a ride to Yale, which was out of bounds. I was the buffer between Scottie's antagonism to her father's interference, and Scott's frustration in having to work in Hollywood, while the daughter he loved was two thousand miles away and speeding merrily, he believed, on her way to damnation. But Scottie *did* give him cause to worry. She did not always tell him when she took weekends away from Vassar, and there were two anguished days when he was telephoning all over the United States to find her.

Scott was using me as a guinea pig for a book he was planning to write "in my old age": *How to Make Education Interesting*. Because I wanted an education and because I wanted to please him, I read every book he prescribed. He insisted that Scottie read the same books, but Scottie was getting an education, and she saw no valid reason to add to her toil.

I offered my own letters from Scott to Mr. Turnbull, but he did not choose to use them, and perhaps *Beloved Infidel* is best buried in my past. There is so much for me still to accomplish in the future.

When I have time I must return to the psychiatrist, Dr. Castillo, of last summer in London. I did not lie on a couch. I talked to him and he listened. And he had some answers. It was interesting to learn some of the truth about myself, to put myself into better focus, to realize that I am no worse, although no better, than any other normal healthy person; that no one is perfect, no one is God; to be calmer, to give at least as much as I receive, to understand why I am the way I am. To accept myself for what I am. To make mistakes and not be crushed by them. To feel pity, not hatred for those who injure me. To accept pain as part of life's package.

The possibilities of the future! For me there is great magic in the unknown. What will the postman bring? Whose voice shall I hear when the telephone rings? What chance encounter will enrich my life? What does tomorrow hide? As Johnny always said and still does, "Anything can happen." I had dreaded getting old. "Can I survive old age?" I had often wondered. But if it is just around the corner, I have not noticed it because something is always happening in my life. There will always be another exciting story to cover, something new with my children.

When I have time I will think about growing old. Scott was grooming me to be a charming old lady, that is what his educating of me in The F. Scott Fitzgerald College of One was all about. Younger people would seek my company because I would be so interesting, and what I feared most for my old age, loneliness, would never come to pass. I am working on being a charming old lady. It is not easy. I have much to correct in my character. Hopefully I repeat a line Scott taught me to love from T. S. Eliot's poem, "The Love Song of J. Alfred Prufrock"—"There will be time . . . time for a hundred indecisions/ And for a hundred visions and re-visions. . . ."

INDEX

207

Everything Happens With
Boys&Girls Together

William Goldman's
bold, shocking novel of our times!